W9-AZU-375

Contents

Unit 1: Revelation

Unit 2: Interpretation and Overview
of the Bible

Unit 3: Revelation in the Old Testament

Unit 4: Revelation in the New Testament

Unit 5: Sacred Scripture and the Life of Faith

Introduction

"In the beginning . . ." (Genesis 1:1).

These are the first words in the Bible, and it is fitting that they should be the first words in this book. The beginning point for any exploration of our faith is discovering that God has revealed himself to us. This course starts by exploring God's Revelation, which is communicated to us through Tradition and Scripture. The course will focus on Sacred Scripture, the Bible. As the editor for this book, I am excited to welcome you to what can be an amazing encounter with the living Word of God.

I imagine that you have at least one Bible in your home. I have three in my home. Two of them belonged to my grandparents. Those Bibles sit in a prominent space on a shelf in my home office. When my grandparents passed away, I asked for their Bibles because, for me, they are a special connection to a part of my past. They remind me of my family and my history. They remind me of the love my grandparents had for each other and passed on to my parents and to me. When I first acquired these Bibles, I sat down and leafed through their pages. I found passages that had been marked important by my grandparents. I discovered old family pictures of my parents and relatives I did not know. I came across documents that were tucked into the Bibles for safe keeping. I do not open these Bibles much anymore because I want them to stay intact. However, I am very aware of these treasured possessions, and I am deeply grateful for them.

The third Bible in my office is the one I use for personal study and for my work. I consult this Bible often. I have important passages marked. I have notes tucked into it. The pages are getting tattered from use. This Bible plays a part in my spiritual and professional life almost every day, always bringing me closer to God.

These three Bibles—the ones I have reverently placed on a shelf and rarely touch anymore and the one I take off the shelf and consult daily—are a good example of what Scripture is in my life. It is a connection to my personal history and the history of the faith I hold so dear. It helps me to know where I come from, what I was created for, and God's enduring goodness in reaching out to me and to all his people to lead us to salvation. My hope is that Scripture can do the same for you—that it will connect your life today to the history of our salvation and to the promise of eternal life, that it will help you to grow in your relationship with God, and that it will guide you in how to live your life and bring the Good News of Jesus Christ to others.

You are going to learn a great deal about God and Scripture during this course, with this book as the starting point. But this book, studied in a single semester, cannot teach you everything there is to know about God's Revelation. Seeking this understanding is a lifelong journey. I constantly discover new insights in my well-worn Bible. My hope is that through this course and lifelong study of Scripture, you too will continue to encounter the living Word of God.

Peace and blessings,
Steven McGlaun
Editor, First Edition

When we study the Bible, what are we really studying? Is it a collection of exciting stories? A book of advice about moral life? A historical artifact?

The Bible is all these things, of course—but it is so much more. When we study the Bible, we study God's Revelation and the history of our salvation. Therefore, before we turn our attention to the Bible in this course, we must look at the many ways God has revealed himself to us.

We start by recognizing that God created us with the deep longing to know him. This is where it all begins: our desire for some eternal truth beyond the everyday details of our own lives. The only source of happiness we need is our love for God, made possible by his love for us. Through the natural world and our own reason—both of which come from God—we can begin to know God. We can find him in all his creation. This is called natural revelation, and it has been affirmed by Sacred Scripture and the teachings of the Church.

If we can find God through his creation, why do we need to study the Bible? Sadly, Original Sin hinders our ability to know God fully through natural revelation. This is why God provided us with Divine Revelation: his communication about himself and his saving plan for us. We can begin our study of Divine Revelation through Sacred Scripture. However, Divine Revelation was fulfilled when God sent his own Divine Son, Jesus Christ, to save us from sin and death.

The enduring understandings and essential questions represent core concepts and questions that are explored throughout this unit. By studying the content of each chapter, you will gain a more complete understanding of the following:

Enduring Understandings

1. When we respond to the invitation to live in communion with God, we become more fully the people he created us to be.

2. We can come to know God through the natural world and through human reason.

3. God's Revelation is communicated through Sacred Scripture and Sacred Tradition.

Essential Questions

1. How does one find true happiness?

2. How can I know and search out God?

3. How has God communicated with humanity?

Chapter 1

The Desire to Know God

Introduction

We are created with a longing, a yearning, for God. Each of us yearns for a life of meaning and truth, which can be fulfilled only by our supreme, good, and loving God. God wants us to know him. It's so easy to become distracted by worldly promises and definitions of happiness, goodness, and beauty. But God continually invites and challenges us to renounce the distortions of this world and fix our eyes on the infinite truth found in him alone. There is only one answer, one choice, if we want to be truly happy in this life and the next. That answer is God—our God who knew us before we were born, knows our thoughts before we speak them, and leads us on the path to salvation.

We begin our study of the Bible by exploring God's continual invitation to us to be in relationship with him. We see in this chapter that just as we have been created with a longing for God, so God also longs to be close to us. Jesus Christ, the Incarnate Son of God, shows us God's great love for humanity and invites us to communion and salvation through God. When we respond to God's invitation to live in communion with him, we find the lasting happiness he created us to experience.

Article 1: We Are Created to Long for God

Hunger . . . thirst . . . yearn . . . crave . . . long . . . need! When we use these words, we describe a desire to fill an emptiness, a void, in our lives. We all have the need to satisfy this inner longing. Because God has written this inner longing into our hearts, we experience a restlessness that only God can satisfy. To be human is to embark on a journey of wandering, as the Israelites did during the Exodus, knowing that our one true direction and destination is God alone.

We Are Religious Beings

Each of us is a religious being. Whether we realize it or not, our **vocation** (from the Latin word meaning "to call") as religious beings is to live fully human lives—lives in which we know, love, and freely choose God. When we say that humans are religious beings, we are saying that we are made by and for God, to live in communion with him. Within the human heart is a place that desires to be filled with God's infinite love. From the moment of conception, we were knitted in our mother's womb with

vocation
A call from God to all members of the Church to embrace a life of holiness. Specifically, it refers to a call to live the holy life as an ordained minister, as a vowed religious (sister or brother), or in a Christian marriage. Single life that involves a personal consecration or commitment to a permanent, celibate gift of self to God and one's neighbor is also a vocational state.

Primary Sources

Saint Teresa of Ávila on the Holy Desire for God

Do you ever feel an unexplainable desire for silence and prayer? God's love draws us to him and calls us to respond to him with love. Sometimes we experience his love as a yearning in our heart. In *The Interior Castle*, Saint Teresa of Ávila, the first female Doctor of the Church, wrote about how God reaches out to us every day. The next time you are in prayer, reflect on the following words of Saint Teresa of Ávila:

> This Lord of ours is so anxious that we should desire him and strive after his companionship that he calls us ceaselessly, time after time, to approach him; and this voice of his is so sweet. . . . His appeals come through the conversations of good people, or from sermons, or through the reading of good books . . . through sicknesses and trials, or by the means of truths which God teaches us at times when we are engaged in prayer; however feeble such prayers may be, God values them highly.

a desire for truth and happiness that only God can satisfy. We find expressions of this desire both in Sacred Scripture and in the lives of the saints.

The Book of Psalms, in the Old Testament, sheds light on our longings that can find meaning and rest only in the knowledge and wisdom of God. Psalm 42 speaks of the quest for God in this way: "As the deer longs for streams of water, / so my soul longs for you, O God. / My soul thirsts for God, the living God" (verses 2–3). The psalmist compares thirst for God to being parched, longing for refreshing and plentiful water. In Psalm 23 we find the longing for a shepherd who gives strength, provides protection, and sets a banquet of love.

The writings of the saints also illustrate humanity's search for God. At all times we move toward God to find completion. Saint John of the Cross wrote about "one dark night, fired with love's urgent longings. . . . O night that has united the Lover with his beloved" (*The Collected Works of Saint John of the Cross*, pages 358–359). John was speaking of his soul's burning desire to be united with God, the Lover. Saint Teresa of Ávila stated, "In the measure you desire Him, you will find Him."

Pray It!

Hear, Receive, Follow

God wants us to know him. He even created us to long to know him. But like most people, you probably have many distractions that interfere with your ability to focus on God. At such times, how can you turn your attention back to God and make time for him? Prayer is always a good place to start. This prayer is short and simple—but if you pray it regularly, you might find that it has a powerful effect:

O God:
Open my ears to hear you
and my heart to receive you,
and strengthen my will
that I may follow you.
Amen.

(*The Catholic Youth Prayer Book,* page 13)

According to both saints, persistent longing and authentic desire are the direct paths to God.

We Are Always Moving toward God

Saint Augustine of Hippo said, "The whole life of a good Christian is a holy desire to see God as He is." We came from God and are constantly journeying back to him. Our ultimate desire is union with him. Because we are religious beings, our whole spiritual journey is characterized by an unceasing craving to know the saving hand of God. When we respond to his invitation to live in communion with him, we become more fully the people he created us to be.

> **What can you do in your everyday life to respond to God's invitation to live in communion with him?**

Article 2: God's Invitation

How often do you interact with friends, family, classmates, and even strangers? We spend much of our time on earth building relationships. Science and our own experiences tell us that healthy relationships are necessary for us to survive and thrive. The heart of any healthy relationship is a strong, intimate closeness or bond. This goal challenges us to become people of compassion and faith. The most important relationship we have is with God. Sacred Scripture reminds us of the critical need to know God and his power to save us (see Philippians 3:8–11).

Just as we constantly yearn to know God, he constantly calls us to relationship with himself. The *Pastoral Constitution on the Church in the Modern World* (*Gaudium et Spes,* 1965) states, "From the very circumstance of his origin man is already invited to converse with God" (19). In other words, we are invited into communion with God to experience the grace of his saving love. God wants to know, love, and hold us. Therefore he continually calls us to himself.

Incarnation
From the Latin, meaning "to become flesh," referring to the mystery of Jesus Christ, the Divine Son of God, becoming man. In the Incarnation, Jesus Christ became truly man while remaining truly God.

Jesus Christ: God's Greatest Invitation

Because God so longs for a relationship with us, he has reached out in a radical way. In the **Incarnation** the Word of God became flesh in the person of Jesus Christ. Through Jesus Christ, God revealed himself to human beings in a new way so we might hear and understand the message of **salvation**. In fact, the name Jesus means "God saves." In and through Jesus Christ, God has "provided the definitive, superabundant answer to the questions that man asks himself about the meaning and purpose of his life" (*Catechism of the Catholic Church* [CCC], 68). The Incarnation of the Son of God is about God's love for humanity. Because of his love for us,

Did You Know?

The Church in the Modern World

© St. Peter's, Vatican City / Bridgeman Images

In 1962, Blessed Saint Pope John XXIII opened the twenty-first Ecumenical Council of the Church, also known as **Vatican Council II**. Like all Ecumenical Councils, Vatican Council II was a gathering of the Church's bishops from around the world, convened by the Pope. Pope John XXIII wanted the Church to respond to the cares and concerns of people in a rapidly changing world. *The Church in the Modern World,* one of the Council's many documents, emphasizes a pastoral concern for the people of the modern era, declaring that their joys, hopes, grief, and anguish must be the Church's as well. With the goal of "scrutinizing the signs of the times" and "interpreting them in the light of the Gospel" (4), the document addresses the dignity of the human person, the need for community in an individualistic world, and our relationship to the universe. It also addresses the Church's role in the formation of people, the sanctity of marriage and family life, and economic and social justice.

God the Father sent his only Son, who is God himself, to invite us into a life-giving relationship with him. By dwelling among us, God further extends his invitation to communion and eternal salvation. Although we build many relationships throughout life, no relationship is greater than the one we have with our God.

> **In what ways is your relationship with God the greatest relationship in your life? How can it become even greater?**

Article 3: Happiness in God Alone

What do I need to be truly happy in this lifetime? All of us ask ourselves this question at some point. Most of us struggle with it throughout our entire lives. In our society the media offers various answers to this question, ranging from expensive homes, cars, and clothing to lives of promiscuous sex and experimentation with drugs and alcohol. Those who seek happiness through these sources discover that they do not get the happiness they thought they would. Why?

The promises of this world are empty, lacking depth and meaning. Some things might provide momentary satisfaction or relief, but they eventually leave us looking for a new fix for our unhappy and aching spirits. We may try to fill the void of unhappiness with the latest smartphone, computer, fashion trend, and so on. Through advertising and popular entertainment, the media has been able to convince people that material goods relieve our dissatisfactions with life. In reality, material goods leave us still looking for true happiness.

According to Saint Augustine, we need not look for happiness anywhere but with God, because our hearts are restless until they find rest in him. In the words of the *Catechism*, God is "our first origin and our ultimate goal" (CCC, 229). He is our beginning and our destiny. We can find happiness and truth only when we live in right relationship with God and commit fully to him. He always

salvation
From the Latin *salvare*, meaning "to save," referring to the forgiveness of sins and assurance of permanent union with God, attained for us through the Paschal Mystery—Christ's work of redemption accomplished through his Passion, Death, Resurrection, and Ascension. Only at the time of judgment can a person be certain of salvation, which is a gift of God.

Vatican Council II
The Ecumenical or general Council of the Roman Catholic Church that Saint John XXIII convened as pope in 1962 and that continued under Venerable Pope Paul VI until 1965.

takes the first step in calling us to this communion with himself. Responding to God's call means we remove the promises and distractions of this world and focus on him to have a clearer sense of his vision and path.

Being fully committed to God means putting our faith in him. The Holy Spirit works in us and helps us to believe by preparing us to receive the gift of faith. God's supernatural gift of faith leads us to choose him with our whole heart and mind, not preferring anything else and not replacing him with anything. When we make this choice, we will naturally want to live a life based on the Beatitudes—recognizing that true happiness is found in God alone. Jesus Christ, God's infinite Word and Wisdom, gave us these Beatitudes as a key for living in true happiness:

> Blessed are the poor in spirit,
>   for theirs is the kingdom of heaven.
> Blessed are they who mourn,
>   for they will be comforted.
> Blessed are the meek,
>   for they will inherit the land.
> Blessed are they who hunger and thirst for righteousness,
>   for they will be satisfied.
> Blessed are the merciful,
>   for they will be shown mercy.
> Blessed are the clean of heart,
>   for they will see God.
> Blessed are the peacemakers,
>   for they will be called children of God.
> Blessed are they who are persecuted for the sake of
>   righteousness,
>   for theirs is the kingdom of heaven.

Blessed are you when they insult you and persecute you and utter every kind of evil against you [falsely] because of me. Rejoice and be glad, for your reward will be great in heaven.

(Matthew 5:3–12)

Have you ever been unhappy even when you got something you really wanted? Why do you think you were still unhappy?

Article 4: Saint Augustine and the Four Objects of Love

Have you noticed that some people get along with everyone? The more friends they have, the more friends they seem to make. This is possible because within our heart and soul is a tremendous capacity to love. The more we love in a genuine way, the more love we have to offer.

Love—sometimes referred to as *caritas*, a Latin term meaning "charity"—is equated with the emotions of affection, reverence, and blessing. Love describes the manifestation of God's presence in creation. Our primary call as Christians is to give and accept love. Underlying

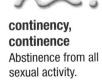

continency, continence
Abstinence from all sexual activity.

 ## Faith in Action
Saint Augustine's Change of Heart

© Galleria degli Uffizi, Florence, Italy / Bridgeman Images

Does it sometimes seem like saints must be holy and virtuous from birth? If so, then you may be surprised to learn about the sinful early life of Saint Augustine, the fourth-century Church Father. Augustine's pagan father was proud of his son's physical ability and cleverness, but his Christian mother grieved because the young Augustine had fallen into sin. For example, he and his friends once stole pears from a neighbor's garden. Augustine later recalled that he was not hungry, and the pears were not even tasty. Rather, he enjoyed the sin itself. He was unrepentantly sinful into adulthood, even having a son with one of his mistresses. He increasingly searched for deeper meaning, but he was not ready to give up his sinful ways, praying, "Grant me chastity and **continency**, but not yet" (*Confessions,* 8.17).

What changed? One day Augustine's conscience would not let him go on like he'd been living, and he wept in his garden as children played nearby. Then he heard a child chant, "Take up and read; take up and read" (*Confessions,* 8.29). He opened his Bible to read: "Let us conduct ourselves properly . . . , not in orgies and drunkenness, not in promiscuity and licentiousness, not in rivalry and jealousy. But put on the Lord Jesus Christ, and make no provision for the desires of the flesh" (Romans 13:13–14). These words made clear to Augustine what he must do, and he finally turned to Christ with all his heart.

much of the Christian understanding of love is the wisdom of Saint Augustine of Hippo, who proclaimed that there are four objects we should love: God, our neighbors, ourselves, and our bodies.

1. God

"You shall love the Lord, your God, with all your heart, with all your soul, and with all your mind" (Matthew 22:37). Jesus Christ identified this as the first Great Commandment. Before we can love anything or anyone, we must first love God, who breathed life into our bodies. But love does not start with us. We are only able to love because God loved us first. Once we respond by giving our full selves to him, the love that flowed from the wounds of Jesus Christ on the cross will inflame our hearts with a fire that cannot be extinguished.

2. Our Neighbors

According to Saint Augustine, if we do not love our neighbors, we do not love God. Loving our neighbors does not mean we always agree with their attitudes and actions. It means we revere and respect our neighbors

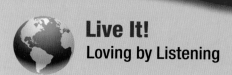

Live It!
Loving by Listening

One way you can love is by listening well. Listening requires more than just physically hearing something. Good listening is a gift that takes time and energy. It demands full presence and attentiveness. It is sometimes difficult to listen, especially when the person speaking is in pain.

Listening also fits in with Saint Augustine's four objects of love. Listening to God in prayer and in his Word is essential in the life of a Christian. Listening to your neighbor is love too. If anyone has ever attentively listened to you when you've had a problem, you know what a wonderful gift it is to share your worries with someone who cares. Listening to yourself—your own fears, needs, hopes, and dreams—is also important, especially in discerning your vocation in life.

Take time each day to show love—for God, others, and yourself—by being an attentive listener.

because God has created every person "in his image" (Genesis 1:27). Recall the second Great Commandment that Jesus proclaimed: "You shall love your neighbor as yourself" (Matthew 22:39).

3. Ourselves

To love ourselves is to love God. Self-love is the realization that God is imprinted on our heart, waiting, wanting us to display his love to the world in a beautiful and magnificent way. Knowing that Jesus Christ gave himself for our salvation points to our infinite worth and value— God himself died for us. But we must be sure that love of self does not become selfish or contrary to God's will. Rather, loving ourselves should empower us to move beyond ourselves and build the Reign of God, where all people can see their own value.

4. Our Bodies

Our body is one of God's great masterpieces. It will be resurrected at the end of time, manifest in God's greatness, goodness, and glory. We must hold our body in high esteem, because it bears God's creative hand. "It is animated by a spiritual soul, and it is the whole human person that is intended to become, in the body of Christ, a temple of the Spirit'" (CCC, 364).

> **Which of these—God, neighbor, yourself, or your body—do you have the most difficulty loving? How can you overcome that difficulty?**

Chapter Review

1. What is the vocation of every human being?

2. How did Saint Augustine summarize the goal of a good Christian?

3. What is the Incarnation? How is it an important event in God's work of salvation?

4. What were the goals of Vatican Council II's document *The Church in the Modern World*?

5. What do we find when we respond to God's call to live in communion with him?

6. What did Jesus give us as a framework or as the keys for living in true happiness?

7. According to Saint Augustine, what are the four objects of love?

Natural Revelation

Introduction

God painted all creation with the truth of his existence. He also created us with the ability to know him by using our ability to think—our reason. Through creation and reason, we can come to know God. This is called natural revelation. Because of natural revelation, we can logically and reasonably deduce the existence of God through the natural order. God shaped all living things as a sign and symbol of his desire to be known through his magnificent universe.

Sacred Scripture calls our attention to our ability to know God through natural revelation. So do the writings of the Church Fathers, the proofs developed by scholastic theologians, and the teachings of recent Church Councils. However, the ability of the human mind to fully know the truth about God through natural revelation has been hindered because of historical and social conditions and the consequences of Original Sin. Something more is needed. God, in his wisdom and goodness, provided Divine Revelation for us. Divine Revelation is God's communication about himself and his plan for humanity, which he made known to us most fully by sending his own Divine Son, Jesus Christ. Natural revelation is the subject of this chapter; you will read about Divine Revelation in chapter 3.

natural revelation
The process by which God makes himself known to human reason through the created world.

Article 5: Sacred Scripture and Natural Revelation

"The heavens declare the glory of God; / the firmament proclaims the works of his hands" (Psalm 19:2). God reveals himself in many and varied ways. We can come to know God by contemplating his wondrous and majestic universe. The process by which God makes himself known through the natural and created order is called **natural revelation**. Within each of us lies the capacity to understand God as the beginning and the end of the universe. From the sun and moon to the trees and changing seasons, from the uniqueness of every person to the endless energy that flows through all living things, all creation proclaims God's existence. Both the Old and New Testaments emphasize natural revelation by calling attention to God's glory in the universe he created.

Natural Revelation in the Old Testament

Sacred Scripture contains countless passages that point to the Christian understanding of natural revelation. In the account of Creation in the Book of Genesis, we learn

Live It!
Seeing God in All Things

When creating a yearbook spread for the senior class, the editor asked a few seniors to submit pictures of their rooms at home to be printed in the spread. The headline asked readers to guess which room belonged to which senior. Not surprisingly, the friends who knew the seniors the best could easily match the rooms with their owners. It makes sense that the way you decorate your room says a lot about you. After all, you are the interior designer.

The same is true with God. All creation is able to tell us something about the Creator, as we come to know God better and better. Take time to consider what the natural world is telling you about God. Make a plan to experience the next sunrise or sunset. Go to a hill or to a shoreline, or any open area, and just take it in with all its colors. Then pause for a moment to see if you can perceive God's hand in it.

about God's creative action over the course of seven days. At the end of each day, after God worked to splash the earth with color and life, he saw how good and beautiful his creations are. The goodness of every created thing points to the Absolute and Supreme Good: God. Light, darkness, water, sky, earth, plants, trees, sun, moon, stars, animal life, and human beings—God's most important creation—all point to God as "the first cause and final end of all things" (CCC, 34).

A passage in the Book of Wisdom describes people who were unable to recognize God from the things they could see. The passage describes as foolish those "who from the good things seen did not succeed in knowing the one who is" (13:1). They didn't recognize that all created things point to the Creator. When we take time to wonder and marvel at the beauty and order of the world, we are able to see the work of God, who is Creator of Heaven and earth.

© Andrey.tiyk / shutterstock.com

Creation itself gives witness to the glory of God, the Creator. What parts of creation cause you to think about God and give thanks to God?

Natural Revelation in the New Testament

Like the Old Testament, the New Testament also sheds light on our understanding of natural revelation. The Acts of the Apostles details the growth of the early Church under the direction of the Holy Spirit. In the Acts of the Apostles, we read Saint Paul's description of a God who "fixed the ordered seasons and the boundaries of their regions" (17:26). Paul offered this description to direct the Athenians to a magnificent truth: God is alive and real, and he continually reveals himself throughout all creation.

The letters of Saint Paul also affirm that God has made himself evident in all creation. In his Letter to the

Romans, Paul writes this about God: "Ever since the creation of the world, his invisible attributes of eternal power and divinity have been able to be understood and perceived in what he has made" (1:20). Acts and Romans, along with many other New Testament writings, point to our capacity to know God through the natural order. Sacred Scripture directs our eyes and heart toward the world and all its inhabitants, enabling us to recognize God's existence and presence.

In light of natural revelation, how can science promote faith?

Faith in Action
The White Violet Center: Caring for God's Creation

© Dieter H / shutterstock.com

The White Violet Center for Eco-Justice was established by the Sisters of Providence of Saint Mary-of-the-Woods in Indiana in 1995. Its mission is to "foster a way of living that recognizes the interdependence of all creation."

From the time that Saint (Mother) Theodora Guerin traveled from France to Indiana in 1840, the Sisters of Providence have been rooted amidst the farms and forests of this midwestern state. Mother Theodora loved her new home in the forest. Having been taught by her mother to use plants and herbs for healing, she used her knowledge to benefit her new neighbors in Indiana. Today the Sisters of Providence recognize reverence for the natural world as an integral part of their charism.

The White Violet Center has become a center of education where the sisters and other experts teach the practical skills necessary for living in harmony with the world that God created and entrusted to us as a sign of his love and care. Every year the center sponsors an Earth Day celebration. The sisters also offer workshops in weaving, using the wool from their own herd of alpacas. The White Violet Center website posts action alerts to encourage involvement in important political decisions that affect the environment. Visitors to the center are welcome to enjoy touring the sisters' well-cultivated organic farmland, walking the bluebird trail, and meeting the alpacas.

Article 6: Natural Revelation and the Wisdom of the Church Fathers

"Creation is a great book. . . . [God] set before your eyes the things he had made. . . . Heaven and earth cry out to you, 'God made me!'" With these words Saint Augustine, an influential **Father of the Church**, proclaimed that the universe and created order point to the existence of God. Saint Augustine invited us to open the "book of creation" and discover the presence of God. Many other Fathers of the Church affirmed the notion of natural revelation—our ability to know God, the Creator and Lord, in and through the magnificence of his creation, informed by our human reason. However, historical conditions and the consequences of **Original Sin** often diminish our ability to fully know God's truth through natural revelation alone. This is why we need Divine Revelation.

Fathers of the Church (Church Fathers)
During the early centuries of the Church, those teachers whose writings extended the Tradition of the Apostles and who continue to be important for the Church's teachings.

Did You Know?

Time Line of the Church Fathers

Father of the Church is a title given to an important teacher in the early Church whose work extended the tradition of the Apostles. Many worked to correct early heresies, but all promoted teachings that are still important for the Church today. The Church has named dozens of Church Fathers, including these saints:

- Saint Athanasius (296–373), Bishop of Alexandria
- Saint Gregory of Nazianzus (325–389), Archbishop of Constantinople
- Saint Basil the Great (330–379), Archbishop of Caesarea in Cappadocia, in modern-day Turkey
- Saint Gregory of Nyssa (335–394), Bishop of Nyssa in Cappadocia, in modern-day Turkey
- Saint Ambrose (340–397), Bishop of Milan
- Saint John Chrysostom (347–407), Archbishop of Constantinople
- Saint Jerome (347–419), of Bethlehem, known for the Vulgate, the first Latin translation of the Bible
- Saint Augustine (354–430), Bishop of Hippo Regius, now Annaba, in modern-day Algeria
- Saint Gregory the Great (540–604), Bishop of Rome

Original Sin
From the Latin
origo, meaning
"beginning" or
"birth." The term
has two meanings:
(1) the sin of the
first human beings,
who disobeyed
God's command by
choosing to follow
their own will and
thus lost their
original holiness
and became
subject to death,
(2) the fallen state
of human nature
that affects every
person born into
the world, except
Jesus and Mary.

The Universe as a Sign of God

Essential to the theology and spirituality of the Church
Fathers is the idea that the universe provides us with
visible evidence of God's existence. Therefore, when we
notice a beautiful sunset, enjoy the changing colors of
a tree, or recognize the cycle of life, we can arrive at a
deeper knowledge of God as both the beginning and the
end of all creation. Saint Gregory of Nyssa, a Church
Father and bishop, recognized that as we come to know
God through the created universe, our desire for God
grows stronger and deeper. According to the Church
Fathers, because the universe shows God's existence, it
draws us into a closer relationship with him.

The Human Being as the Image of God

Many Church Fathers—especially Saints Athanasius,
Gregory of Nazianzus, Gregory of Nyssa, and Augustine of Hippo—paired the idea that God can be known
through natural revelation with the belief that humanity
is the summit of creation. In other words, the Church
Fathers saw human beings as the high point of God's
creative action in the world. After all, the Book of Genesis tells us that God created us in his image. To look at
humans in all our complexities is to see God. He is the
fashioner of our souls. Saint Irenaeus made this point
in a well-known saying: "Man fully alive is the glory of
God."

Seeing God Revealed in All Creation

Saint Augustine emphasized, "Even the tiniest insect cannot be considered attentively without astonishment and
without praising the Creator." The Church Fathers truly
recognized the imprint of God on everything he created,
especially on human beings. Nothing created by God, not
even the smallest bug, is insignificant. God's existence
and glory are manifested in the smallest to the largest of
his creations. We can know him through the work of his
hands. This is the fruit of the scriptural understanding
of natural revelation. The Church Fathers proclaimed

the undeniable truth of God revealed in nature. When we recognize God's Revelation in all creation and listen to God's call in the deepest parts of our being, we can be certain that God exists and that he is the origin and the end of all things.

> **How does a seemingly insignificant insect or plant point to the undeniable imprint of God on creation?**

Pray It!

God's Presence in Creation

Do you feel spiritually awed by mountains or thunderstorms? Many people find it easy to experience God when they contemplate a wonder of nature. The following prayer can help you to remember that God is the author of all creation:

God,
Help me to see that all creation flows from you.
You reveal yourself in the wind,
in the stars and planets of the night sky.
All plants and animals remind me of your glory.
Although my life is sometimes chaotic,
I marvel at the order in the universe.
The majestic mountains, the forests,
and the vast beaches that line our oceans
give witness to the peace and harmony you place within creation.
Remind me often that I am your child,
for you created me in your image and likeness.
Help me to develop my capacity to love,
seek the truth, and use my freedom wisely.
And as I continue to see the beauty and wonder of all your creation,
may it lead me to a deeper longing for you.
Amen.

Middle Ages
Also known as the medieval period, the time between the collapse of the Roman Empire in the late fifth century AD and the beginning of the Renaissance in the fourteenth century.

scholastic theology
The use of philosophical methods to better understand revealed truth. The goal of scholastic theology is to present the understanding of revealed truth in a logical and systematic form.

Doctor of the Church
A title officially bestowed by the Church on saints who are highly esteemed for their theological writings, as well as their personal holiness.

Article 7: Natural Revelation and Scholastic Theology

New, rational arguments to demonstrate the existence of God emerged during the **Middle Ages**, particularly in the twelfth, thirteenth, and fourteenth centuries. These centuries saw the beginning of **scholastic theology**, an approach to the study of God that uses philosophical methods to better understand revealed truth. Grounded in Sacred Scripture and in the Church Fathers' understanding of natural revelation, scholastic theology also relies heavily on the use of logic. The great scholastic theologians of the Middle Ages maintained that we can use our minds to develop logical, convincing arguments to attain truth and certainty about God and the human experience. Two of these great thinkers were Saint Anselm of Canterbury and Saint Thomas Aquinas.

The goal of scholastic theology is to present the understanding of revealed truth in a logical and organized form. Scholastic theology continues to be an energizing force behind current arguments regarding the genuineness of God's existence.

Saint Anselm of Canterbury: One Proof of God's Existence

Saint Anselm of Canterbury, a **Doctor of the Church**, monk, and scholastic theologian wrote a prayer, or meditation, called *Proslogion,* he proposed an argument that uses reason alone to assert the existence of God. His argument is as follows:

1. God is "that than which nothing greater can be thought."
2. It is greater to exist in reality than to exist merely in the mind.
3. Then God must exist in reality, not only in mind and understanding.

Today scholars still study Saint Anselm's argument.

Saint Thomas Aquinas: The Five Proofs

Saint Thomas Aquinas, a Dominican friar, is arguably the most influential scholastic theologian. He too was named a Doctor of the Church. He is best known for his work called *Summa Theologiae. Summa Theologiae* is a twenty-one–volume work on theology and faith. One of Aquinas's many accomplishments in philosophy and theology is his five proofs of God's existence. According to Aquinas, the reality of God can be proved, or logically demonstrated, in five ways.

contingency
A state in which something relies or depends on something else.

First Proof: The First Mover

The first proof or argument is known as the First Mover. It begins with the idea that the universe constantly moves. Because everything is always moving and changing, human beings can logically see a need for a First Mover, who set everything in motion and still guides the actions of humanity. We call that First Mover God.

Second Proof: Causality

The second proof of God's existence is referred to as Causality, or First Efficient Cause. By reflecting on the cycle of life, we realize that all things are caused by something else. We equally realize that nothing can create itself. Therefore common sense tells us there must be an Ultimate Cause or First Efficient Cause, which is uncaused, not created by something else. This uncaused First Cause is God.

After reading this section, what do you think is significant about the two objects Saint Thomas Aquinas is holding in this painting?

Third Proof: Contingency

The third proof is based on a theory of **contingency**. This argument states that the universe contains many contingent things—that is, things that came into existence because of something else. But if everything is contingent on something that already existed, there

© National Gallery, London / Art Resource, NY

must have been a time in the past when nothing existed. Yet we know that things do exist. If they exist, they cannot exist without a Necessary Being. A Necessary Being is one who creates but is not created. That Necessary Being, which gives life to all beings, is God.

Fourth Proof: Perfection

The fourth proof begins with our understanding of perfection. Most of us can point out the imperfections of the world and humanity. In naming imperfections we acknowledge that there are varying degrees of beauty, goodness, and knowledge. But how do we recognize perfect beauty, goodness, and knowledge? According to Aquinas, we know perfection because there is one All-Perfect Being, God, who sets the infinite standard for wisdom and truth.

Fifth Proof: Intelligent Being

The fifth and final proof points out that the world is characterized by remarkable order. This proof begins by recognizing that many things in the universe have no intelligence of their own. Yet despite their lack of intel-

Primary Sources

Know the Cause by Examining the Effect

Have you studied cause and effect in your science classes? For example, you might have learned that a motionless object will not move unless something exerts force on it. Saint Thomas Aquinas used similar logic to explain natural revelation. He pointed out that everything we witness in nature can lead us to understand its divine cause, even when the cause is hard to perceive directly:

> When an effect is more apparent to us than its cause, we come to know the cause through its effect. Even though the effect should be better known to us [because it is easier for us to witness], we can demonstrate from any effect that its cause exists, because effects always depend on some cause, and a cause must exist if its effect exists. We can therefore demonstrate that God exists from what is not evident to us on the basis of effects which are evident to us.

(Aquinas, *Summa Theologiae*)

ligence, they still act toward and achieve their end. One can then deduce that if things that lack intelligence still fulfill their purpose, there must be something intelligent that does have knowledge of their end and directs all things to their appropriate conclusion. This something can be seen as the intelligent designer behind our complex universe. We name this Intelligent Designer and Magnificent Architect God.

All five of Aquinas's proofs logically point to the existence of God as the First Mover, First Cause, Necessary Being, Model of Perfection, and Intelligent Being. In the words of the *Catechism*, each argument emphasizes that we "can come to know that there exists a reality which is the first cause and final end of all things, a reality 'that everyone calls "God"'[2]" (34).

How can God be both the cause and the end of everything?

Article 8: Natural Revelation: Vatican Council I to the Present

Church history echoes with the assertion that God "can be known with certainty from the created world by the natural light of human reason[3]" (CCC, 36). At various points in the Church's history, the reality of natural revelation has encountered opposition. At these times the Church has benefited from the wisdom of the **Magisterium** and from noted theologians in affirming the role of natural revelation in helping people to experience the existence of God.

In December 1869 Vatican Council I, the twentieth **Ecumenical Council** of the Church, was convened. Before it was cut short due to outside circumstances, the Council closely examined the relationship between faith and reason. Some claimed that human reason lacks the capacity to grasp religious knowledge. Many throughout the world were challenging the Church's teaching that God can be known in and through creation, informed by

Magisterium
The Church's living teaching office, which consists of all bishops, in communion with the Pope, the bishop of Rome.

Ecumenical Council
A gathering of the Church's bishops from around the world to address pressing issues in the Church. Ecumenical Councils are usually convened by the Pope or are at least approved by him.

conscience
The "inner voice,"
guided by human
reason and Divine
Law, that enables
us to judge the
moral quality of a
specific action that
has been made,
is being made,
or will be made.
This judgment
enables us to
distinguish good
from evil, in order
to accomplish
good and avoid
evil. To make good
judgments, one
needs to have
a well-formed
conscience.

human reason. In its constitution *Dei Filius* (1870), the Council affirmed, "God, the first principle and last end of all things, can be known with certainty from the created world by the natural light of human reason" (2).

The philosopher Emmanuel Kant (1724–1804) is noted for saying, "Have the courage to use your own reason!" This motto, along with the assertions of Vatican Council I, gained the attention of the philosopher and theologian John Henry Cardinal Newman (1801–1890). Cardinal Newman developed a theory known as the convergence of probabilities. This theory says that a number of probable hints, or indicators, point to the existence of God. These indicators range from the mystery of our world to our frequent experiences of beauty and goodness, from the voice of **conscience** to the enjoyment of freedom. The theory also says that no single indicator necessarily proves the existence of God. Instead, when these hints are combined, they produce a powerful argument. The strength of these probable indicators, taken together, points us to the same conclusion: God exists.

Pierre Teilhard de Chardin (1881–1955) was a French theologian who was a member of the Society of Jesus, also called the Jesuits. The Jesuits are a group of priests and religious brothers who follow the ideas and spirituality of Saint Ignatius of Loyola. Teilhard was educated in theology and science. As both a mystic and a scientist, he sought to reconcile the world of religious thought with the rapid growth of scientific knowledge during his lifetime. One of his most significant contributions to the Church's understanding of natural revelation is the belief that creation reveals the sacred face and blazing heart of God.

Karl Rahner (1904–1984), another Jesuit theologian, largely influenced the Catholic understanding of natural revelation. His work during Vatican Council II, and his many writings, presented the idea that whenever we experience a limitation in knowledge, freedom, or perfection, we have an underlying awareness of God as Absolute Mystery. To help us understand God as mystery, Rahner used the image of a horizon. When we gaze at the horizon, we are not directly looking at it, because it is not something we can actually see. The horizon is where the sky and sea only appear to meet. It is beyond us, but it is the background of everything we see. Just as we do not see the horizon directly, we are unable to see God directly. Nonetheless he is always there. As Absolute Mystery, he forms the backdrop for our lives. Rahner believed that we come to know God through the deep mystery and complexity

© Iakov Kalinin / shutterstock.com

of the universe. Natural revelation, paired with human reason, helps us to become aware of a God of awesome depth who wants to be known.

Can you think of another metaphor, besides the image of the horizon, to explain God's mystery?

Karl Rahner spoke of God as the "horizon of being." How would you explain what this means to someone who has never heard the phrase?

Chapter Review

1. What is natural revelation?

2. How does the Book of Wisdom support the concept of natural revelation?

3. Why is natural revelation alone insufficient for us to know God fully?

4. How do the Church Fathers explain human beings' place as the summit of creation?

5. What was the goal of scholastic theology?

6. List and give a brief explanation of the five proofs for the existence of God given by Saint Thomas Aquinas.

7. What did the Pope and bishops reassert at Vatican Council I about the relationship between faith and reason?

Divine Revelation

Introduction

As we have seen, God makes himself known to us in many ways through the natural order, informed by our God-given intellect. However, we can only know God in a limited way through natural revelation. That is why, in the fullness of his love, he has also freely chosen to reveal himself and his plan for humanity more directly. This is called Divine Revelation.

We study Divine Revelation in a course about the Bible because Sacred Scripture contains the written accounts of God's Revelation to the Jewish People and the first Christians. But we also must recognize that the Bible itself is not the fullness of Divine Revelation. The definitive and most exquisite moment in the Revelation of God took place when the Word of God, the Second Person of the Trinity, became flesh. Jesus Christ is the fullness of Divine Revelation and salvation. He forged a new path for all of us to follow. This is the same path the Apostles and their successors, the bishops, have followed. Guided by the Holy Spirit, the Church is called to continually teach and live the mysteries revealed by Christ. Together Sacred Scripture and Sacred Tradition are the means by which Divine Revelation is transmitted to every generation.

Article 9: Salvation History: God's Revelation

Many of us are lucky enough to have storytellers in our families. From these people we learn our family history. We may hear about how our parents fell in love and how our grandparents survived tough times. We may also hear stories of pain and conflict within the family, caused by selfishness and greed. If we listen carefully, these stories help us to understand who we are, whom we can model our lives after, and what family pitfalls to avoid.

But we are also part of a much larger and more important history. The Church calls this **salvation history**. Salvation history tells us how God's saving hand has been at work in and through human history. In a general sense, we can say that all human history is salvation history. By this we mean that the one true God—Father, Son, and Holy Spirit—has been present and active in the lives of all his people since the beginning of time. But salvation history is more precisely understood as the pattern of specific events in human history in which God clearly revealed his presence and saving actions. Salvation was accomplished once and for all through Jesus Christ, a truth **foreshadowed** and revealed throughout the Old Testament.

At the heart of salvation history is **Divine Revelation**. Over time God revealed the fullness of his loving plan to save the human race from our bondage to sin and death. "God has revealed himself to man by gradually communicating his own mystery in deeds and in words" (CCC, 69). Divine Revelation, also called supernatural Revelation, is our window into the wisdom and knowledge of God. Although Divine Revelation happened in a gradual way, the Father chose to fully disclose himself and his plan through the life, Passion, Death, Resurrection, and Ascension of his Divine Son, Jesus Christ. He did this so we can share in his divine nature and his eternal life. God alone has revealed to us the central mystery of the Christian faith—the mystery of the **Trinity**—by revealing

salvation history
The pattern of specific events in human history in which God clearly reveals his presence and saving actions. Salvation was accomplished once and for all through Jesus Christ, a truth foreshadowed and revealed throughout the Old Testament.

foreshadow
To represent or prefigure a person before his or her life or an event before it occurs.

Divine Revelation
God's self-communication through which he makes known the mystery of his divine plan. Divine Revelation is a gift accomplished by the Father, Son, and Holy Spirit through the words and deeds of salvation history. It is most fully realized in the Passion, Death, Resurrection, and Ascension of Jesus Christ.

Trinity
From the Latin *trinus,* meaning "threefold," referring to the central mystery of the Christian faith that God exists as a communion of three distinct and interrelated Divine Persons: Father, Son, and Holy Spirit. The doctrine of the Trinity is a mystery that is inaccessible to human reason alone and is known through Divine Revelation only.

himself as Father, Son, and Holy Spirit. There will be no new Revelation until Jesus Christ comes again in glory.

As salvation history has unfolded, God has continually invited us into communion with the Blessed Trinity through both actions and words. Salvation history tells us about God, who heals, refreshes, transforms, speaks to, reveals himself to, and saves us. God revealed his name to our ancestors in ways beyond human imagination—from the time he disclosed his divine name to Moses in the **theophany** of the burning bush to the time the angels heralded the name of Jesus Christ, God Incarnate.

Out of love for us, his children, God has provided the definitive and complete answer to our universal questions about the meaning and purpose of our lives. God reveals himself especially in Jesus Christ, who is himself God, to help us know and love him beyond our own ability to do so. Yet despite his Revelation of himself, God remains a mystery, one that we can never fully grasp. He stretches our hearts and minds so there is immeasurable space for divine knowledge and love, yet human language can never capture the magnificence of our transcendent God.

Live It!
God's Hand in My History

If we believe God's saving hand has been active throughout all of history, then that means it has been active in our own individual lives as well. God is often present to us through the people and events in our lives. Prayerfully reflecting on this can be a good spiritual exercise.

One way to do this is by charting your own personal history as a journaling activity. Begin by reflecting on your life. Then tell your story in terms of the people or events that have brought you closer to God. Remember that our relationship with God is not always sweet and rosy, but even the events we might have perceived as negative at one time can strengthen our relationship with God. How do you see God's hand working in your life?

In the words of John Henry Cardinal Newman, "As prayer is the voice of [human beings] to God, so revelation is the voice of God to man." Divine Revelation is the voice of God, who has revealed himself as Truth and Love. He is trying to get our attention and attract our souls. God wants us to know truth, beauty, goodness, and peace. He knows these can be found only in his revealed Word of Life, Jesus Christ. Divine Revelation is about God's love for his most perfect creations: each of us.

How is God trying to get your attention?

theophany
God's manifestation of himself in a visible form to enrich human understanding of him. An example is God's appearance to Moses in the form of a burning bush.

Article 10: Salvation History in the Old Testament

Salvation history, as recorded in Sacred Scripture, reveals God's love for his people. Sacred Scripture—the Old and New Testaments—roots us in God's Divine Revelation to those who have gone before us. This is why we study the Bible: to learn about God's self-communication to us and his countless saving actions on our behalf. Every time we read or hear the Word of God, we are led ever deeper into the mystery and wonder of God. Let's first look at how the Old Testament, the words of our ancestors in faith, reveals the truth of God.

Old Testament Highlights

Salvation history begins with our first parents, whom we know by the symbolic names of Adam and Eve. Even though all his creation continually provides evidence of his existence, God wanted to further manifest himself to our first parents. "He invited them to intimate communion with himself and clothed them with resplendent grace and justice" (CCC, 54). Even when Adam and Eve turned away from God in sin, God remained faithful to them and promised them his salvation (see Genesis 3:15). The sin of Adam and Eve is called Original Sin. It led to the loss of original holiness, made humans subject to death, and made sin universally present in the world.

covenant
A solemn agreement between human beings or between God and a human being in which mutual commitments are made.

The account of Noah and the Flood is an important part of salvation history. Why did sin become so widespread? How does the story of Noah give us hope?

This universally present sin led to further sin among God's people. Their sins resulted in broken communities and families and in their separation from God. Yet despite their sinful actions, God still heard the cries of his People and offered them the hope of salvation.

Salvation history continues with the account of Noah. We learn how sin was spreading throughout the whole world, making all people wicked and corrupt. God intended to destroy his creation through a great Flood. However, God gave Noah, the one remaining good and righteous man, instructions to build an ark that would save him and his family from disaster. Both the instructions and the rainbow that appeared at the end of the Flood symbolize God's **covenant** with all living beings—a covenant nourished by God's self-disclosure. This covenant will last until the end of time.

Generations after the Flood, salvation history tells us, God scattered and divided humanity. He did so because of human pride, symbolized by the building of the Tower of Babel. Then God began his plan to reconcile all humanity with himself by calling a special people to be his light to the nations. Thus he entered into a covenant with the **patriarch** Abraham. God appeared to Abraham in a vision, promising him descendants more numerous than the stars. God made this promise even though Abraham's wife, Sarah, was unable to have children. Because Abraham was a man of great faith and righteousness, he obeyed God. His obedience resulted in a bloodline of charismatic patriarchs, including Isaac and Jacob. It also helped Abraham to gain land that yielded in abundance.

© Bequest of Lisa Norris Elkins, 1950 / Bridgeman Images

Salvation history continues with the well-known account of Moses and the Exodus. After freeing the Israelites from slavery in Egypt, God entered into a covenant with these descendants of Abraham, who were now known as the Israelites. At Mount Sinai, God gave Moses the Law as the people's part of the covenant. The Law is summarized in the Ten Commandments. Christians call this Law the Old Law, and we call this covenant the Old Covenant. This covenant gave the people an identity as the Chosen, Holy Children of God. Through Divine Revelation, God promised to remain faithful to the covenant and never to cease calling the Israelites to be faithful.

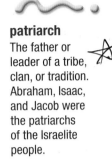

patriarch
The father or leader of a tribe, clan, or tradition. Abraham, Isaac, and Jacob were the patriarchs of the Israelite people.

Faith in Action
Story of a Soul

© Paul Matthew Photography / Shutterstock.com

Saint Thérèse of Lisieux, known as the Little Flower of Jesus, was a Carmelite nun and a woman of profound wisdom. Her life on this earth was brief, but she became known to the world through her autobiography, *Story of a Soul*. Her superiors had recognized her unique holiness and directed her to write it. In the book she shares with us the many ways God revealed himself to her simple soul. She describes a path, called "the little way," in which she explains how every charitable action performed for God is a manifestation of God's existence. In *Story of a Soul,* she describes her fear that she could not measure up to the holiness of the great saints of the Church. But instead of giving up, she writes, she looked for "some means of going to heaven by a little way which is very short and very straight, a little way that is quite new." Her "little way" of practicing true charity is one factor that earned her the title Doctor of the Church.

The manner in which God made himself known to Saint Thérèse is known as private revelation. This is distinct from Divine Revelation. Private revelations help people to live more fully at certain times in history, but they do not add to or change Christ's definitive Revelation.

prophet
A person God chooses to speak his message of salvation. In the Bible, primarily a communicator of a divine message of repentance to the Chosen People, not necessarily a person who predicted the future.

Although God revealed his will and plan to Adam, Eve, Abraham, and Moses, one obstacle continued to stand in the way of God's plan: humanity's tendency to sin, as a result of Original Sin. The Israelites repeatedly turned away from the covenant and the Law. In response, God revealed himself to the **prophets**, people like Isaiah, Jeremiah, and Ezekiel. He called the prophets to speak God's Word and to announce the "radical redemption of the People of God, purification from all their infidelities, a salvation which will include all the nations[4]" (CCC, 64).

Further Hints of Salvation

In addition to the historical accounts just described, we also find hints of salvation in the group of Old Testament books called **wisdom literature**. Wisdom literature, as you might imagine, refers to Israelite writings that extol

Pray It!

Help Me to Know You, Jesus

It can be hard to imagine the awesomeness and immensity of God. Focusing on building a relationship with Jesus Christ, his Son, is sometimes easier. We know that Jesus is the fullness of Divine Revelation, the Second Divine Person of the Trinity. But because he became man, we sometimes find Jesus easier to talk to—knowing that he experienced human joy, sorrow, and fear, just as we do. Use this prayer to ask Jesus to help you know him. Then talk to Jesus about your day, sharing your joys and frustrations like you would with any friend.

Jesus, the Good Shepherd:
Open my eyes,
    that I might see your glorious light.
Open my mind,
    that I may know your truth.
Open my heart,
    that I might receive your healing touch.
And open my ears,
    that I might hear you say,
      "I love you."
Amen.

(*The Catholic Youth Prayer Book,* page 13)

the virtue of wisdom and give practical advice on what it means to be wise. Wisdom literature speaks of a God who intervenes and discloses himself in the events of people's lives. We find God's divine wisdom crying "aloud in the street" (Proverbs 1:20), trying to catch the attention of his beloved children.

Wisdom is sometimes personified in the wisdom literature. The word *personify* means to describe something as one might describe a human being. You can find examples in Proverbs 1:20–21 and Wisdom 6:12–14. This personification of wisdom is fully realized in Jesus Christ, the Son of God, who is the Wisdom of God (see 1 Corinthians 1:30).

wisdom literature
The Old Testament books of Proverbs, Job, Ecclesiastes, Sirach, and the Wisdom of Solomon.

> **Which events from salvation history do you want to read about again in the Old Testament, or perhaps read for the first time? Why?**

Article 11: Jesus Christ: The Fullness of All Revelation

> And the Word became flesh
> and made his dwelling among us
> and we saw his glory,
> the glory as of the Father's only Son,
> full of grace and truth.
> (John 1:14)

> And a voice came from the heavens, saying, "This is my beloved Son, with whom I am well pleased."
> (Matthew 3:17)

As you can see in these two quotations from the Gospels, Sacred Scripture reveals that Jesus Christ is the Son of God. This title describes the unique and eternal relationship between God the Father and Jesus Christ, the Second Divine Person of the Trinity. Jesus Christ is the only Son of the Father, and he is God himself. He is the perfect image of the Father and is the fullness of Divine Revelation (see John 14:8–11). As the *Catechism* explains: "God has revealed himself fully by sending his own Son, in whom he has established his covenant for ever. The Son is his Father's definitive Word; so there will be no further Revelation after him" (73). Jesus Christ is "the Father's one, perfect, and unsurpassable Word. In him he has said everything; there will be no other word than this one" (65). Because Christ, the Son of God, humbled himself in taking on our humanity, we have been invited into communion with the Blessed Trinity in a whole new way.

The Definitive and Transforming Word

All salvation history, as contained in Sacred Scripture, speaks of one single Word, a transforming Word. This Word is the Second Divine Person of the Trinity, God himself, who came to dwell among us by assuming a human nature. The same Word who created the universe and revealed himself to the sacred writers of Sacred Scripture is Jesus Christ. All of Sacred Scripture, therefore, bears witness to Jesus Christ—the First and Last, the definitive Word of Revelation.

In the life of Jesus Christ, described in the Gospels, we especially see the glory of God. The Word being born in a lowly stable, the Word welcoming the sinner, the Word healing pain and naming demons, the Word washing the feet of friends, the Word hanging on a cross, and the Word rising from the dead—these all reveal a God who chose to reveal himself by taking on our humanity. In the Gospels we learn how God's Word, by revealing himself in the flesh, came to nurse our pain, bandage our limitations, and counsel our souls. There is no greater Word, and no greater Word can ever be imagined.

Full of Grace and Truth

Wouldn't it be nice if God's grace and truth came with an instruction manual? Good news—we already have one. Because he is the definitive Word of God, we can think of Jesus Christ as our instruction manual for interpreting all creation and its final end. When we study the life of Jesus

Christ, who reveals the New Covenant, we come to know the fullness of salvation. We cannot fully understand this plan in our lifetime. But by developing a relationship with Jesus Christ, we come to know his free offer of grace, which enlightens the human mind and heart.

The Gospels use many images to convey the truth of Jesus' identity as the culmination of Divine Revelation. Shepherd, Friend, Savior, Doctor, Bread, Vine, Gate, and Light—all these images point to Jesus, the Son of God, who perfectly reflects and reveals his Father. He is the Word that can free us from all that enslaves us.

© Netfalls - Remy Musser / Shutterstock.com

Like Saint Patrick of Ireland, let us bind ourselves to Christ, the Eternal Word of God:

> I bind to myself today
> The virtue of the Incarnation of Christ with that of his Baptism,
> The virtue of His Crucifixion with that of His Burial,
> The virtue of His Resurrection with that of His Ascension,
> The virtue of His Coming on the Judgment Day.
> (from "Saint Patrick's Breastplate")

How do the images for Jesus used in the Gospels help you to understand who he is?

In this Greek icon, the top letters—*IC XC*—are abbreviations for the Greek spelling of Jesus Christ. The three letters in the halo—*O W N*—are an abbreviation for "He Who Is." What does this title tell us about Jesus Christ?

Article 12: The Church and the Transmission of Divine Revelation

"What I say to you in the darkness, speak in the light; what you hear whispered, proclaim on the housetops."
(Matthew 10:27)

Do you know what Jesus was asking of the Apostles in this quotation from Matthew? Jesus Christ, the fullness of Divine Revelation, commanded the Apostles to tell all people and all nations what they heard and saw regarding

Sacred Tradition

Tradition comes from the Latin *tradere*, meaning "to hand on." Sacred Tradition refers to the process of passing on the Gospel message. It began with the oral communication of the Gospel by the Apostles, was written down in Sacred Scripture, and is interpreted by the Magisterium under the guidance of the Holy Spirit.

Apostolic Succession

The uninterrupted passing on of apostolic preaching and authority from the Apostles directly to all bishops. It is accomplished through the laying on of hands when a bishop is ordained in the Sacrament of Holy Orders as instituted by Christ. The office of bishop is permanent, because at ordination a bishop is marked with an indelible, sacred character.

the salvation of God. He entrusted them with the gift of the Holy Spirit to empower them to authentically teach and interpret the sacred truths revealed through his teachings and actions during his earthly life and through the events of the **Paschal Mystery**—Jesus' Passion, Death, Resurrection, and Ascension. As they moved from village to village, city to city, the Apostles helped more and more people believe in Jesus Christ through their preaching and writing, inspired by the Holy Spirit. This handing on, or transmission, of the truths Jesus Christ taught is known as **Sacred Tradition**. By the power of the Holy Spirit, Sacred Tradition will continue to be transmitted to each new generation until Christ returns in glory.

Through the process of **Apostolic Succession**, the original Apostles have passed on their authority to their successors, the bishops of the Church. Every bishop of the Church can trace his special authority back to the original Twelve Apostles in an unbroken chain of succession through the laying on of hands in the Sacrament of Holy Orders as instituted by Christ. The office of bishop is permanent because this Sacrament marks a bishop with an indelible, sacred character. In the Sacrament of Holy Orders, the Holy Spirit empowers a bishop with the gifts needed to fulfill his role in the Church, including the gift of authentically teaching and interpreting Sacred Scripture and Sacred Tradition. As true successors to the Apostles who are guided by the Holy Spirit, the bishops, in communion with the Pope, witness to, and develop a deeper understanding of, God's self-revelation in the Church's life, doctrine, and worship.

Tradition helps us to understand the Revelation of Jesus Christ found in Scripture. Through Tradition and the leadership of the bishops as teachers and interpreters, the Church proclaims the redemption found in Jesus Christ. It is through her life, teachings, and liturgy that she "perpetuates and transmits to every generation all that she herself is, all that she believes⁵" (CCC, 78).

In fulfilling this mission, the Church is guided by the Holy Spirit. The God who spoke to people of the past continues to communicate with men and women through the Holy Spirit. The Holy Spirit ignites the hearts of believers with a fire. Jesus sent the Holy Spirit as our Advocate when the hour of his glorification arrived (see John 14:15–17), and the Holy Spirit continues to enliven and manifest all that has been revealed in Jesus Christ, the Word Made Flesh. The Holy Spirit proceeds from the Father and the Son, guides the Church into the fullness of God's revealed truth, and opens the hearts and minds of God's people to know the truth he has revealed and to faithfully live as his own people.

Paschal Mystery
The work of salvation accomplished by Jesus Christ mainly through his Passion, Death, Resurrection, and Ascension.

How can you be more open to the power of the Holy Spirit in your own life of faith?

Article 13: Scripture and Tradition: The Two Pillars of God's Revelation

What exactly is the difference between Sacred Tradition and Sacred Scripture? Why do Catholics have beliefs and practices that are not in the Bible? Earlier in this chapter, you learned that Sacred Tradition is the handing on, or transmission, of the truths Jesus Christ taught us. Put more simply, Sacred Tradition teaches us the fullness of Divine Revelation. It began with the preaching of the Gospel by the Apostles, was written in Sacred Scripture, continues to be handed down and lived out in the life of the Church, and is interpreted by the Magisterium under the guidance of the Holy Spirit. Notice that Sacred Scripture developed from Sacred Tradition. However, the Bible alone does not communicate everything God reveals through Sacred Tradition. In conversation with Scripture, Tradition passes on the message of the Gospel to be lived out in the life of the Church.

© Duncan Walker / iStockphoto.com

At the Last Supper, Jesus commanded the Apostles to "do this in memory of me" (Luke 22:19). The Apostles fulfilled this command even at the cost of their lives.

redemption, redemptive
From the Latin *redemptio,* meaning "a buying back," referring, in the Old Testament, to Yahweh's deliverance of Israel and, in the New Testament, to Christ's deliverance of all Christians from the forces of sin.

As Catholics we are blessed in recognizing that God has chosen to disclose the truths of Revelation through both Sacred Tradition and Sacred Scripture. "There exists a close connection and communication between Sacred Tradition and Sacred Scripture," both of them "flowing from the same divine wellspring" *(Dogmatic Constitution on Divine Revelation [Dei Verbum,* 1965], 9). They communicate the whole of God's **redemptive** and reconciling love. Together "Sacred Tradition and Sacred Scripture make up a single sacred deposit of the Word of God" (10). This deposit of the Word of God enables the Church to contemplate God, the source of everything she is, does, and believes.

Are you beginning to see how Sacred Scripture and Sacred Tradition are intimately bound? They are two pillars of strength that hold up the Church as a light for all to know the mystery of Christ. These two pillars—the written, inspired Word of God and the living transmission of the Word of God—effectively communicate the

Did You Know?

© Victorian Traditions / shutterstock.com

Mary, the Mother of God

Within the Tradition of the Church lies a special devotion to the Blessed Virgin Mary. Devotion to the Blessed Mother is found in liturgical feasts and in prayers like the Rosary. Because of the teachings of the Apostles, we have come to realize the significant role Mary played in salvation. By saying yes to God's call to be the mother of his Son, Mary opened the doors to Heaven. She miraculously conceived by the power of the Holy Spirit, and she gave birth to Jesus Christ, the Eternal Son of God Made Flesh. Thus Mary remained a virgin through the conception and birth of Jesus and throughout her entire life. Mary is honored as the *Theotokos,* Greek for "God-bearer"—a title affirming that as the mother of Jesus Christ, who is God himself, Mary is the Mother of God. Sacred Scripture and Sacred Tradition lift up Mary as a model of humble faith and amazing courage.

whole of God's Revelation. Neither pillar can be understood without the other. Therefore each is "to be accepted and venerated with the same sense of loyalty and reverence" (*Divine Revelation*, 9).

The Deposit of Faith

The ***Deposit of Faith*** is a term we use to describe the heritage of faith contained in Sacred Scripture and Sacred Tradition. The task of interpreting the Deposit of Faith is entrusted to the Magisterium. The Magisterium—the "living teaching office of the Church" (*Divine Revelation*, 10)—is made up of the Pope and all the bishops in communion with him under the guidance of the Holy Spirit. Both individually and collectively, the bishops of the Church have the unique obligation and right to authentically teach and interpret Scripture and Tradition. Thus the Magisterium, rooted in its teaching authority and moved by the Holy Spirit, defines the **dogma**, or doctrine, of the faith.

Faith is necessary for our salvation. Our faith rests in Jesus Christ and the One who sent him. "For God so loved the world that he gave his only Son, so that everyone who believes in him might not perish but might have eternal life" (John 3:16). The Deposit of Faith contained in Sacred Scripture and Sacred Tradition nurtures our faith with the sacred truth revealed by God.

Sacred Tradition Is Faithful to Sacred Scripture

As you can see, it is not accurate to say that some Catholic beliefs and practices are not faithful to the Bible. Everything that is part of Sacred Tradition manifests what was disclosed through Jesus' teachings and actions during his earthly ministry and during the events of the Paschal Mystery. Nothing the Church teaches or proclaims ever contradicts the truth of Jesus Christ. In the words of the *Catechism*, Sacred Tradition and Sacred Scripture make "present and fruitful in the Church the mystery of Christ, who promised to remain with his own

Deposit of Faith
The heritage of faith contained in Sacred Scripture and Sacred Tradition. It has been passed on from the time of the Apostles. The Magisterium takes from it all that it teaches as revealed truth.

dogma
Teachings recognized as central to Church teaching, defined by the Magisterium and considered definitive and authoritative.

'always, to the close of the age'[6]" (80). What an amazing Church to be a part of!

How do you understand the difference between tradition and Tradition?

Article 14: The Vocation of All

Saint Vincent of Lérins stated: "Keep the talent of the Catholic faith inviolate and unimpaired. What has been faithfully entrusted, let it remain in your possession, let it be handed on." By virtue of our Baptism, we are all called to treasure our faith as a priceless gem. We are to hold it in the treasure chest of our lives. We are also to share the gem with others. In this way we can bring forth the light and radiance of Jesus revealed through Sacred Scripture and Sacred Tradition. The Church "cannot err in matters

Primary Sources

Saint John Chrysostom on Sacred Tradition

© HIP / Art Resource, NY

You might wonder why the Church's Tradition is as important for our faith as Sacred Scripture is. After all, Scripture is the result of divine inspiration—but is Tradition? Let's consider an insight from Saint John Chrysostom. Chrysostom was an early Church Father and Doctor of the Church known for his wonderful preaching, his work in liturgical theology, and his fierce arguments against political and Church abuse:

> "Therefore, brethren, stand fast and hold the traditions that you have been taught, whether by word or by our letter" [2 Thessalonians 2:15].

From this it is clear that they [the early Church] did not hand down everything by letter, but there was much also that was not written. Like that which was written, the unwritten too is worthy of belief. So let us regard the tradition of the Church also as worthy of belief.

(Homily IV on 2 Thessalonians)

of belief" (*Dogmatic Constitution on the Church [Lumen Gentium, 1964]*, 12), because the Holy Spirit guides her in the ways of truth and righteousness. Gifted by Apostolic Succession and led by the universal call to holiness, the entire Church—which includes each one of us—must speak what she has heard, in the light and from the housetops.

© Christopher Futcher / shutterstock.com

How do you speak the truth of your faith in your own life?

We all share in the responsibility to learn about God's revealed truth and to share it with others. Besides in classes at school, how do you continue to learn about your faith?

Chapter Review

1. What is Divine Revelation?

2. What is salvation history?

3. What is Original Sin, and what are some of the consequences of Original Sin?

4. What is Sacred Tradition?

5. What is the relationship between Sacred Scripture, Sacred Tradition, and Revelation?

6. What is the Deposit of Faith?

7. What is the Magisterium? What is the Magisterium's responsibility in regard to Sacred Scripture and Sacred Tradition?

Through natural revelation and Divine Revelation, we can fulfill our deep longing to know God. We study Sacred Scripture, the inspired Word of God, because it reveals who God is and his plan for our salvation. Human authors wrote the sacred books of the Bible in the language and styles of their own times, but they did so under the inspiration of the Holy Spirit. That means God is the ultimate and supreme author of the Bible, which is free from error with regard to the truths he reveals for our salvation.

The early Church identified seventy-three books that provide us with authentic Revelation and truth and therefore belong to Sacred Scripture: forty-six Old Testament books and twenty-seven New Testament books. The Magisterium, the teaching office of the Church, is solely responsible for authentically interpreting Scripture to understand the truth God reveals to us. The Church interprets Sacred Scripture in light of her Tradition, the inspiration of the Holy Spirit, and the cultural context of the human authors of the sacred books.

Both Testaments are essential for helping us to understand the Incarnation of God's Word. The Old Testament beautifully reveals God's saving action in the lives of the Israelites before the coming of Christ. In the New Testament, we learn that Jesus Christ is the New Covenant who fulfills God's covenant with the Jewish People.

The enduring understandings and essential questions represent core concepts and questions that are explored throughout this unit. By studying the content of each chapter, you will gain a more complete understanding of the following:

Enduring Understandings

1. The collection of books in the Bible was written over a long period of time by human authors who were inspired by God.

2. Biblical exegesis helps us to understand the meaning of Sacred Scripture.

3. The Old Testament recounts the relationship between God and the ancient Israelites.

4. The New Testament focuses on the mission of Jesus Christ and the development of the early Christian communities.

Essential Questions

1. Who wrote the Bible?

2. How are we supposed to read Sacred Scripture?

3. What can Christians learn from the Old Testament?

4. How can study of the New Testament enrich one's faith life?

Chapter 4

Understanding Sacred Scripture

Introduction

In Sacred Scripture we find the account of God's saving hand at work in human history and experience. God is the Bible's sole and supreme author. Without error, Sacred Scripture teaches and proclaims the truths God wishes to reveal for the sake of our salvation. The Holy Spirit inspired the human authors of the sacred books, who used their God-given human knowledge and intelligence to communicate the particular truths entrusted to them. Even though it is written in the language and styles of particular times and cultures, all of Sacred Scripture reveals to us the truth of who God is and of his work of salvation.

The canon of the Bible consists of forty-six Old Testament books and twenty-seven New Testament books. The contents of the canon were discerned based on their authentic Revelation and truth. Inspired by God, inerrant in truth, defined in number, and appearing in different translations, the texts of both the Old and New Testaments lead us to right understanding of God's Incarnate Word.

Article 15: Divine Inspiration and Biblical Inerrancy

Writers and artists sometimes talk about a time when they were inspired. This usually means that a person or event prompted them to create something unique or helped them to write especially well. Maybe you have felt that way while working on a project or school assignment.

But the Bible's inspiration is unique. The Holy Spirit, the Third Person of the Trinity, inspired the human authors who wrote the Bible's books. We call this **Divine Inspiration** because God himself is the ultimate author of Sacred Scripture. Thus the books of Sacred Scripture "without error teach that truth which God, for the sake of our salvation, wished to see confided to the Sacred Scriptures" (*Dogmatic Constitution on Divine Revelation [Dei Verbum, 1965]*, 11).

Divine Inspiration
The divine assistance the Holy Spirit gave the authors of the books of the Bible so the authors could write in human words the message of salvation God wanted to communicate.

The Author of Sacred Scripture

God chose ordinary and often unsuspecting people to write the books of the Bible. The Holy Spirit "breathed into" (the literal meaning of *inspired*) human beings the ways and truths of God. Does this mean that the human authors were only human word processors, recording words the Holy Spirit dictated to them? Not at all! They kept full use of their human knowledge and creativity. The Bible's human authors were true authors. But in a marvelous way, God acted in them and through them as they wrote about the origins of creation and sin, the relevance of wisdom and prophecy, and the saving work of Jesus Christ, the Eternal Son of God Made Flesh.

Within the words of Scripture, therefore, lies the delicacy of God's wisdom. His wisdom is absolute and without error. Even though human authors wrote the words, God is the ultimate author, and the saving truths he willed us to know are inerrant (that is, without error). In other words, the books of the Bible teach us the truths of our faith accurately and without mistake. This is called **biblical inerrancy**.

**biblical
inerrancy**
The doctrine
that the books of
Sacred Scripture
are free from error
regarding the
truth God wishes
to reveal through
Scripture for the
sake of our salva-
tion.

Through the Medium of Human Words

In Sacred Scripture we come to know the amazing works of God: the Father, Son, and Holy Spirit. We are able to understand God's Revelation because in Sacred Scripture he speaks to us using human words. It is a sign of God's tremendous respect for us that he uses human language and symbols to share his saving grace.

Yet we must keep in mind the ways culture and time affect the Bible's words. The human authors used the languages, feelings, assumptions, and communication styles of their times and cultures. We need to study all these factors to understand what the authors intended to communicate. As we do so, we must also realize that the human authors themselves may not have been aware of the deeper truths God was communicating through them. Understanding only what the human authors intended to communicate is not enough. For a correct interpretation of Sacred Scripture, we must also look for the truth that God wanted to reveal to us through the authors' words. As the *Catechism* explains, "Sacred Scripture must be read and interpreted in the light of the same Spirit by whom it was written[1]" (111).

> **What inspires you? What does it mean to be inspired by God?**

Live It!
Serving as Lector

Each time we gather to celebrate Mass, we hear the Word of God. Lectoring, or proclaiming the sacred Word during Mass, is one way some members of the assembly are called to participate. Lectors proclaim the first and second readings. In preparation, lectors immerse themselves in the Scripture passages by reading and praying with them. Perhaps God is calling you to serve as a lector in your parish or school chapel. Pray about it and, if you are interested, let your pastor or campus minister know.

Article 16: From the Spoken to the Written Word

Communication is essential to the survival of the human race. We have spent several thousand years developing new ways to exchange stories, thoughts, and feelings. Today our technological advances allow us to communicate through phones, e-mails, text messages, websites, television and radio shows, and in so many other digital ways. We have developed these methods to help us connect with one another. However, even with these new ways to connect, there are still three basic forms of communication: nonverbal actions, the spoken word, and the written word. These three types of communication were instrumental in the development of Sacred Scripture as we know it today.

It All Starts with an Experience

Before anything can ever be spoken or written, human beings must have an experience. Central to the experiences of people during Old Testament times was their relationship with God. They experienced God as creator, liberator, and covenant maker. They also experienced God as warrior, father, beloved spouse, dancing wisdom, and herald of hope. Then, grounded in the heritage and wisdom of the past, the people of the Gospels personally saw and interacted with the Word Made Flesh, Jesus Christ. They gathered around Jesus with attentive ears and hearts, hearing and loving his healing words. Their journey was different from that of the people of the Old Testament. Yet both groups were instructed to tell the world about God's saving action.

From Experience to the Spoken Word

The Israelites originally handed down their experience of God orally—that is, by word of mouth. During Old Testament times, few people could read and write. Consequently the people relied heavily on hearing and passing on the spoken words of their ancestors. Some of the methods they used were prophesying, preaching,

oral tradition
The handing on of the message of God's saving plan through words and deeds.

written tradition
Under the inspiration of the Holy Spirit, the synthesis in written form of the message of salvation that has been passed down in the oral tradition.

telling stories, and reciting poetry. Accounts of God's wonderful work on behalf of humanity were shared in families, social groups, and other gatherings. The Israelites also handed down their experience of God through the manner in which they worshipped and kept the covenants he made with them. This handing on of truth-filled, wisdom-filled words and deeds from generation to generation is called **oral tradition**.

In New Testament times, methods of communication were developing dramatically. More people were learning to read, and written communication was becoming more common and more accessible. Still, the spoken, proclaimed Word of Jesus was powerful and transforming. Indeed he sent his followers with the charge to proclaim the Word of God. In the Gospel of Mark, Jesus says, "Go into the whole world and proclaim the gospel to every creature" (16:15). The Acts of the Apostles describes how the Holy Spirit came to the Apostles in "tongues as of fire" (2:3) so they could speak to all people about God's great love. Notice that both passages emphasize speaking rather than writing.

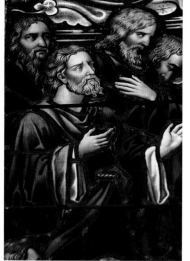

© Leah-Anne Thompson / iStockphoto.com

The Apostles preached the Good News to others after Jesus' Ascension. How do you see the Good News being shared today?

From the Spoken Word to the Written Word

In both Old and New Testament times, people wanted to preserve God's message of salvation for later generations. This is how the **written tradition** began. Through the inspiration of the Holy Spirit, people wrote down God's Revelation to his children. The early Christians were especially concerned about protecting and safeguarding the message of Jesus Christ. Many who had known Jesus personally were being persecuted and put to death for their faith. The early Christians did not want to lose the perspective and testimonies of these witnesses to the life and mission of our Lord and Savior, Jesus Christ.

Let's look at the Gospels as an example of this pro-gression from original experience to spoken word and then to written account:

1. **The life and teachings of Jesus** Jesus, the Son of God, walked the earth, teaching and preaching the truth of salvation.

2. **The oral tradition** The Apostles, enlightened by the Holy Spirit, traveled throughout the Roman Empire, preaching and teaching. They handed on to their hearers all that Jesus had revealed.

Pray It!

Praying with the Psalms

It can be uplifting and comforting to pray with the psalms, especially when we don't know where to begin. Pray with Psalm 23 from *The Revised Grail Psalms* (see the Faith in Action sidebar in this chapter). This psalm has helped people to find peace and encouragement for centuries:

The LORD is my shepherd;
there is nothing I shall want.
Fresh and green are the pastures
where he gives me repose.
Near restful waters he leads me;
he revives my soul.
He guides me along the right path,
for the sake of his name.
Though I should walk in the valley of the shadow of death,
no evil would I fear, for you are with me.
Your crook and your staff will give me comfort.
You have prepared a table before me
in the sight of my foes.
My head you have anointed with oil;
my cup is overflowing.
Surely goodness and mercy shall follow me
all the days of my life.
In the LORD's own house shall I dwell
for length of days unending.

© Brooklyn Museum of Art, New York, USA /
Bridgeman Images

3. **The written Gospels** Under the guidance
of the Holy Spirit and without error, the
Evangelists wrote down the Gospels to syn-
thesize the oral teachings of the Church, as
well as some earlier writings, regarding the
Incarnate Word of God, Jesus Christ.

From experience to speech to writing, salvation history has been recorded and handed
on. The spoken and written traditions have
communicated the deep seed of God's wisdom for more than two thousand years. These
traditions continue to pave the way into each new
millennium and each new day.

**Enlightened by the Holy Spirit, the Apostles
preached the faith. How does the Holy Spirit inspire
you to spread the Gospel message?**

Article 17: When Did It Happen? When Was It Written?

Have you ever had an experience that seemed insignificant at the time but later you realized its importance? We
may not recognize the saving action of God until we have
time to reflect on all that has happened to us. This was
equally true for the writers of the Bible.

The ancient Israelites and first Christians often
did not write down their personal experiences or their
ancestors' dealings with God. They did not understand
the larger implications of these experiences. Through
the intervention and inspiration of the Holy Spirit, the
writers of biblical texts began to recognize the need to
write down their people's experiences of God manifested
in creation, freedom, covenant, and Incarnation. This is
why many of the biblical books were written down years,

even centuries, after the events they describe. The following chart gives some examples:

Books	Period Covered	Date Written
Genesis	Creation–1500 BC	900–500 BC
Exodus	1500–1250 BC	900–500 BC
Prophetic Books	922–300 BC	865–300 BC
Gospels	5 BC–AD 30	AD 62–100
Paul's Letters	AD 51–100	AD 51–100

In addition, most books do not appear in the Bible in the order in which they were written. A number of Paul's letters (Romans, First and Second Corinthians, Galatians, Philippians, Colossians, and First and Second Thessalonians) were most likely written around AD 50–60—before the Gospels of Matthew, Mark, Luke, and John were written (AD 62–100). However, it makes sense to place the Gospels first in the New Testament, because they are eyewitness accounts of Jesus' life. Paul's letters cover the life of early Christians after the Death and Resurrection of Jesus Christ.

We must not become too concerned with the historical dates or arrangement of the sacred books. Instead we should pay attention to the overarching truth and cohesive picture of our compassionate God woven through the words of Sacred Scripture. It is good to have a sense of history and accuracy. It is better to know the ultimate, never ending, triumphant love God offers his people.

How can studying history help us to understand Sacred Scripture? How can it hinder our understanding?

Article 18: Setting the Canon of Scripture

Did you know that the Bible is one of the bestselling books of all time? The Bible continues to be the most widely read book in the world. It is the sacred text for

canon

The collection of books of the Bible that the Church recognizes as the inspired Word of God.

Christians: a collection of *biblia sacra* (Latin for "sacred books"). The **canon** of the Bible is the official collection of inspired books. It is an integral part of the Church's Tradition. The canon of the Catholic Bible is composed of forty-six Old Testament books and twenty-seven New Testament books. In these sacred books—composed by human authors under the inspiration of the Holy Spirit—we find God's self-Revelation to human beings. Sacred Scripture thus lays the foundation for the beliefs, practices, and customs of the Catholic faith.

But how do we know which ancient texts are sacred books that properly belong in Sacred Scripture? Three councils of the Church were instrumental in discerning the canon of Sacred Scripture as we know it today. They were the Council of Hippo (393), the Council of Carthage (397), and the Ecumenical Council of Trent (1543–1563). These councils contributed something unique to the discussion about the authenticity of particular books. Most interesting is that each council, in its own way, arrived at the same conclusive list of inspired books that belong in the canon of the Bible. It was not until the Ecumenical Council of Trent that an infallible

Did You Know?

Understanding the Gospel Writers' Context

Learning when a book of the Bible was written can help us to interpret it. For example, Mark probably wrote the first Gospel sometime between AD 65 and 70. At that time the faith of Christians was being tested by Roman persecution. This may be why Mark's Gospel emphasizes Jesus' faithfulness to his mission even when he was misunderstood and persecuted.

Or consider John's Gospel, likely the last Gospel, written sometime between AD 90 or 100. At this time many Jewish Christians were rejected by Jews who did not believe Jesus was the Messiah. These Jewish Christians were no longer allowed to worship in the synagogues. The Gospel of John emphasizes the importance of believing in Jesus and describes conflicts between Jesus and Jewish leaders who did not believe in him. John probably wanted to encourage the Jewish Christians to remain faithful despite rejection and conflict.

definition regarding the books included in the canon was declared.

Four Standards Used to Determine the Canon of Scripture

Occasionally the popular media and works of literature place before us stories about newly discovered "gospels." The contents of these gospels often contradict the truths we read in Sacred Scripture and the fundamental beliefs of Christianity. For this reason, it is important for us to understand how the Church identified the authentic canon.

In her earliest centuries, the Church identified which writings belong in the list of sacred books by examining each book in the light of Sacred Tradition. The early bishops, successors to the Apostles, used four standards to discern the validity of a book. A book had to pass all four standards to be considered divinely inspired and canonical (that is, part of the sacred canon). These four standards especially governed the New Testament writings.

1. Apostolic origin: The first standard required the book to be based on the preaching and teaching of the Apostles and their closest companions.
2. Community acceptance: Was the book accepted and received by all major Christian communities in the Mediterranean world? If Christians accepted it universally, then it passed this second standard.
3. Use in early Christian worship: The third standard revolved around the early Christian community's use of a text. Was the book being used in Christian liturgical celebrations? Most important, was it used when the faithful gathered for the **Eucharist**, also called the Mass? If early Christians were weaving a book into their worship, the early bishops concluded that it enhanced the prayer lives of the people.

Eucharist, the
The celebration of the entire Mass. The term can also refer specifically to the consecrated bread and wine that have become the Body and Blood of Christ.

Gnostic
Referring to the belief that salvation comes from secret knowledge available to only a select few.

Psalter
The Book of Psalms of the Old Testament, which contains 150 Psalms.

4. Consistency: The final standard involved delving deeply into the book to see whether its message was consistent with other Christian and Hebrew, or Jewish, writings.

When we know the standards the bishops used to determine the canon of the Bible, we can begin to see why some books were not selected. For instance, the **Gnostic** gospels were rejected because they placed little importance on the suffering and Death of Jesus. Christ's suffering and Death are essential for understanding God's full plan of salvation. These key events in his life must be emphasized so we can come to know God's redemptive work. Because the early Church undertook this discernment process so carefully, we can rest assured that the canon of Sacred Scripture is the true, authoritative record of God's saving plan.

> **Now that you know how the canon of Scripture was set, how does this enhance or otherwise change your understanding of the Bible?**

Article 19: Different Translations: The Same Revelation

Hebrew, Greek, Aramaic, Latin, Spanish, French, Mandarin, Russian, English—the world is filled with many languages and dialects. Translating one language to another is daunting, complex work at any time. But this task is especially challenging for individuals who translate the Bible from its original languages of Hebrew, Aramaic, and Greek. Because we place such high value on the inspired words in the Bible, translations are always completed by many people working with numerous ancient texts. The people who work on a particular translation bring their expertise and knowledge of the language to the task. The result is a diversity of biblical translations, but the truths of Divine Revelation are the same.

An early Greek translation of the Old Testament, called the Septuagint, and the New Testament, which was written in Greek, were used for many centuries in the early Church. After Saint Jerome translated the Old and New Testaments into Latin in the late fourth century AD, the Church used that translation—known as the Vulgate—for well over a thousand years. As a result of Vatican Council II, the Vulgate was revised to reflect new understandings of linguistics, history, and culture. This *Nova Vulgata*, or Neo-Vulgate (both *nova* and *neo* mean "new"), was published in its entirety in 1979. Today the Neo-Vulgate is the Church's official Latin text of the Bible.

Faith in Action
Faithfully Translating the Book of Psalms

© CEFutcher / iStockphoto.com

"Every translation is an interpretation." This saying means that one language can never precisely translate into another. Even so, Bible translators recognize their responsibility to translate the Word of God as exactly as possible. Certain books of the Bible pose special challenges for translators. For example, the Book of Psalms is a book of poetry. The original Hebrew has a certain rhythm, and a good translator will try to preserve that rhythm. But how?

Several decades ago, Joseph Gelineau, a French Jesuit priest, prepared a French translation of the psalms. The psalms were very rhythmic and easily sung. In response to Father Gelineau's work, the Ladies of the Grail, a Catholic women's group in England, undertook an English translation of the psalms that everyone could sing easily. Working with scholars and musicians, these faithful women translated the psalms from Hebrew into English. The result was the much-loved Grail **Psalter**, which was released in 1963.

With advances in biblical scholarship, a revised translation became necessary. This work was undertaken by the monks of Conception Abbey in Missouri. The revised translation, approved by the Vatican in 2010, closely reflects the original Hebrew, Greek, and Latin texts of Sacred Scripture. Eventually all liturgical books in the English-speaking world will include psalms from this official translation. In the years to come, you will be hearing and singing treasured psalms from the *Revised Grail Psalter* in your own parish.

If you go to your local bookstore today, of course, you might have a hard time finding the Latin edition. But you will find many different versions, or translations, of the Bible in many other languages—there are dozens of English translations alone. Usually each particular version, or translation, exists to serve a particular purpose. One translation's purpose might be to stay as faithful as possible to the original words, for the sake of accuracy. Another translation might use more contemporary words and phrases to promote easier understanding. A translation intended for children might use simpler words whenever possible. For this reason we consider several translations to be trustworthy and sound.

Among those, four Catholic biblical translations are widely used among modern English-speaking communities: the *New American Bible, Revised Edition (NABRE); the New Revised Standard Version, Catholic Edition (NRSV); the New Jerusalem Bible (NJB);* and the *Good News Translation in Today's English Version, Second Edition (GNT).* Despite differences in the language they use, these four translations present one message of God's saving love.

Primary Sources

The Church's Guidance on Translating Sacred Texts

How do translators of Sacred Scripture and Church writings know where to start? For one thing, they spend years studying the original languages and the art of translation, and they also become experts in ancient literary techniques, history, and culture. The Church has also provided clear rules for translators of Scripture and liturgical books. We find one important rule in "Liturgiam Authenticam," a 2001 instruction from the Congregation for Divine Worship and the Discipline of the Sacraments (an office in the Vatican):

> It is not permissible that the translations be produced from other translations already made into other languages; rather, the new translations must be made directly from the original texts, namely the Latin, as regards the texts of ecclesiastical [Church] composition, or the Hebrew, Aramaic, or Greek, as the case may be, as regards the texts of Sacred Scripture. (24)

Do you know which translation of the Bible is used most often by Catholics in the United States? The *New American Bible, Revised Edition* (NABRE) translation is probably used most widely. The NABRE, the translation used for most Bible passages in this book, is the same translation that appears on the website of the United States Conference of Catholic Bishops. The NABRE is also the translation used in readings from the Lectionary for Mass and the Book of the Gospels that we hear during Mass.

Even so, the NABRE is not used universally by English-speaking Catholics. Although the NABRE is the approved lectionary text for the United States, the NRSV is the approved lectionary text for Canada. The NJB is widely used outside the United States, and many throughout the world find it to be a wonderful asset to prayer because of its poetic nature. The GNT is used in many schools because it employs a more basic vocabulary and is more conversational in style. You can see the differences in these four biblical translations by examining their texts of Matthew 5:13–16.

Which of the following translations of the same passage do you find most appealing, and why?

Different Translations of Matthew 5:13–16

New American Bible, Revised Edition

The Similes of Salt and Light

"You are the salt of the earth. But if salt loses its taste, with what can it be seasoned? It is no longer good for anything but to be thrown out and trampled underfoot. You are the light of the world. A city set on a mountain cannot be hidden. Nor do they light a lamp and then put it under a bushel basket; it is set on a lampstand, where it gives light to all in the house. Just so, your light must shine before others, that they may see your good deeds and glorify your heavenly Father."

New Revised Standard Version

Salt and Light

"You are the salt of the earth; but if salt has lost its taste, how can its saltiness be restored? It is no longer good for anything, but is thrown out and trampled under foot.

"You are the light of the world. A city built on a hill cannot be hid. No one after lighting a lamp puts it under the bushel basket, but on the lampstand, and it gives light to all in the house. In the same way, let your light shine before others, so that they may see your good works and give glory to your Father in heaven."

New Jerusalem Bible

Salt for the Earth and Light for the World

"You are salt for the earth. But if salt loses its taste, what can make it salty again? It is good for nothing, and can only be thrown out to be trampled under people's feet.

"You are light for the world. A city built on a hill-top cannot be hidden.

No one lights a lamp to put it under a tub; they put it on the lamp-stand where it shines for everyone in the house.

In the same way your light must shine in people's sight, so that, seeing your good works, they may give praise to your Father in heaven."

Good News Translation

Salt and Light

"You are like salt for the whole human race. But if salt loses its saltiness, there is no way to make it salty again. It has become worthless, so it is thrown out and people trample on it.

"You are like light for the whole world. A city built on a hill cannot be hid. No one lights a lamp and puts it under a bowl; instead it is put on the lampstand, where it gives light for everyone in the house. In the same way your light must shine before people, so that they will see the good things you do and praise your Father in heaven."

Chapter Review

1. What is Divine Inspiration?

2. Who is the ultimate author of Sacred Scripture? Explain the relationship between the ultimate author and the human authors of Scripture.

3. What is the relationship between Divine Inspiration and biblical inerrancy?

4. What is the total number of books in the official canon of the Bible? How many make up the Old Testament? How many make up the New Testament?

5. List the three stages of the formation of the Gospels.

6. What standards did the early bishops use to discern which books belong in the canon of the Bible?

Chapter 5

Interpreting Sacred Scripture

Introduction

In Sacred Scripture—the Old Testament and New Testament—we begin to know the truth of who God is and what his plan is for our salvation. The truth God reveals in Sacred Scripture must be interpreted throughout time. The authentic interpretation of Scripture is entrusted to the Magisterium, the teaching office of the Church. The Magisterium interprets the meaning of a particular text within the Tradition and teachings of the Church and in the light of the Holy Spirit, who inspired its writing.

The task of biblical interpretation focuses on two levels of meaning in Sacred Scripture: the literal sense and the spiritual sense. Assisted by the work of biblical scholars, the Church also considers the literary forms found in the Bible, as well as the cultures and conditions in which the sacred books were written. She teaches us how to relate the truths of Divine Revelation to science and history, explaining, "There can never be any real discrepancy between faith and reason[2]" (CCC, 159). Above all the Church articulates an authentic understanding of salvation grounded in Jesus Christ, who is the fullness of Revelation because he is God himself.

Article 20: A Vocation to Interpret and Teach

Do you talk with friends (or even strangers) about your religious beliefs? If so, you have probably discovered that many people have strong feelings about religious beliefs, especially about what the Bible teaches about certain things. Understanding the truth that God wants to reveal in Scripture is very important, but we can find it to be a tremendous challenge. This is why God has not left us on our own in interpreting the Bible. With the grace of the Holy Spirit, the Magisterium of the Church provides us with the proper guidance and wisdom.

The Authority of the Magisterium

As you learned in chapter 3, the Magisterium is the living, teaching office of the Church—the bishops in communion with the Pope. Jesus Christ himself gave the Magisterium the sole authority to authentically interpret the words of Sacred Scripture. The Holy Spirit guides the Magisterium in this task of safeguarding and explaining the truths revealed in the Bible. This involves prayerfully listening to the same Spirit who inspired the human

Live It!
Sacred Scripture and Personal Prayer

Reading the Bible as part of personal prayer and reflection is an important way to grow in faith. When we read a Bible passage, we must consider it in the context of the history of our salvation. We must also consider the intention of the original author and what God intends to reveal. The guidance of the Magisterium can help us to grow in our understanding of God's love for us, communicated through his words and deeds in Scripture, and of how we can respond to him with love in the way we live each day. Choose a particular book from Sacred Scripture, and do some research to find out what the Church says about it. Start by checking your personal Bible to see if it includes an introduction to that book. The Vatican website *(www.vatican.va)* also has an English text of the Bible that includes introductions and notes.

authors of the Bible. As the *Catechism* explains, "What comes from the Spirit is not fully 'understood except by the Spirit's action'[3]" (CCC, 137). Under the guidance of the Magisterium, the Church seeks to hear and understand what God reveals through the words of Sacred Scripture. Above all we must pay close attention to determine the truths God intended to communicate for the sake of our salvation.

Interpreting and explaining Sacred Scripture is a grave responsibility, and many who are not bishops also engage in this work. Those who do biblical interpretation, such as scholars and priests, are called to follow the Magisterium's principles for interpretation. At all times the interpreters' research, teaching, and preaching are subject to the judgment of the Magisterium. Biblical interpreters serve the Church by helping us to gain a better understanding of the meaning of Sacred Scripture. The principles of interpretation are helpful to all—especially students like you—who read and seek to understand the Bible.

Guidance from the Church

Over the last century, the work of biblical interpretation has expanded to include a variety of academic disciplines as ways to begin to understand Sacred Scripture. In this chapter we explore several of these principles of interpretation. But they are only a starting point. As the Church continually reminds us, we must not study Sacred Scripture as if it were just another literary work or historical artifact. We must use these methods of interpretation as mere lenses to help us see and develop an ever deeper understanding of God's Revelation in Sacred Scripture. Let's look at three important documents in which the Magisterium examines some methods of interpretation:

- *Divino Afflante Spiritu* (1943)—In this encyclical Pope Pius XII allowed a limited use of modern methods of biblical analysis. The teaching authority of the Church began to recognize the need to examine literary techniques and forms as a way to study their influence on the deeper meaning of biblical passages.

- *Dogmatic Constitution on Divine Revelation (Dei Verbum*, 1965)—This dogmatic constitution from Vatican Council II further explored the relationship between literary techniques and the intended meaning of the Word of God. The Council also strongly emphasized the need to study the cultures in which the books of the Bible were written. These studies can help us to understand what God wants to communicate to us. The Council cautioned biblical scholars that all study of a particular text must be situated within the whole history of salvation.

- *Interpretation of the Bible in the Church* (1993)—The Pontifical Biblical Commission, an office in the Vatican, built on the teachings of *Divino Afflante Spiritu* and *Divine Revelation* by laying out several approaches and methods of interpretation, including historical and literary studies. The Pontifical Biblical Commission explained the senses of Scripture (literal and spiritual, including allegorical, moral, and anagogical). It further developed guidelines for Catholic interpretation of Sacred Scripture, including the role of Tradition, the task of the interpreter, and the relevance of other theological disciplines.

As you can see from these documents, one role of the Magisterium is to guide all the faithful in bringing to light all that God reveals for our salvation. The Magisterium, as the servant of the Word of God, is strengthened in this work by its direct link to the Apostles. We trust in the Holy Spirit, who directs the Magisterium in its interpretation of Sacred Scripture and guides the efforts of all the faithful to understand and share the message of Scripture. As Saint Thomas More, an English martyr under King Henry VIII of England, stated so well: "The Church of Christ has always, and never fails in, the right understanding of Scripture, so far as is necessary for our salvation."

**biblical
exegesis**
The critical
interpretation and
explanation of
Sacred Scripture.

The Magisterium interprets Sacred Scripture without error. How does this confirm or change your thinking about the Bible?

Article 21: Biblical Exegesis

Many people wonder, "Why do I have to read the Bible? I have nothing in common with the people of the Bible. Times have changed." It is true that times have changed, but we still struggle with the same issues people faced then: jealousy, idolatry, disbelief, hypocrisy, selfishness, and so on. Although we may not recognize the similarities between ourselves and our ancestors in faith, closer study of Scripture helps us to understand the events it portrays and relate those events to our lives today.

The process of interpreting and explaining a passage from Sacred Scripture is called **biblical exegesis**. Biblical exegesis involves thoughtful and rigorous interpretation of Scripture and what God is communicating to us through his Word. Biblical exegesis dispels the myth that

Pray It!

The Guidance of the Holy Spirit

A good practice when reading Scripture is to pray to the Holy Spirit for guidance. Pray the following prayer to the Holy Spirit the next time you pray with Scripture:

Come, Holy Spirit, fill the hearts of your faithful.
Enkindle in them the fire of your love.
Send forth Your Spirit, and they will be created,
And you will renew the face of the earth.
Let us pray:

Lord, by the light of the Holy Spirit, you have taught the hearts of the faithful. In the same Spirit, help us to relish what is right and always rejoice in your consolation. We ask this through Christ our Lord. Amen.

the people and lessons of the Bible are outdated. Instead, it affirms that the inspired Word of God continues to speak to us and guide us.

That is why thorough biblical exegesis must always be done with an awareness of the larger truths revealed through all of Sacred Scripture—the unity of its content and teachings. A given biblical passage can be fully understood only within the complete picture of both the Old and New Testaments. The Scripture scholar discovers the deeper meaning of Sacred Scripture when he or she takes into account the unity that exists in all truth. This is especially true for the truths of faith. There is coherence among them, so understanding one truth helps us to better understand the others. This unity in doctrine is known as the **analogy of faith**.

> **How can biblical exegesis help us to make sense of a biblical event or custom that we might not understand today?**

analogy of faith
The coherence of individual doctrines with the whole of Revelation. In other words, as each doctrine is connected with Revelation, each doctrine is also connected with all other doctrines.

exegete
A scholar specializing in critical explanation of biblical texts.

Article 22: Biblical Scholars: Bridging the Gap between Yesterday, Today, and Tomorrow

Biblical exegesis is primarily the work of biblical scholars—men and women with advanced degrees in biblical studies. Although any of us can strive to develop an understanding of the Word of God in the Bible, these professionals are fluent in Greek, Aramaic, or Hebrew (or all three), and they often specialize in particular areas of exegesis. For example, one scholar might be an expert in the cultural beliefs of biblical people, and another might have a deep knowledge of Paul's letters and their contexts. Biblical **exegetes** also teach Bible study and create Bible study resources such as dictionaries, professional journals, and commentaries.

An early Church Father, Saint Fulgence of Ruspe, stated, "Study your heart in the light of the Holy Scriptures, and you will know therein who you were, who you are, and who you ought to be." Biblical scholars work hard to bridge the gaps between the people of yesterday, today, and tomorrow. Enlightened by the Holy Spirit, they must study both what the human authors wanted to communicate and what God intended to reveal to us through their writing. They study the culture and context in which the writer of a particular book of the Bible lived so that they can more fully develop our understanding of the meaning of Scripture and the intentions of each sacred writer. Scholars must also examine the literary genres and techniques commonly used in the time and culture of each writer. All these tasks aid the study of a given passage and uncover the levels of meaning behind the words.

Most important, an authentic interpretation of Sacred Scripture is grounded in the Tradition and teachings of the Church. It is carried out "in the light of the same Spirit by whom it was written[4]" (CCC, 111). For this reason, biblical scholars must also follow the guidance of the Magisterium, be conscious of Sacred Tradition, and be mindful of the unity of all Church teachings.

Did You Know?

© Bettmann/Corbis / AP Images

Bible Commentaries

Bible commentaries are a particularly significant contribution of biblical scholarship. Such commentaries draw on the tireless studies of biblical scholars to examine the meaning of the stories and lessons of Sacred Scripture. From a study of the cultures in which the stories were written to a discussion of their significance today, biblical scholars have provided resources that aid in spreading the truth and wisdom of God's Word. Two popular and reputable Bible commentaries are *The Collegeville Bible Commentary* and *The New Jerome Biblical Commentary*.

They need to pay attention to the whole of Revelation written in Sacred Scripture. In these ways, biblical scholars can challenge us to know our past, recognize where we stand today, and envision where we ought to be tomorrow.

> **What aspect of the work of biblical exegetes do you find most interesting, and why?**

Article 23: The Senses of Scripture

The goals of biblical study are to discover meaning, depth, and truth and to help us understand Sacred Scripture. Exegetes work continually to develop and explain an ever deeper and clearer understanding of the meaning of the Bible.

In *Summa Theologiae,* Saint Thomas Aquinas laid the foundation for modern biblical interpretation. He recognized that Sacred Scripture is packed with rich language. This language communicates special meaning with regard to actual events and people, faith, just action, and everlasting life. Aquinas taught us to study Sacred Scripture by focusing on its two different senses, or levels of meaning: specifically, the literal sense and the spiritual sense.

The Literal Sense

To determine the literal sense, we look at what the words of Scripture actually say—that is, the obvious meaning of the text. Discovering the literal sense of a passage is a key task of biblical exegesis. The interpreter examines the actual events being spoken about. The interpreter also considers key people and other details described in the text. Through cultural and literary exploration, the exegete seeks deeper understanding of the life, times, and writing styles of God's Chosen People. The literal sense lays the framework for all other senses of Scripture.

allegory
A literary form in which something is said to be like something else, in an attempt to communicate a hidden or symbolic meaning.

Christological
Having to do with the branch of theology called Christology. Christology is the study of the divinity of Jesus Christ, the Son of God and the Second Divine Person of the Trinity, and his earthly ministry and eternal mission.

The Spiritual Sense

The spiritual sense goes beyond the literal sense of the words to consider what the realities and events of Scripture signify. The spiritual sense can be broken into three categories: allegorical sense, moral sense, and anagogical sense.

- **Allegorical sense** An **allegory** is a type of symbolism in which one thing points us to a deeper meaning or truth. Specifically, to consider the allegorical sense of a Scripture passage, we look at how the people, events, and things in the literal sense point to the mystery of Christ. In other words, we examine their **Christological** significance.

- **Moral sense** Fundamental to the moral sense of Sacred Scripture is the search for what it means to live a just and ethical life. The moral sense helps us to understand how a particular passage instructs us to live in right relationship with God, neighbor, self, and the earth.

- **Anagogical sense** The anagogical sense considers "realities and events in terms of their eternal significance⁵" (CCC, 117). In what way does the passage lead us toward our future heavenly home?

The *Catechism* quotes a medieval poem to help us remember these senses of Scripture: "The Letter [literal sense] speaks of deeds; Allegory to faith; / the Moral how to act; Anagogy our destiny⁶" (118). This quotation shows us the importance of studying Sacred Scripture from every angle. We must study the meaning of words and events, the lessons regarding the role of Christ in salvation, the teachings about moral and just living, and our vocation to be with God always. The literal sense and all three spiritual senses open the door to the deeper truth God wants us to know in Sacred Scripture.

Senses of Sacred Scripture in the Exodus Account

Still not sure what the literal and spiritual senses of Scripture help us to understand? Let's apply what you have learned to the crossing of the Red Sea in the Book of Exodus (see 14:10–31).

- **Literal sense** The literal sense tells us that God delivered the Israelites by working through Moses to part the Red Sea. God did this so the Israelites could cross, and then he closed the sea to drown Pharaoh's army.

- **Allegorical sense** Just as Moses, through God's power, led the Israelites from slavery to freedom, so too are we freed from the slavery of sin, death, and evil by the power of God manifested in Jesus Christ, the New Moses.

- **Moral sense** Just as God destroyed Pharaoh's sinful power in the Red Sea, so too does Christ destroy Original Sin in the waters of Baptism so that we may live good and moral lives based on the New Law revealed in the Beatitudes.

- **Anagogical sense** Just as the Israelites entered the Promised Land through the waters of the Red Sea, so also do we enter the Promised Land, our heavenly home, by passing through the waters of Baptism.

Primary Sources

Making Sense of Scripture

In *Divino Afflante Spiritu* (1943), Pope Pius XII explains how studying the senses of Sacred Scripture and its literary forms can help us to interpret details that seem inaccurate or puzzling in some Scripture accounts:

> Not infrequently . . . when some persons reproachfully charge the Sacred Writers with some historical error or inaccuracy in the recording of facts, on closer examination it turns out to be nothing else than those customary modes of expression and narration peculiar to the ancients, which used to be employed in the mutual dealings of social life and which in fact were sanctioned by common usage. (38)

redact
To edit or adapt written material to serve a particular purpose.

literary forms (genres)
Different kinds of writing determined by their literary technique, content, tone, and purpose.

Would you find it easier to examine the literal sense or the spiritual sense of a biblical passage? Why?

Article 24: Literary Analysis of Scripture

To better understand the meaning the Bible's human authors intended to convey, biblical scholars analyze the Bible as a literary document. For example, they might seek to discover other written or oral sources the biblical writers may have known about or even used as they wrote their books. Exegetes work to understand how the authors **redacted**, or edited, other writings to create the sacred books of the Bible. In addition, scholars look at a book's internal structure to consider how its author organized the text and to look for clues about the author's purpose and main points. Using these and other forms of literary analysis, biblical interpreters strive to help us learn both what the human authors wanted to communicate and what God wanted to reveal to us through them.

By now you might be thinking that only biblical scholars have the knowledge and skill needed to interpret the Bible. But any one of us can begin to study the Bible as a literary document by considering the **literary forms** we find in it. From poetry to parables, from Creation accounts to the Gospels, we encounter many forms of literature in the Bible. Literary forms, also called literary genres, refer to different styles of writing found in Sacred Scripture. The study of literary forms can give us insight into the meaning the sacred writers intended to convey. We must know which literary form we are reading and realize that each form has its own rules for interpretation. The following chart describes nine significant literary forms found in the Bible. Can you think of others?

Literary Forms in the Bible

Type	Explanation	Example
Creation accounts	Explanations of how something came into existence	Adam and Eve, Noah, Tower of Babel
Psalms	Hymns or songs of prayer that express praise, thanksgiving, petition, lamentation, or a historical memory of God's action on behalf of the Chosen People	Book of Psalms
Prophetic oracles	Counsel and wisdom given by God	Prophetic books
Historical books	Accounts of the saving action of God in human history	First and Second Samuel, First and Second Kings
Wisdom literature	Collections of sayings and teachings about how to live a good and wise life, a life pleasing to God	Books of Proverbs, Ecclesiastes, Wisdom
Parables	Brief stories told by Jesus to exemplify moral or religious lessons	Mustard Seed, Prodigal Son
Letters (epistles)	Letters to early Christians to pass on wisdom, correction, and community information	Letters of Paul
Apocalyptic literature	Descriptions of the end times, prophecies of catastrophic upheavals on earth, and promises of a New Creation	Books of Daniel, Revelation
Gospels	Accounts of real events and teachings from Jesus' life that give deeper insight into the meaning of his life and mission	Books of Matthew, Mark, Luke, John

Learning about the literary forms found in the Bible is an important part of our study of the Bible. But we must always remember that Sacred Scripture is not just another form of literature. We must always read it in light of the Incarnate Word, Jesus Christ, who through the Holy Spirit opens our minds to help us understand what truths God wanted to reveal to us by means of the writing of the human authors.

How does recognizing the literary form of a Bible passage help you to understand its meaning?

Article 25: Archaeology: Another View of Sacred Scripture

The Indiana Jones movies give us the idea that biblical archaeology is a grand adventure, even a dangerous one. The truth, of course, is that biblical archaeology rarely involves daring brushes with villains. The world becomes excited every time a biblical location or artifact is found, but archaeology offers us an even quieter and more profound excitement. Simply put, biblical archaeology can lead us to a deeper understanding of the Word of God. Archaeologists help to ground us in the historical authenticity of the Bible by finding and studying the probable locations of many key biblical events. Through archaeology we have even been able to locate early copies of sacred books and other writings of the time. We can walk where peoples of the Bible walked, see the objects they used, and study the very manuscripts they themselves wrote and read.

Locating Biblical Places and Events

If you ever have the opportunity to visit Israel, you will notice that the Israeli national parks are different from U.S. national parks. Most of Israel's national parks are archaeological excavations, or digs. The last several decades have seen a dramatic increase in the number of digs in Israel. The result has been the discovery of many ancient texts, artifacts, and buildings. Archaeologists have even found entire cities that date back to the time of Christ and earlier. These discoveries have helped us to understand more clearly what life was like in biblical times.

© Brian Singer-Towns / Saint Mary's Press

For example, archaeologists have unearthed the ancient Roman city of Sepphoris. This city, rebuilt in the first century AD, was only about an hour's walk from Jesus' small village of Nazareth. It is entirely possible that Jesus visited Sepphoris as a young man. Maybe he even worked there with Joseph, his foster father. In Sepphoris Jesus would have learned about Greek and Roman culture and witnessed firsthand how, in his words, "the rulers of the Gentiles lord it over them" (Matthew 20:25).

Discovering Ancient Writings

Particularly important archaeological finds include the discovery of ancient texts, both biblical and nonbiblical. We do not have an original version of any biblical book. This is why scholars are always searching for the earliest copies. The most important modern discovery of ancient biblical texts is the Dead Sea Scrolls. These documents are important to biblical study because they contain copied fragments from nearly every book in the Old Testament. The Dead Sea Scrolls are believed to have been written and preserved by a Jewish religious community, possibly called the **Essenes**. They lived sometime between the first century BC and the first century AD. The Dead Sea Scrolls were discovered in the late 1940s in caves in the Qumran region, near the northwest shore of the Dead Sea. The scrolls are perhaps the only surviving copies of biblical documents made before AD 100. They also recount information about the beliefs and customs of the Jewish People of the time.

Archaeologists continue to uncover sites across the Holy Land that further our understanding of biblical life and times. College students from around the world volunteer to help in this work.

Essenes
A group of pious, ultraconservative Jews who left the Temple of Jerusalem and began a community by the Dead Sea, known as Qumran.

Nag Hammadi manuscripts
Fourth-century writings, discovered in 1945 near the village of Nag Hammadi in Upper Egypt, that are invaluable sources of information regarding Gnostic beliefs, practices, and lifestyle. Gnosticism was an early Church heresy claiming that Christ's humanity was an illusion and the human body is evil.

fundamentalist approach
The interpretation of the Bible and Christian doctrine based on the literalist meaning of the Bible's words. The interpretation is made without regard to the historical setting in which the writings or teachings were first developed.

Also important is the discovery of ancient nonbiblical religious texts like the fourth-century **Nag Hammadi manuscripts**. Found in 1945 near the village of Nag Hammadi in Upper Egypt, these manuscripts describe the beliefs, practices, and lifestyle of a sect of people called the Gnostics. Gnosticism was an early Church heresy claiming that Christ's humanity was an illusion and that the human body is evil. Scholars had long thought these manuscripts were destroyed in the early centuries of the Church, as part of efforts to stamp out all heresies. These and other nonbiblical texts help us to understand the religious beliefs of other nations and peoples during biblical times.

How does knowing about the original copies of ancient writings shape your understanding of the canon of Scripture?

Article 26: Sacred Scripture in Relation to Science and History

We live in a time of great inquiry and discovery. We are constantly expanding our understanding of science, history, and other areas of knowledge. Every day new discoveries challenge the ways we think and how we view the world. It is easy, therefore, to presume that faith could conflict with science and history.

However, the Catholic Church teaches us how faith, science, and history can coexist and can inform one another. The academic disciplines of math, science, psychology, sociology, history, and literature are wonderful gifts that must be valued and used responsibly. There is a harmony between these academic pursuits and the truths revealed throughout Sacred Scripture. God instilled in us eager imaginations and inquisitive minds. He created us with the ability to come to a fuller understanding of faith and belief. Our minds were not given to us so that we could consider ourselves superior to his mysterious ways.

Looking at the Whole Picture

You are probably beginning to see how many different lenses we have to examine "what meaning the sacred authors really intended, and what God wanted to manifest by means of their words" (*Divine Revelation*, 12). Guided by the teaching authority of the Church, academic endeavors such as science and history can help us to break down the barriers of an overly literalist or **fundamentalist approach** to Scripture. These different lenses can also free us from an approach that is limited to symbolic understanding. We want to look at the whole picture.

Faith in Action
Manuscripts and Medieval Monks

© The Board of Trinity College, Dublin, Ireland / The Bridgeman Art Library

The illustration below is from the Gospel of Luke in the Book of Kells. This beautiful illuminated manuscript of the Gospels was produced by the monks of Kells, Ireland, around the year AD 800. In an illuminated manuscript, the text is embellished with intricate initials, borders, and illustrations. In medieval Europe, centuries before the printing press was invented, monks copied and illuminated texts by hand, using carefully prepared parchment, gold and silver foil, and colorful inks. In the scriptorium of a medieval monastery, these copyists spent long hours painstakingly copying the Bible, as well as writings of the Church Fathers and other important religious and secular works.

In the Middle Ages, waves of barbarian invaders disrupted trade routes and sacked major cities across Europe, destroying many vital texts in the process. This destruction effectively reduced communication, learning, and literacy. Irish monks—whose monasteries were somewhat protected from these disruptions by the English Channel, separating Ireland from the mainland—played a vital role in preserving and handing on the Bible and key documents of the early Church. This is why many historians give special credit to Irish monastic communities for helping to preserve Western culture and reintroduce vital Church texts to the rest of Europe and eventually the world.

contextualist approach
The interpretation of the Bible that takes into account the various contexts for understanding. These contexts include the senses of Scripture, literary forms, historical situations, cultural backgrounds, the unity of the whole of Sacred Scripture, Sacred Tradition, and the analogy of faith.

The Church supports a **contextualist approach**. In this approach the literal sense of Scripture is informed by scientific and historical knowledge. This knowledge helps us to recognize the deeper symbolic meaning of the spiritual senses of Scripture. A contextualist approach simply teaches us how to relate the truths of faith to science. If we study Sacred Scripture in a contextualist manner, we realize that there is no real conflict between faith and reason. The truths revealed in the Bible will never conflict with the truths we learn by studying science and history.

God acts in and through history, so there is a strong and consistent historic basis for the Old and New Testaments. This is particularly the case with the Gospels. However, the Church does not propose that the Bible's purpose is to present historical and scientific facts. Some biblical accounts may not be clearly supported by historical experiences or accurate historical references. But this does not mean Scripture is in error or that our scientific explorations are wrong.

Reconciling Mystery with Science and History

As human beings we are educated according to theories of learning and data collecting. Our world has not taught us to deal with human limitations. It has not taught us to deal with truth that is so deep and broad that our limited minds cannot fully comprehend it. This is what Catholics mean by absolute mystery—and mystery is exactly what we encounter in Sacred Scripture. Saint Gregory the Great, a pope and Doctor of the Church, explained, "Holy Scripture by the manner of its language transcends every science, because in one and the same sentence, while it describes a fact, it reveals a mystery."

Science and history, combined with literary analysis and many other academic disciplines, are avenues for understanding Divine Revelation. However, we must always remember that they have limitations that must be respected and understood. God has given us the mind to pursue these avenues. Therefore all that is unveiled and proven through these avenues will sing in unison with the words of Sacred Scripture, leading to the infinite Incarnate Word, Jesus Christ. If science and faith conflict, it means we have an inadequate understanding of one or both of them.

> **How does your understanding of a mystery of our faith differ from the way you view a scientific or historical mystery?**

Article 27: Look at Sacred Scripture from Every Angle

As you can see, to grasp the truth of Sacred Scripture, we must look at the Bible from every angle, using every lens available to us. Guided by the Church's Magisterium, we must continually study Scripture to reach an authentic knowledge of God's self-Revelation. The fields of archaeology, history, science, and literary analysis can help the Church to understand God's Revelation in Scripture. In this way, we can glory in the riches of Divine Wisdom disclosed in the sacred words of the Bible.

> **Why is it appropriate to think of academic disciplines as lenses for viewing and understanding Sacred Scripture?**

Chapter Review

1. Who has been entrusted with the responsibility of authentically interpreting Sacred Scripture?

2. What is biblical exegesis? What should an exegete be attentive to when interpreting Scripture?

3. Why is it important to know the literary genres when interpreting a particular book or passage of Sacred Scripture?

4. What are the literal and spiritual senses of Scripture?

5. Why does the Church teach that there can be no conflict between religious truth and scientific and historical truth?

6. Briefly describe the contextualist approach for interpreting the Bible.

7. What is biblical archaeology and what benefits can it have for understanding Sacred Scripture?

Overview of the Old and New Testaments

Introduction

We can think of the Old and New Testaments as a single tapestry, throughout which the artist has woven a unifying presentation of salvation history. Our faith is not based solely on the teachings of the New Testament, but has its foundation in the Old Testament. We call the Old Testament "old" not because it is outdated but simply because it relates the teachings and events before the coming of Jesus Christ. It is not an antique of the past but rather a beautiful revelation of God's saving action in the lives of the Israelites. The New Testament, especially the Gospels, records the Good News of Jesus Christ, the New Covenant, who fulfilled the Old Covenant made between God and the Jewish People.

This chapter describes the many categories of books found in Sacred Scripture and explores how they form a cohesive picture of salvation history. We read each Testament in light of the other, because both are the true Word of God. We must study both to understand the Incarnation of God's Word and his plan for our salvation.

Hebrew people
The descendants of Abraham and Sarah who became known as the Israelites after the Exodus and who later were called Judeans or Jews.

Article 28: The Old Testament: *Old* Does Not Mean "Out of Date"

What does the word *old* mean to you? Your response might include some of the following words: *boring, unattractive, lackluster, disposable,* and *out of date.* Associating such concepts with the term overlooks an important dimension of "oldness": that the old paves the way for the new and that, often, we need the old to appreciate and understand the new.

The same is true for Sacred Scripture. The Old Testament is not out of date or insignificant. It contains the Scriptures that are sacred to the Jewish People. As Christians we also venerate it as the true Word of God because it is the foundation of our identity as a people, a family of faith, profoundly touched by the Incarnation of God. The Old Testament contains the Revelation of God that lays the framework for our Christian faith.

The Old Testament is the account of a loving and communicative relationship between God and the **Hebrew people**. The Hebrew people were also called the Israelites and, later, the Jews. The time frame of the Old Testament spans from the Creation of the world to the kingdom of the Maccabees, two centuries before the birth of Jesus. The Old Testament describes the covenant that God made with the Jewish People and recounts how he remained faithful to them, always willing to take sinners back, even when they succumb to the temptations of the world. Egypt and Mesopotamia, two major centers of culture and life in the ancient Near East, form the backdrop for the events we read about in the Old Testament.

Why are the books of the Old Testament sacred for Christians as well as Jews? In the words of the *Catechism:* "The Old Testament is an indispensable part of Sacred Scripture. Its books are divinely inspired and retain a permanent value,[7] for the Old Covenant has never been revoked" (121). In the Old Testament writings, all peoples encounter foundational teachings on the meaning of life, morality, right relationship with God, and the mystery of salvation. We must not discard these writings and teachings. Instead we must read, venerate, and integrate them into our spiritual lives. The Revelation of God in the Old Testament will forever be valuable and vital. It never loses its worth and it is always pertinent to the human experience.

At World Youth Day in 2000, Pope Saint John Paul II challenged young people and the entire Church to

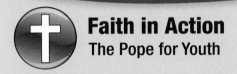

Faith in Action
The Pope for Youth

© Forum / UIG / Bridgeman Images

Pope Saint John Paul II (Karol Wojtyła, 1920–2005) was the visible head of the Church for nearly twenty-seven years. Elected at age fifty-eight, this native of Poland was the youngest Pope to be elected during the twentieth century and the first non-Italian Pope to be elected since the 1500s.

Karol's early life was not easy. His mother died in childbirth when he was eight. He lost his older brother, a doctor, to scarlet fever. Then his father died. By age twenty-one, he had lost every one of his family members. In 1939, shortly after Karol had entered a local university, World War II began with the Nazi invasion of Poland. Karol's university was closed. For four years he did hard manual labor in a stone quarry. Gradually Karol began to realize that he might be called to the priesthood. But because the Nazis had closed the seminary, he studied for the priesthood at the home of the archbishop of Krakow and was ordained in secret.

Father Wojtyła met often with youth groups, even accompanying them on ski trips and hikes, perhaps remembering his own youthful sorrows and pleasures. Even after he was elected Pope, Saint John Paul II continued to devote much of his time to ministering to young people. Most notably he launched World Youth Day, celebrated internationally every two or three years. This special gathering of Catholic youth celebrates the life of the Word of God, Jesus, among the youth of today.

Pope Saint John Paul II died in April 2005. He was beatified on May 1, 2011, and was canonized on April 27, 2014. We celebrate his feast day on October 22, the anniversary of his inauguration as Pope in 1978.

"open wide the doors to Christ." In the same spirit, we recognize that the Old Testament opens wide the doors and windows to the most perfect manifestation of Revelation, Jesus Christ, God's Incarnate Son. Jesus' entire life embodied the promise made between God and his people in the Old Covenant. Jesus, the New Covenant, who is God himself, fulfills the prophecies of the Old Testament and brings to fruition the hopes and expectations of a broken and sinful people. The books of the Old Testament give us only an initial, incomplete understanding of salvation history—but they do bear witness to God's entire plan of loving goodness. The truth is that the Old Testament contains "a storehouse of sublime teaching on God and of sound wisdom on human life, as well as a wonderful treasury of prayers; in them, too, the mystery of our salvation is present in a hidden way"[8] (CCC, 122). The ancient words of the Old Law, as written in the Old Testament, are not out of date. In fact, they truly prepare us for the Gospel. The Old Law is the first stage of revealed Law.

> **What is one thing about the Old Testament you hope to explore in depth in this course?**

Article 29: The Canon and Structure of the Old Testament

Did you know that Catholics and Protestants use different versions of the Old Testament? The Catholic Bible includes seven Old Testament books excluded from the Protestant Bible. These books are called the deuterocanonical (Greek for "second canon") books. The books are Tobit, Judith, First and Second Maccabees, Wisdom, Sirach, and Baruch. The Church's decision to include these books in the Old Testament is part of Apostolic Tradition. The Catholic Church has long relied on the Greek translation of the Old Testament, called the Septuagint, which contained the deuterocanonical books. The Protestant reformers rejected the Septuagint as the basis for the Old Testament, affirming the Hebrew translation instead. This is why Protestant Bibles generally do not contain the seven deuterocanonical books (except sometimes as an appendix).

The chart "The Canon of the Old Testament" lists the forty-six books of the Old Testament. Let's look more closely at the types of books we find there.

Pray It!

More Desirable Than Gold

Long before the birth of Christ, the Psalms emphasized the importance of becoming intimately familiar with God's Word. Today you too can praise the Word of God with these words from Psalm 19:

The law of the LORD is perfect,
    refreshing the soul.
The decree of the LORD is trustworthy,
    giving wisdom to the simple.
The precepts of the LORD are right,
    rejoicing the heart.
The command of the LORD is clear,
    enlightening the eye.

. . . .

More desirable than gold,
    than a hoard of purest gold,
Sweeter also than honey
    or drippings from the comb.
By them your servant is warned;
    obeying them brings much reward.

. . . .

Let the words of my mouth be acceptable,
    the thoughts of my heart before you,
LORD, my rock and my redeemer.
                                (Psalm 19:8–9,11–12,15)

Torah
A Hebrew word meaning "law," referring to the first five books of the Old Testament.

Pentateuch
A Greek word meaning "five books," referring to the first five books of the Old Testament.

Law of Moses
The first five books of the Old Testament, which are also called the books of law or the Torah. God gave Moses the tablets summarizing the Law (see Exodus 31:18), which is why it is also called the Law of Moses, or the Mosaic Law.

Types of Books in the Old Testament

The Old Testament books can be divided into four categories. These four categories are the books of law (or Pentateuch), the historical books, the prophetic books, and the wisdom books.

- **The books of law** The name "books of law" refers to the first five books of the Old Testament. These five books teach about Creation and sin. They provide us with inspirational accounts of people of faith, as well as the history, teachings, and laws of the Chosen People of Israel. The books of law are also called the **Torah** (from Hebrew, meaning "law"), the **Pentateuch** (from Greek, meaning "five books"), or the **Law of Moses**.

- **The historical books** The historical books tell about the many trials and triumphs of Jewish history before Christ. They recount the lives of various leaders, including kings, judges, warriors, and prophets. In the historical books, we can trace the saving action of God in the lives of the Israelites.

- **The prophetic books** The prophetic books proclaim the messages of visionary religious reformers whom God called to challenge the people of Israel to stop their idolatrous practices, to act justly, and to care for the people. In addition to calling the people to repent, these prophets also proclaimed a message of hope and consolation.

- **The wisdom books** In the wisdom books, we find poetry that is steeped in emotion, as well as practical advice on what it means to be wise. These books focus on the themes of wisdom, self-control, patience, honesty, diligence, suffering, praise, thanksgiving, and respect for elders.

The Canon of the Old Testament	
CATEGORIES	
The Books of Law	
Genesis	Numbers
Exodus	Deuteronomy
Leviticus	
The Historical Books	
Joshua	Second Chronicles
Judges	Ezra
Ruth	Nehemiah
First Samuel	Tobit
Second Samuel	Judith
First Kings	Esther
Second Kings	First Maccabees
First Chronicles	Second Maccabees
The Prophetic Books	
Isaiah	Obadiah
Jeremiah	Jonah
Lamentations	Micah
Baruch	Nahum
Ezekiel	Habakkuk
Daniel	Zephaniah
Hosea	Haggai
Joel	Zechariah
Amos	Malachi
The Wisdom Books	
Job	Song of Songs
Psalms	Wisdom
Proverbs	Sirach
Ecclesiastes	

A Seamless Garment and a Compass

The forty-six books of the Old Testament are a seamless garment. Each book is unique, but together they form one cloth woven from God's redeeming and liberating love. The Old Testament includes histories, genealogies, laws, customs, rituals, wise sayings, poetry, and prophecies—all grounding us in the Old Covenant made between God and the Jewish People, and all pointing us to the New Covenant Jesus made. We can also think of the Old Testament as our compass, pointing us in one direction only: on the pathway to Jesus Christ.

Salvation history is filled with accounts of empires' vying for control of the ancient Middle East. How many of the empires on this map have you heard of?

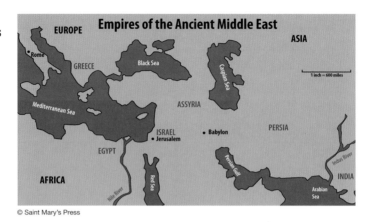

© Saint Mary's Press

How can studying the Old Testament enrich your life of Christian faith?

Article 30: The New Testament: Why Is It Called "New"?

The New Testament is called "new" because God the Father radically broke into the human condition by sending his only Son, Jesus Christ, to initiate a New Covenant with his people. God had never before revealed or manifested himself in such a way. Certainly he had acted in amazing ways in the Old Testament. But by taking on human nature, he opened the doors to a new day, a new Revelation, a new freedom. Vatican Council II explained:

> The word of God, which is the power of God for the salvation of all who believe (see Rom. 1:16), is set forth and shows its power in a most excellent way in the writings of the New Testament. For when the fullness of time arrived (see Gal. 4:4), the Word was made flesh and dwelt among us in His fullness of grace and truth (see John 1:14). (*Dogmatic Constitution on Divine Revelation*, 17)

The New Testament centers on the words and actions of Jesus Christ and all that he accomplished for the sake of our salvation through his Passion, Death, Resurrection, and Ascension. It also describes how the early Christian communities received and applied his teachings. It covers the time period from approximately

4 BC to AD 100. The New Testament's twenty-seven books tell us about God's fullest Revelation through the Incarnation.

Hellenism
The acceptance of Greek culture, language, and traditions.

Politics and Religion

Jesus' life and mission took place in Palestine, also called the Holy Land. In New Testament times, Palestine was divided into three major provinces: Judea, Samaria, and Galilee. Jesus was born in Judea, ministered in Galilee, and invited the "unclean" of Samaria into the circle of salvation. Through his actions Jesus spread his message of hope and reconciliation to all of Palestine.

The society in which Jesus and the early Christian communities lived was quite diverse in religious practices. It was governed by Roman rule and was also profoundly affected by **Hellenism**, the influence of Greek culture. There were many religious groups, or sects, within the Jewish community alone. These included the Pharisees, Sadducees, Essenes, Herodians, and Zealots. Each group emphasized a different way to live the Jewish faith. The Pharisees were the educated interpreters of the Law of Moses. The Sadducees strictly adhered to

Live It!
When Necessary, Use Words

The Christian faith spread because the early Christians listened to the call to go out and spread the Good News of Jesus Christ. In many cases they shared the Gospel with people who had never even heard of Jesus. The call to spread the Good News is part of your Christian vocation too! You may think that most people you encounter have already heard of Jesus, but that does not mean your work is done.

We are called to preach the Gospel to everyone at all times. This does not mean you have to go out on the street corner and preach to strangers. The manner in which you act can witness your faith to others. Advice that has been credited to Saint Francis says, "Preach the Gospel at all times; when necessary, use words." With this in mind, strive to do every act with great care, knowing that it can be a witness to someone of your love for Jesus Christ. How can you start today?

the Torah and preserved the sanctity of the Temple. To prepare for the coming of God, the Essenes withdrew to a life of solitude and prayer. The Herodians were political leaders who collaborated with the Roman Empire. The Zealots were a revolutionary group concerned with the restoration of Jewish independence. Despite these divisions, however, nearly 90 percent of the Jewish population did not belong to any sect. Collectively these people are known as the great majority. Jesus ministered to all Jews, but he focused much of his time and energy on the great majority.

The Gospels: The Heart of All Scripture

We call the Gospels the heart of the Christian message because they provide the "principal witness for the life and teaching of the Incarnate Word," Jesus Christ (*Divine Revelation*, 18). In them we find accounts of healing, driving out of demons, and washing of feet. We see the breaking of bread, crucified love, and an empty tomb. We learn from Jesus whenever we read about his miracles, his concern for the poor and marginalized, his prayer life, the way he loved others, the way he accepted the Father's

Did You Know?

Different Jewish Groups During Jesus' Time

Society during the time of Jesus and early Christianity was diverse in culture, economic status, religious beliefs, and political thought. Several different Jewish groups existed during this period, the most prominent being the Pharisees, Sadducees, Essenes, Herodians, and Zealots.

Pharisees A Jewish religious group who strictly observed and taught the Law of Moses.

Sadducees A group of powerful and often wealthy Jews who were connected to the Temple priests and often disagreed with the Pharisees.

Essenes A group of pious, conservative Jews who left the Temple of Jerusalem and founded a community beside the Dead Sea, known as Qumran.

Herodians A group of Jewish leaders, including the Temple high priests and Jewish royal families, who collaborated with the Roman governors.

Zealots People who banded together during the time of Christ to violently resist Roman occupation.

will in the garden, and of course his Passion, Death, Resurrection, and Ascension. The central object of the Gospels as well as the entire New Testament is Jesus Christ, the Incarnate Son of God, and the beginning of his Church, guided by the Holy Spirit, whom he sent.

> **If a friend asks you where to begin studying the Bible, would you recommend starting with the Gospels? Why or why not?**

Article 31: The Canon and Structure of the New Testament

The twenty-seven unique books in the New Testament introduce us to the life and teachings of Jesus Christ and the growth of the early Church. We often group the books of the New Testament into the following five categories: the Gospels, the Acts of the Apostles, the Pauline letters, the non-Pauline letters, and the Book of Revelation.

- **The Gospels** The Gospels tell us about the life, ministry, and teachings of Christ, as well as his Passion, Death, Resurrection, and Ascension.

- **Acts of the Apostles** Written by Luke the Evangelist, Acts picks up where the Gospels leave off. We learn about Pentecost: the day when the Holy Spirit descended on the Apostles, with Mary present among them. Acts also tells us about the early Christian community under the leadership of Saint Peter and Saint Paul, guided by the Holy Spirit.

- **The Pauline letters** Paul and his disciples wrote the Pauline letters to early Christian communities he helped form. The letters offer empowering advice, teaching, community news, and pastoral encouragement and support.

- **The non-Pauline letters** The non-Pauline letters serve essentially the same function as the letters Paul wrote, but other authors wrote them, including James, Peter, John, and Jude.

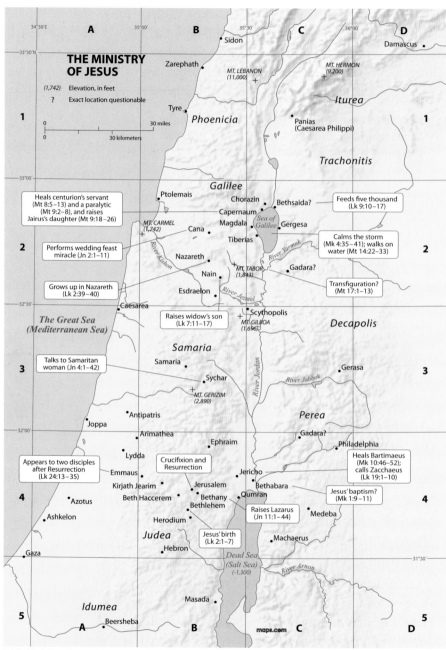

THE MINISTRY OF JESUS

34°30'E   **A**   35°00'   **B**   35°30'   **C**   36°00'   **D**

33°30'N

(1,742) Elevation, in feet
? Exact location questionable

0 ———————————— 30 miles
0 ———————————— 30 kilometers

1

Sidon

Damascus

Zarephath

MT. LEBANON (11,000)

MT. HERMON (9,200)

Iturea

Tyre

Phoenicia

Panias (Caesarea Philippi)

Trachonitis

33°00'

Galilee

Ptolemais

Chorazin

Bethsaida?

Feeds five thousand (Lk 9:10–17)

Heals centurion's servant (Mt 8:5–13) and a paralytic (Mt 9:2–8), and raises Jairus's daughter (Mt 9:18–26)

Capernaum

Sea of Galilee

MT. CARMEL (1,742)

Cana

Magdala

Gergesa

Tiberias

Calms the storm (Mk 4:35–41); walks on water (Mt 14:22–33)

2

Performs wedding feast miracle (Jn 2:1–11)

River Kishon

Nazareth

River Yarmuk

Nain

MT. TABOR (1,843)

Gadara?

Grows up in Nazareth (Lk 2:39–40)

Esdraelon

River Jezreel

Transfiguration? (Mt 17:1–13)

32°30'

Caesarea

Raises widow's son (Lk 7:11–17)

Scythopolis

MT. GILBOA (1,696)

Decapolis

The Great Sea (Mediterranean Sea)

Samaria

Samaria

Gerasa

3

Talks to Samaritan woman (Jn 4:1–42)

Sychar

River Jordan

River Jabbok

MT. GERIZIM (2,890)

Antipatris

Perea

32°00'

Joppa

Arimathea

Ephraim

Gadara?

Philadelphia

Lydda

Crucifixion and Resurrection

Jericho

Heals Bartimaeus (Mk 10:46–52); calls Zacchaeus (Lk 19:1–10)

Appears to two disciples after Resurrection (Lk 24:13–35)

Emmaus

Bethabara

Jesus' baptism? (Mk 1:9–11)

4

Kirjath Jearim

Jerusalem

Qumran

Azotus

Beth Haccerem

Bethany

Bethlehem

Raises Lazarus (Jn 11:1–44)

Medeba

Ashkelon

Herodium

Judea

Jesus' birth (Lk 2:1–7)

Machaerus

Gaza

Hebron

Dead Sea (Salt Sea) (-1,300)

River Arnon

31°30'

Idumea

Masada

5

Beersheba

maps.com

A   **B**   **C**   **D**

© Saint Mary's Press, Thomas Nelson, and maps.com

Jesus spent his entire earthly life in a relatively small geographic area. Use the scale on this map to estimate how many miles north to south and east to west he walked.

- **Revelation:** A Jewish-Christian prophet named John most likely composed the Book of Revelation for late-first-century Christians. Revelation offers words of support to those enduring persecution because of their Christian beliefs. It speaks of the second coming of Christ at the end of time, known as the **Parousia**.

Parousia
The second coming of Christ as judge of all the living and the dead, at the end of time, when the Kingdom of God will be fulfilled.

The Canon of the New Testament	
CATEGORIES	
Gospels	
Matthew	Luke
Mark	John
Acts	
Acts of the Apostles	
Pauline Letters	
Romans	First Thessalonians
First Corinthians	Second Thessalonians
Second Corinthians	First Timothy
Galatians	Second Timothy
Ephesians	Titus
Philippians	Philemon
Colossians	
Non-Pauline Letters	
Hebrews	First John
James	Second John
First Peter	Third John
Second Peter	Jude
Revelation	
Book of Revelation	

To fully comprehend all that the books of the New Testament tell us, we study the context in which they were written: from the history and political divisions of the time period to the culture and religious practices of its people. We must know this time and place if we want to truly understand all that was written in the books of the New Testament and revealed in Jesus Christ, the fulfillment of all God's promises of salvation.

How can studying the Bible's historical and cultural context help us to grow in our understanding of God's plan of salvation?

Article 32: The Unity of the Old and New

Sacred Scripture is truly a gift to all humanity. An integral part of that gift is the Old Testament, which we must never discard even though we now also have the New Testament. All salvation history recorded in the Old Testament still has—and will always have—inherent value and importance. We need it so we can understand the life and mission of Jesus Christ. The New Covenant is founded upon the Old, and the Old Covenant illuminates the way to the New.

Both the Old and New Testaments are therefore vital to help us see the big picture of God's gift of grace and redemption. The Church reminds us of the unity of the Old and New Testaments: "the New Testament lies hidden in the Old and the Old Testament is unveiled in the New[9]" (CCC, 129). For this reason, Christians under-

Primary Sources

The Unity of the Old and New Testaments

In the early centuries of the Church, some Christians neglected to study the Old Testament. A few even sought to remove the Old Testament from Sacred Scripture. In response, Saint Jerome—the first great Bible scholar—explained that we must study both the Old and New Testaments to fully understand the saving power of God in Christ:

> For if, as Paul says, Christ is the power of God and the wisdom of God, and if the man who does not know Scripture does not know the power and wisdom of God, then ignorance of Scripture is ignorance of Christ. (Saint Jerome, *Commentary on Isaiah*)

This is one reason why a reading from the Old Testament, chosen to correspond to the Gospel reading, is the first reading of the Liturgy of the Word at most Sunday Masses. This reinforces a unity of the Old and New Testaments that has been affirmed by the Church since the time of the Apostles.

stand that "the unity of the two Testaments proceeds from the unity of God's plan and his Revelation. The Old Testament prepares for the New and the New Testament fulfills the Old; the two shed light on each other; both are true Word of God" (140).

> **Why do we say that Sacred Scripture is a gift to all humanity?**

Chapter Review

1. What is the proper understanding of the word *old* in "Old Testament"?

2. How are the Catholic Bible and the Protestant Bible different?

3. List the seven deuterocanonical books.

4. What are the four categories of books found in the Old Testament? Briefly explain the type of books in each category.

5. What is the "big picture" painted by both the Old Testament and New Testament together?

6. Name four Jewish groups (sects) present in the New Testament and describe something unique about each group.

7. What are the five categories of New Testament books? What role did each play in spreading the message of Jesus Christ?

Unit 3

Revelation in the Old Testament

As you have learned, the Old Testament includes four categories of writing: the books of law, the historical books, the prophetic books, and the wisdom books. In this unit, we examine each of these categories more closely.

Genesis and Exodus are the first two books of law. *Genesis* means "origin" or "beginning," and that is exactly what we find in the Book of Genesis: the Creation of the universe, our first parents, Original Sin, and God's covenant with his Chosen People. The Book of Exodus picks up a few centuries later to describe how God, through Moses, freed the Israelites from slavery in Egypt. We learn about Moses' encounter with God on Mount Sinai, where God introduced his Law, summarized in the Ten Commandments.

The historical books tell us of the Israelites' arrival in the Promised Land, the judges who protected them, and the first kings. Unfortunately, the Israelites continually fell into sin and forgot to be faithful to God. The prophetic books contain the words of the prophets God commissioned to call his people back to the covenant. The prophets warned about God's wrath if the people continued to stray—but after God allowed his people to be conquered and exiled as punishment, the prophets reassured them that God continued to love them and call them back to himself. The prophets also heralded the coming of a messiah. Finally, the wisdom books are unique writings that help us to find universal truth and meaning in the mysteries of life.

The enduring understandings and essential questions represent core concepts and questions that are explored throughout this unit. By studying the content of each chapter, you will gain a more complete understanding of the following:

Enduring Understandings

1. The Books of Genesis and Exodus describe God's covenant of love and fidelity.

2. The historical books recount ancient Israelite history and demonstrate how God interacted in the Israelites' lives and in the lives of their leaders.

3. The prophetic books contain the words of the people whom God commissioned to call the Israelites back to the covenant.

4. The wisdom books help people of faith to find meaning in the mysteries of life.

Essential Questions

1. How can Scripture help us to understand God's desire to be in relationship with us?

2. Why is it important for Christians to understand ancient Israelite history?

3. How might prophetic voices both encourage and challenge us?

4. How can the wisdom books help us in everyday life?

7

The Book of Genesis

Introduction

We begin our study of the Old Testament with the Book of Genesis, an important book because it explains our origins as people of faith. Genesis starts with the Creation of the universe and concludes with God's faithfulness to the patriarchs of the covenant. This book helps us to envision the social and historical circumstances of the Near East in the early part of the second millennium BC, roughly 2000 to 1500 BC. Does that mean we can study Genesis as a detailed, chronological account of history? Not at all—the focus of Genesis is not painstaking historical accuracy. Rather, we are meant to study it as an account steeped in the truths of God's saving love for his people.

Genesis is the first of the five books of law, also called the Pentateuch. The five books of the Pentateuch are Genesis, Exodus, Leviticus, Numbers, and Deuteronomy. They introduce us to God as the source of all creation. In particular, the Book of Genesis explains the role of humans in the origin of sin and its many devastating effects. It tells us about God's desire to be in communion with his people, and it emphasizes the lasting effect of the covenant God formed with Abraham. We learn that God is a God of history who is always faithful to his promise of covenant love.

Article 33: Creation: In the Beginning

I believe in one God,
the Father almighty,
maker of heaven and earth,
of all things visible and invisible.

(*Roman Missal*)

Notice the energy and the sense of purpose implied by the movement in this painting. What do you think the artist was saying about Creation?

Are these words familiar to you? They are from the **Nicene Creed**. We profess this creed every Sunday at Mass. This passage expresses our belief that God is the principle source of all creation. The Nicene Creed echoes the words and events of Sacred Scripture, especially the Book of

© Alinari / Art Resource, NY

Genesis. The beginning of Genesis tells us how God created the world and all its inhabitants in seven figurative days. The Genesis accounts of Creation reveal God's infinite wisdom and his plan of loving goodness, which is ultimately fulfilled in Christ, the New Creation. That is, God's creative action in and through the natural order points toward, and is fulfilled in, the Incarnation.

The Primeval History

The accounts of Creation, together with the accounts of Adam and Eve, Cain and Abel, Noah and the Flood, and the Tower of Babel (see Genesis, chapters 1–11), are called the **primeval history**. The term refers to the time before the invention of writing. Through the inspiration of the Holy Spirit, the accounts in the primeval history were written long after the events they portray occurred. Even so, they communicate the truth without error precisely because they were written under the guidance of the Holy Spirit. Thus, when we read the accounts of

Nicene Creed
The formal statement or profession of Christian belief originally formulated at the Council of Nicaea in 325 and amplified at the Council of Constantinople in 381.

primeval history
The time before the invention of writing and recording of historical data.

Creation and other events in Genesis, chapters 1–11, we must consider what truths the Holy Spirit is conveying through the words of human authors.

Salvation History Begins: Two Accounts of Creation

Did you know that Genesis begins with not one, but two accounts of Creation? The first account (see 1:1–2:4) is an orderly description of God's creative activity, structured as a seven-day week. The second account (see

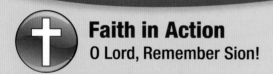

Faith in Action
O Lord, Remember Sion!

© SeanPavonePhoto / shutterstock.com

The peoples who live in the lands described in the Bible, what we now call the Middle East, trace their origins to several ancient cultures. For centuries three of these groups—Jews, Christians, and Muslims—have shared and occasionally fought over the Holy Land, especially the city of Jerusalem, which has special significance for all three religions.

Into this uneasy mix of religion and culture came the Sisters of Our Lady of Sion. (*Sion*, or *Zion*, is another word for Jerusalem.) This community of vowed women was founded in 1843 by two Jewish brothers in France who had converted to Catholicism and become priests. One of the brothers, Fr. Alphonse Ratisbonne, brought the sisters to Jerusalem to establish a school and an orphanage. Both were open to children of all faiths. The mission of the Sisters of Our Lady of Sion is to "witness by their life to God's faithful love for the Jewish People and to his fidelity to the promise he revealed to the Patriarchs and Prophets of Israel for all humanity" (CCJ Hillingdon News Archive).

Today some of the Sisters of Our Lady of Sion lead a contemplative life of prayer and work within their religious community, while others minister actively among the people. But all continue to work to build bridges of understanding among all faith traditions through their work in education, nursing, and social justice all around the world. Their former school in the Holy Land is now a guest house open to all people, a popular venue for ecumenical and interreligious discussions.

2:4–25) is where we learn about the creation of the first man, Adam, and the first woman, Eve. These two well-known accounts probably came from different Israelite religious traditions and were combined by the final author of Genesis, under the guidance of the Holy Spirit. The two accounts complement each other in revealing the nature of God, the holiness of Creation, and human nature and purpose.

The two Creation accounts are not meant to convey historical or scientific fact. Rather, they use figurative, or symbolic, language to tell us about the beginning of salvation history. The seven magnificent days of Creation in the first account show us that the universe was created out of love and has inherent goodness, beauty, and order that reflect God's own nature. Over and over we read that he looked upon what he created and saw how good it was. This first account teaches us that the world is fundamentally good. God did not create anything that is flawed or evil. This understanding of Creation is very important for us as God's people because it shows that God created the universe out of love. This account also reveals the awesome creative power of God: he needs only to will something, and whatever he wills becomes reality.

The second account of Creation focuses on the nature and destiny of the human person. It begins with the creation of Adam. God formed Adam from the dirt and breathed life into him (see Genesis 2:7). The description of how God breathed life into Adam is a figurative way to explain that we human beings participate in God's own divine life. God also created a beautiful garden for the man to live in and care for, and God himself walked in this garden (see 3:8). These details tell us that God created us for a life of beauty, peace, and joy in full communion with him. God also created a suitable partner for the man: Eve, a woman made from the man's own flesh. This account teaches us that God created men and women as loving partners for one another. We learn that the two sexes are meant to complement and fulfill each other.

Both Creation accounts teach us about the unique dignity that human beings enjoy. In the first Creation account, we read, "God created mankind in his image; / in the image of God he created them; / male and female he created them" (Genesis 1:27). The human person—each of us—is created in God's image, which means that only we, of all his creatures, have moral freedom, intellect, and an eternal soul. In the second Creation account, we read that God shared his own breath in giving human beings life—a sign of our sharing in divine life. But God also made Adam responsible for caring for the garden and allowed him to name all the animals. All of these details symbolize that human beings are called in a unique way to participate in God's creative work, especially in caring for his Creation.

The *Catechism of the Catholic Church (CCC)* reminds us that although "the work of creation is attributed to the Father in particular, it is equally a truth of faith that the Father, Son, and Holy Spirit together are the one, indivisible principle of creation" (316). Both Creation accounts point to this truth. Through them we also discover that the creation of the universe was the freely chosen work of God alone. Nothing forced him to create the universe, and he had no assistance.

Saint Bonaventure, a Franciscan theologian and Doctor of the Church, pointed out that God is present at all times and in all things: "In everything, whether it is a thing sensed or a thing known, God himself is hidden within." The two Creation accounts proclaim that light, darkness, sea, sun, living creatures, human beings, and all the rest of creation bear the mark of our God. The glory of God lies within everything in creation. Sometimes God's glory is visible. At other times it is invisible. But creation was not an accident. God orchestrated it. He is the originator, sustainer, and redeemer of all creation.

What does it mean to be called to participate in God's creative work? How do you respond to this call?

Article 34: Original Sin and God's Response

How would you explain sin to a friend? If you say that it means doing something that disobeys God or hurts another person, you would be close. We are created to live according to God's precepts and laws. That means we are created to be in right relationships with God and others. Unfortunately, our selfish desires get in the way of these right relationships. Holy people throughout the centuries have defined sin as missing the mark, falling short, brokenness, wrongdoing, misdeeds, and an offense against truth. The *Catechism* defines *sin* as "an utterance, a deed, or a desire contrary to the eternal law[1]" (1871).

We learn about the beginning of sin in the account of the first humans, Adam and Eve, who disobeyed God by eating the forbidden fruit (see Genesis 3:1–24). Their choice to give in to the devil's temptation and disobey God marks the first sin in salvation history. Their sin is called Original Sin; we often refer to it as "the Fall." Through Original Sin the first humans lost their original holiness and became subject to death. Original Sin also describes the fallen state in which all the descendants

Did You Know?

Mortal Sin and Venial Sin

There are two kinds of sin: venial and mortal. Sin is considered venial when it is less serious and reparable by charity. It damages our relationship with God but does not destroy it. Mortal sin is a grave offense against God. It is called *mortal,* meaning "deadly," because it separates us from God's grace. Three conditions must be met for a sin to be mortal: (1) it must concern a grave matter; (2) the person committing it must have full knowledge of the evil of the act; (3) it must be freely and deliberately committed. Mortal sin destroys within us the virtue of charity, which helps us to love God and our neighbor. Without repentance a mortal sin leads to eternal death. But through the Sacrament of Penance and Reconciliation, a person who has committed mortal sin can receive God's mercy and forgiveness and return to a right relationship with him.

of Adam and Eve, with the exception of Jesus and his mother, Mary, are deprived of original holiness and justice.

The Lasting Influence of Original Sin

© Cameraphoto Arte, Venice / Art Resource, NY

Like many Bible accounts, the account of Cain and Abel is not just about the distant past but is also about us today. Jealousy provoked Cain to murder his brother Abel. How has jealousy led to violent words or actions in your life and in the world today?

Cain and Abel were the sons of Adam and Eve. Genesis tells us that Cain and Abel had a tumultuous relationship filled with sibling rivalry and jealousy (see 4:1–15). One religious practice during Old Testament times was to offer sacrifices to God. Because much of life revolved around the land, including the raising of animals and growing of crops, people usually sacrificed their best animals and produce to God as a sign of their love and fidelity. But whereas Abel offered his best animal to God, Cain presented some meager produce. God was pleased with Abel's offering. This angered Cain, so he murdered his brother out of resentment and jealousy. Affected by the Original Sin of his parents, Cain freely chose to act contrary to God's Law.

The cycle of sin continued. In the account of Noah and the Flood (see Genesis, chapters 6–9), we learn that human beings continued to fall prey to sinful and evil ways. God was saddened by this reality, so he decided to cleanse his creation through a great Flood that would last forty days and nights. Out of love God gave Noah, a good and righteous man, instructions to build an ark to save himself and his family. In faith Noah followed God's instructions and was saved, along with the others on his ark, from the mighty waters of the flood. Afterward

God promised never again to destroy humankind with
a flood. He placed a rainbow in the sky as a sign of his
covenant with Noah and all living beings. This covenant
with humanity will last as long as the world endures.

As Noah's descendants grew numerous and settled in
different places, however, the influence of sin took deeper
root in the lives and actions of the people. In the account
of the Tower of Babel (see Genesis 11:1–9), we learn how
some power-hungry people attempted to build a tower
to reach the heavens. Longing to be like God and lured
by the desire to be famous, they forgot their relationship
with God. Nothing could stop them from building this
self-serving tower of pride—nothing except the hand
of God. To stop the people from building the tower, he
confused their speech and caused them to speak different languages. By making it impossible for these sinful
people to communicate, God effectively prevented them
from carrying out their plan.

God's Constant Protection

If these accounts of Adam and Eve, Cain and Abel,
Noah, and the Tower of Babel described only sin and
punishment, they would seem pretty bleak, wouldn't
they? Happily, in these accounts we also find reassurance
about God's protection and friendship. We know that
God could have created the universe and the first human
beings and stopped there, content to allow us to experience him through his creation. But he didn't. He revealed
himself to Adam and Eve and invited them into a deep
and close relationship with himself. Despite their sin and
fall, God still promised them that he would save humanity from sin and death, and he created covenants with
them and their descendants. From this we know that
God punishes his children justly, but he always continues
to love and protect us. For example, after banning Adam
and Eve from the garden, he spared them humiliation by
giving them clothes to wear. God forced Cain to wander
the earth, but he also placed a special mark on him so no

Semitic
A term referring to Semites, a number of peoples of the ancient Near East—the region commonly known today as the Middle East—from whom the Israelites descended.

Near East
In biblical times the region commonly known today as the Middle East, including the modern countries of Iraq, Iran, Syria, Lebanon, Israel, and Jordan.

one would harm him. To save the righteous, God gave Noah instructions on how to build the ark.

One act of disobedience, one assertion of pride, one Original Sin led to sins too numerous to count. Each offense against God breeds another offense. But Saint John of God assures us, "Just as water extinguishes fire, so love wipes away sin." God's love, as revealed in Jesus Christ, is the only way to end the cycle of sin and evil. Jesus Christ redeemed humanity and broke the bonds of Original Sin. The waters of Baptism cleanse us of Original Sin and unite us with Christ.

Do you see God inviting you to a deeper relationship with him, no matter how many times you sin?

Article 35: Abraham: Model of Faith

Whom do you look up to as a model of faith? For Christianity, Judaism, and Islam, one of the great models of faith in God is Abraham. Abraham was first known as Abram. Abram experienced many hardships, but through an act of faith he entered into a covenant relationship with God that changed everything for him and his descendants. Abram and his wife, Sarai, were **Semitic** nomads wandering the highlands of the **Near East**. God asked Abram to leave everything behind and set out for an unknown territory. God promised him:

> I will make of you a great nation, and I will bless you; I will make your name great, so that you will be a blessing. I will bless those who bless you and curse those who curse you. All the families of the earth will find blessing in you. (Genesis 12:2–3)

This passage from Genesis is the first mention of God's promise to the people of Israel. Abram took Sarai, his nephew Lot, and all their possessions and left for a strange land, Canaan, not knowing where God was leading them.

Stars of the Sky

For many years Abram and Sarai traveled in Canaan and other lands. They had no children, and Sarai was past child-bearing age. In Semitic culture children were seen as a sign of prestige and blessing from God. God spoke to reassure Abram: "Look up at the sky and count the stars, if you can. Just so . . . will your descendants be" (Genesis 15:5). Despite God's promise, however, Sarai continued to be childless. She finally offered her servant, Hagar, to Abram as a concubine so he might father an heir by her. Under this arrangement any child of Hagar would legally belong to Sarai.

Abram finally agreed to Sarai's plan and fathered a son, Ishmael, by Hagar. But as you can imagine, this led to bad feelings between the two women. At one point the pregnant Hagar ran away from the harshness of her mistress. In the wilderness a messenger of God appeared

Pray It!

Faith in God

Abraham had tremendous faith in God. He was willing to surrender everything and trust God completely. It's not easy to give up something that God calls us to let go of. Abraham was asked to leave his homeland, to trust that God would give him a child born of a wife who could not have children, and later to sacrifice this son. Sometimes the things God asks of us aren't easy to do. But just as Abraham's faith got him through difficult situations, faith helps us surrender to God's will too. What is God calling you to sacrifice? If you are struggling with his will for you, turn to him in prayer. This prayer is one place to start:

Jesus,
Sometimes I know exactly what you want me to do,
but I don't have the courage to do it.
I am tired of being held back by fear.
Help me stand up straight
and be whom you made me to be—
faithful, strong, and unafraid.
Amen.

(*The Catholic Youth Prayer Book*, page 13)

to her. At his command she returned to submit to Sarai, fortified by God's promise that her unborn son, Ishmael, would grow to manhood wild and free.

When Abram was ninety-nine years old, God again spoke with him and established his Covenant with Abram and his descendants:

> For my part, here is my covenant with you: you are to become the father of a multitude of nations. No longer will you be called Abram; your name will be Abraham, for I am making you the father of a multitude of nations. I will make you exceedingly fertile; I will make nations of you; kings will stem from you. I will maintain my covenant between me and you and your descendants after you throughout the ages as an everlasting covenant, to be your God and the God of your descendants after you. (Genesis 17:4–7)

God also told Abraham that Sarai's new name would be Sarah, and he promised to bless her with a son. God fulfilled his promise: Sarah bore Abraham a son, Isaac. Through Abraham, God chose to make his covenant, by which he formed his people. Through this covenant, God later revealed his Law to his people through Moses.

Several years after the birth of Isaac, Abraham's faith was tested again. Abraham believed God wanted him to sacrifice Isaac, his most prized gift and sign of the covenant. Filled with sadness and great distress, but trusting that God fulfills his promises, Abraham prepared to sacrifice his son. Seeing Abraham's unshakable faith, God intervened and stopped the sacrifice.

What amazing faith Abraham had! He left behind his home, journeyed with his wife to a new land, and accepted a new identity. Moreover he

Sarah overheard God telling Abraham that she would conceive and bear a child in her old age. Sarah laughed at this prediction, but she did indeed give birth to Isaac, whose name means "laughter."

© Erich Lessing / Art Resource, NY

was willing to offer God the son he had longed for. In Abraham we find true faith, a faith willing to risk all for the love of God. Because of Abraham's faithfulness and complete trust in God, he and Sarah were blessed with countless descendants.

What examples of inspiring faith do you find in the world today?

Article 36: The Covenant Continues with Abraham's Descendants

God continued his covenant with Abraham's descendants, Isaac and Jacob. Together with Abraham, Isaac and Jacob are known as the patriarchs. These men led their tribal families and, together with their wives, ruled over a great number of children, servants, and livestock. The Book of Genesis gives us an idea of how challenging life was during this time. At the same time, Genesis emphasizes God's saving power to rescue the patriarchs and their families from dangers of all kinds.

Primary Sources

"Do We Commit Original Sin?"

We usually think of sin as something we do, such as using God's name in vain, cheating on a test, or skipping Sunday Mass. But Original Sin is different: it is a human state of being, not a personal action. The bishops of the United States explain:

> Do we commit Original Sin? . . . Each of us inherits Original Sin, but it is not a personal fault of ours. It is a [state of] deprivation for each of us of original holiness and justice. This inheritance leaves us in a world that is subject to suffering and death, as well as in an environment in which the accumulated sins and failings of others disturb peace and order. (*United States Catholic Catechism for Adults*, page 70)

The bishops also remind us of God's plan of salvation: "Though Original Sin has had far-reaching consequences, of greater consequence has been God's mercy to us through the Death and Resurrection of Jesus Christ" (page 70).

Promised Land
The land (Canaan) God promised to the children of Abraham.

After Abraham's death his son Isaac assumed the role of patriarch. Isaac and his wife, Rebekah, were the parents of two feuding and imperfect twin sons, Esau and Jacob. Esau, the firstborn twin, went on to father the line of Abraham's descendants who did not live directly under the covenant. Jacob, born second, represented God's plan to create a Chosen People more numerous than the "stars of the sky" (Genesis 22:17). From the moment of their birth, Esau and Jacob lived in conflict with each other. This rivalry reached a critical point when Jacob, with Rebekah's help, stole from Esau the dying blessing of their father, usually reserved for firstborn sons.

Jacob, having supplanted his brother Esau by stealing Isaac's blessing, became the patriarch at his father's death. Though he was at times an ambitious schemer, Jacob proved to be a repentant brother, good father, and successful herder. With his two wives, Leah and Rachel, and their maidservants, he fathered twelve sons and one daughter. God spoke to Jacob in a dream to renew the covenant promise he made to Abraham. After an encounter with a mysterious messenger of God, with whom Jacob wrestled all through the night, God changed Jacob's name to Israel, which means "God-wrestler" or "one who struggles with divine beings." This is why all of Jacob's descendants became known as Israelites. When we refer to the Twelve Tribes of Israel, we are talking about a confederation of twelve Hebrew clans of faithful people who traced their origin to the patriarch Jacob. The names of Jacob's descendants became the names of the Twelve Tribes who settled in the **Promised Land**.

Among Jacob's sons, his favorite was Joseph. This favoritism, combined with Joseph's ability to interpret dreams, caused great jealousy among his eleven brothers. The brothers conspired to sell Joseph as a slave to a passing merchant. He ended up in Egypt, where he rose to power by interpreting dreams for a series of important people. After Joseph interpreted Pharaoh's dreams, the Egyptian ruler made him his second in command. Years later, during a time of famine in Canaan, Joseph's brothers came west to Egypt in search of food. After testing them, Joseph revealed his identity to them and forgave them, and he and his brothers were reconciled. The brothers brought Jacob and their families to Egypt to live. This is how the Israelites came to settle in Egypt, where Pharaoh eventually enslaved them.

God Keeps His Promises

Over and over again, the Book of Genesis shows us how God transcends the brokenness of humanity so that all may know his promise of reconciliation and peace. From the account of an old and infertile couple (Abraham and Sarah) to the tale of trickery and deception between two brothers over birthright (Jacob and Esau) to the account of Joseph, the favored son of Jacob who was sold into slavery by his eleven jealous brothers—we see that nothing stands in the way of the fulfillment of God's covenant promises. Jacob's family became a large tribe, and his large tribe became twelve even larger tribes. God's promise of numerous descendants of Abraham was being fulfilled. Despite the intended and unintended obstacles we humans continue to create, Genesis reassures us that God will still guide us, like a parent, to the Promised Land.

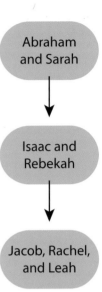

What barriers, intended or unintended, have you put up between yourself and God?

Article 37: The Continuing Role of Patriarchs

The vocation of mother and father to a people in faith was portrayed in the lives of the Old Testament patriarchs and holy women. This vocation was continued in the Christian era through Christ's call of the Twelve Apostles and the work of the early Church Fathers. The leaders in both the Old and New Covenants were channels for God's plan of loving goodness. God entrusted them with spiritual leadership. Even when these leaders made mistakes, we see that God transformed their mistakes into stepping-stones toward the Reign of Heaven. What is so amazing is that the spiritual fathers and mothers of the past, who embody both the beauty and darkness of humanity, fanned the flame of God's promise of eternal joy.

Why should we learn about our spiritual fathers and mothers in Sacred Scripture? How can their example deepen our faith today?

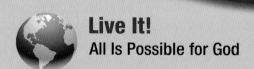

Live It!
All Is Possible for God

Have you noticed that some people God picks for his work seem unqualified for the task? Sometimes the people he calls are physically unable to do what he is asking of them? For example, Sarah, the woman God selected to be the mother of his Chosen People, was elderly and infertile. Sarah laughed at the idea that God chose her for this task. Yet in the end her condition didn't get in the way of God's will.

God can manifest his power through any person or situation. You too have been chosen by God for a unique and special call. Do you feel unsure of what tasks and role he is calling you to? Do you sometimes feel unworthy or incapable of doing what he asks of you? Don't let fear or uncertainty hold you back from responding to God's call. You have been chosen. Pray regularly to seek God's will. When he makes it known to you, you can rest assured he will give you the grace to accomplish it.

Chapter Review

1. How do the two accounts of Creation in Genesis complement each other in revealing the nature of God?

2. How are the effects of Original Sin evident in the lives of Adam and Eve's descendants?

3. What do the accounts of human sinfulness in the Book of Genesis show us about God's mercy and compassion?

4. What is the difference between a venial sin and a mortal sin?

5. What were the terms of the covenant between God and Abraham?

6. What is a patriarch? Name the patriarchs in the Old Testament.

7. What were the Twelve Tribes of Israel, and what was their origin?

The Book of Exodus

Introduction

Slavery—liberation—trust. The Book of Exodus is a captivating account of these three powerful themes. The Book of Exodus covers the period from about 1500 to 1250 BC. It tells of a people, the Israelites, who were enslaved by the ruling dynasty of Egypt. God responded to the Israelites' suffering by calling Moses, a holy and courageous man, to lead them to freedom. On God's behalf, Moses challenged the forces of the Egyptian pharaoh and ultimately was able to lead the Israelites through the waters of the Red Sea. The Israelites followed Moses into the wilderness, only to experience forty years of hardship on their journey to the Promised Land.

After enduring persecution and slavery, followed by the challenges of desert travel, the Israelites reached Mount Sinai. When God presented them with the Ten Commandments there, they formed an identity as the Chosen People of God, a holy nation governed by God's Law. The Book of Exodus tells of a God who saves all his people from the snares of the world. It speaks of a compassionate God who sustains us even in the most difficult situations, a God who longs to be in a covenant relationship with his children.

Article 38: A People Enslaved

> I have witnessed the affliction of my people in Egypt and
> have heard their cry . . . , so I know well what they are suf-
> fering. (Exodus 3:7)

pharaoh
A ruler of ancient
Egypt.

The Lord spoke these words to Moses when his people,
the Israelites, were enslaved. No specific record of the
Israelites' enslavement has been found in Egyptian historical documents, but we know that slavery and persecution were part of the experience of the Israelites in
Egypt because these details are recounted in the Book of
Exodus.

To understand the events described in Exodus, it is
important to know the situation of the Israelites in Egypt.
In the Book of Genesis, we learn that Jacob's family came
to Egypt in search of food during a famine. After Jacob's
descendants enjoyed welcome and peace in Egypt for
several generations, the Egyptian **pharaoh** began to see
the growing number of Israelites as a threat. He ordered
that the Israelites be enslaved. The Egyptian leadership
forced the Israelite people into harsh and inhumane
work. At some point, the pharaoh ordered the deaths of
all male Israelite babies, hoping to eventually eradicate
the Israelite people, sometimes also called the Hebrews.
This action resulted in the unexpected adoption of Moses
and his hidden identity among the Egyptian ruling class.

Young Moses

To save her infant son from the order to kill newborn
Hebrew boys, Moses' mother, an Israelite, placed him
in a basket and floated it down the Nile River. There
Moses was discovered by Pharaoh's daughter. She enlisted
Moses' mother—not knowing she was the baby's biologi-
cal mother—to care for the infant Moses. In this way,
Pharaoh's daughter adopted Moses, and he grew up in
Pharaoh's house.

After Moses reached adulthood, he saw an Egyptian
striking an Israelite slave. In defense of the slave, Moses
killed the Egyptian and hid the body in the sand. When

© Look and Learn / Bridgeman Images

Pharaoh's order to kill all the Hebrew male babies failed because of courageous and resourceful women: the midwives, Moses' mother and sister, and even Pharaoh's daughter.

Moses' actions became known, he feared for his life and fled to the land of Midian. There he encountered the daughters of Reuel, a priest of Midian. Moses stayed with Reuel (also called Jethro) and married his daughter Zipporah.

From his imminent death to his life as a prince of Egypt, from murder to a new life in Midian, the early years of Moses' life reveal the mysterious and glorious work of God. God took an infant and led him on a journey that brought him to a personal encounter with God and a commission to be an instrument of his will.

Why might Pharaoh's daughter have adopted the infant Moses? Was it just luck, or do you perceive God's hand at work?

Article 39: Moses and the Exodus

What a remarkable life Moses led up to this point! Yet even these events of his early life were not as profound as what happened next. While Moses tended sheep for his wife's family near Mount Horeb, the mountain of God, God addressed him from a burning bush and revealed his sacred, divine name: **Yahweh**, often translated as "I am who I am" (Exodus 3:14). God had heard the cries of his children enslaved in Egypt. He called Moses to return to Egypt as his voice of truth and arm of justice. As a humble and a courageous man, Moses embodied the hopes and aspirations of God's holy people to live no longer under the darkness of Pharaoh's reign but rather to walk freely in the light of God's Reign.

The Ten Plagues

Sent by God and assisted by Aaron, his brother, Moses stood up to Pharaoh, saying, "Let my people go" (Exodus 5:1). Pharaoh, whom Egyptian culture considered to be divine, could not simply give in to another god's demands. Angry, he ordered even harsher treatment of the enslaved Israelites. Again at the command of God, Moses and Aaron confronted Pharaoh about his idolatrous and abusive ways. Again he did not heed their message. Through Moses and Aaron, God even worked the wonder of turning a staff into a snake. Still Pharaoh refused to back down. He could not let his own perceived divine status be challenged.

To show who the true God was, God unleashed ten plagues on Pharaoh and Egypt. The plagues were meant to dismantle the authority of the Egyptian empire and to bring about the freedom of the Israelites. God never abandoned his plan of salvation, and he refused to allow the arrogance of one man to direct the fate of a good and righteous people. Beginning by turning water to blood,

Yahweh
The most sacred of the Old Testament names for God, which he revealed to Moses. It is frequently translated as "I AM" or "I am who am."

Pray It!

Your Will Be Done, Lord

The Bible is full of people God called to do his will. Moses is one example of a person God called to be a prophet and to speak his Word. However, Moses lacked confidence, and he said to the Lord: "If you please, my Lord, send someone else!" (Exodus 4:13).

Like Moses, we may not feel worthy or capable of responding to God's will for us. It may be a challenge that takes us beyond our comfort zone. We just need to trust God and allow him to work through us. God provided Moses with what he needed to accomplish his will—namely, Aaron's support—and he will provide what you need too. Pray and ask God to make his will known to you.

Father,
Help me to know what your will is for me.
Give me good judgment to know what you are calling me to do
and the grace necessary to accomplish your will.
Amen.

the first plague, God exerted his identity as the one true God, demanding that his people be set free. Eight more plagues followed: frogs, gnats, flies, a pestilence affecting livestock, festering boils, a hailstorm, locusts, and a three-day darkness. Pharaoh managed to endure all nine plagues and still refused to free the Israelites.

After the ninth plague, God told Moses: "One more plague I will bring upon Pharaoh and upon Egypt. After that he will let you depart. In fact, when he finally lets you go, he will drive you away" (Exodus 11:1). On the night of the tenth plague, God directed the Israelites to slaughter a one-year-old male lamb (now called the Passover, or Paschal, lamb) and to place some of the

Faith in Action
The Martyrs of Compiègne

© Musee des Beaux-Arts, Nantes, France /
Bridgeman Images

The Chosen People were enslaved in Egypt because they were Hebrews. The Catholic Church also has a long history of men and women who have endured suffering and persecution because of their faith. They include the Martyrs of Compiègne: sixteen members of a Carmelite community in France who were killed by guillotine in 1794 during the French Revolution (1789–1799).

The French Revolution ended with a period known as the Reign of Terror. It got this name because Robespierre, a political leader and opponent of the traditional God of Christianity, ordered the deaths of anyone opposing his political or religious ideals. A new law called the Civil Constitution of the Clergy made the Catholic Church subordinate to the French government. The Carmelites of Compiègne, like many other holy men and women in France, were condemned as traitors because they would not denounce God. They knelt and chanted the hymn *Veni Creator Spiritus* (Come, Holy Spirit) and renewed their baptismal and religious vows as they joyfully went to the guillotine one by one. Because of their beautiful example of faith in the face of martyrdom, they were beatified by the Church in 1906. They are sometimes known as Blessed Teresa of Saint Augustine and Companions. Many books and websites recount the story of the Martyrs of Compiègne, as does a well-known opera titled *Dialogues of the Carmelites*.

lamb's blood on the doorposts of the houses where the Israelites gathered. They were to roast the lamb and eat it with bitter herbs and unleavened bread (that is, bread made without yeast). On that night, they were told, the Lord would descend upon Egypt and strike down every firstborn human and beast. But he reassured them: "The blood will mark the houses where you are. Seeing the blood, I will pass over you" (Exodus 12:13).

To this day, the events surrounding the tenth plague are known as the **Passover**, because the Lord passed over all houses marked with the blood of the sacrificial lamb, as he promised the Israelites. But he entered the Egyptian houses not marked with this sign of faith and killed the firstborn children and animals within—including the firstborn son of Pharaoh. To this day, as God commanded, the Israelites celebrate the Passover meal every year to remind them of their escape from slavery through his power.

Passover
The night the Lord passed over the houses of the Israelites marked by the blood of the lamb, and spared the firstborn sons from death. It also is the feast that celebrates the deliverance of the Chosen People from bondage in Egypt and the Exodus from Egypt to the Promised Land.

The Exodus

Pharaoh was grief stricken over the loss of his son, the symbol of his prosperity and power. He finally relented, even begging Moses and the Israelites to leave Egypt, as God said he would. In a spirit of vengeance, however, Pharaoh changed his mind and sent his chariots to pursue the Israelites. Trapped between the Red Sea and the wrath of Pharaoh, the Israelites cried out to Moses, "Were there no burial places in Egypt [such] that you brought us to die in the wilderness?" (Exodus 14:11). Moses responded, "The LORD will fight for you; you have only to keep still" (14:14). Moses stretched his arms over the sea, and "the LORD drove back the sea with a strong east wind all night long and turned the sea into dry ground" (14:21). The Israelites were able to cross on dry land to reach safety. In a final act of destruction, the sea flowed back into place just as the Egyptians attempted to cross in pursuit.

This account of the Israelites' escape from Egypt shows us the saving power of God. We see that God

manna
The breadlike food that God miraculously provided for the Chosen People during their wandering in the desert.

Ten Commandments
Sometimes called the Decalogue, the list of ten norms, or rules of moral behavior, that God gave Moses and that are the basis of ethical conduct.

keeps his promises to his people, even when a situation appears hopeless and impossible. His offer of liberating love and sanctifying grace remains steadfast and will never be subject to a world designed to humiliate the human spirit.

> **How does your faith in God help you through times when life feels hopeless and impossible?**

Article 40: Building Identity and Trust in the Wilderness

Are you familiar with the saying "Out of the frying pan, into the fire"? It describes getting out of one problematic situation only to encounter a new one, sometimes even worse. Likewise, you might think the Israelites' troubles were over now—but liberation from Egyptian slavery and the crossing of the Red Sea were just the start of their difficult journey.

During the Exodus, on the way to the Promised Land, the Israelites had to cross a vast wilderness, a desert where their fate seemed uncertain. Food and water were scarce, and the natives were hostile. Under these less than ideal conditions, the Israelites immediately forgot God's liberating action, which he had already demonstrated in their Exodus from slavery. They also forgot his promise to protect them even in the darkest times.

Disgruntled by the harsh conditions of the desert and disillusioned by the leadership of Moses, the people questioned, "Is the LORD in our midst or not?" (Exodus 17:7). They complained and began to idealize their previous life in Egypt—forgetting the harsh treatment of Pharaoh, ignoring the God who listens to their cries, and discounting the courage of Moses in accepting the call to lead them to freedom. Yet God did not forget his promises. When the people were hungry, God rained down **manna**, little flakes that the people could collect and then boil or bake into a substance like bread. When they were thirsty, God drew water from a rock. When they were afraid,

God protected them. Still they questioned the presence of God.

In all their struggles and complaints, the Israelites were forced not only to work together but also to build a community based on trust in God's saving power. Some were called to assist Moses as leaders. Part of their role was to help the people remember God's wondrous deeds in the Exodus and recognize God's saving presence in their midst. These leaders empowered the Israelites, a forgetful people, to move forward with trust and hope in the ways of the Lord. They reminded the people of a God who never forsakes his promises.

As you can see, the people were traveling an unclear road with many twists and turns. Yet God never left them. He drew them together as a family and gave them a new identity. He brought them from the depths of slavery and called them to a new land to be his Chosen People who still sing of his greatness.

When twists and turns in your life cause you to question God's presence, how do you keep faith?

© Gejra / shutterstock.com

Traveling through the desert forced the Israelites to rely on God for survival. How does life today make it easy for us to forget that we also need to rely on God?

Article 41: The Covenant with Moses

Slavery was followed by freedom, which was followed by wandering in the desert. God had gradually worked to create a people with a new identity and sense of mission, and it was finally time for God to seal their identity. This new identity coalesced at the foot of Mount Sinai. Mount Sinai is the sacred ground where God formed a covenant with his Chosen People. This covenant includes laws and obligations known as the **Ten Commandments**, which continue to govern our relationship with God and with one another.

From Liberation to Covenant

Sinai Covenant
The covenant established with the Israelites at Mount Sinai that renewed God's covenant with Abraham's descendants. The Sinai Covenant establishes the Israelites as God's Chosen People.

Enslavement had stripped the Israelites of their identity and forced them to live under the law of Pharaoh. Brought through the waters of the Red Sea to Mount Sinai, the Israelites entered a covenant with God. At Mount Sinai, Moses climbed the mountain. There God directed him to tell the Israelites that the Lord brought them safely to this place and that if they keep the covenant, they will be the Lord's holy nation.

Moses returned to the people and shared the Lord's offer of his covenant. Within the framework of this **Sinai Covenant**, God declared himself to be their God, a God of fidelity, love, and justice. Recalling the covenant between God and Abraham, the Lord promised that the Israelites would be his "treasured possession among all peoples . . . a kingdom of priests, a holy nation" (Exodus 19:5–6). In return they must be a righteous, moral people who live according to his Law. God promised that after the Israelites agreed to the terms of the covenant, they would dwell in the Promised Land—as Exodus describes it, "a land flowing with milk and honey"

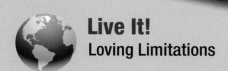

Live It!
Loving Limitations

When someone says you are not allowed to do something, do you immediately want to go out and do it? Most of us dislike having limitations put on us. The problem is that sometimes what we want is not always good. Some limits are necessary. Sometimes limitations are even the most loving thing one person can provide for another.

For example, a mother tells her child not to leave the yard and run into the street. Why? Does she want to keep her son or daughter from having a good time? Of course not. She makes this rule because she loves her child and does not want the child to get hurt. In a similar way, God gives Commandments to guide us, not to restrain us. He does this because he loves us. Pick one of the Ten Commandments that seems restrictive, and write down some positive things that come from following it.

(33:3)—and they would know a God whose "mercy is from age to age" (Luke 1:50).

The Ten Commandments

On the third day at Mount Sinai, God again summoned Moses to the mountaintop. There God gave him the Ten Commandments. Deliv-

© John Said / iStockphoto.com

ered to the Israelites by Moses but "inscribed by God's own finger" (Exodus 31:18), the Ten Commandments are the first stage of revealed law, conveying God's expectations of his people. In this sense, the Ten Commandments express the Israelites' covenant relationship with God. They also summarize the Law of God in the entire Torah, the books of law.

Even today the Ten Commandments remain a framework to help us build a more just society, and they teach us how to live in right relationship with God. They tell us what it means to be God's people and follow his

The Ten Commandments teach us how to live in right relationship with God and with one another. Can you think of a way that each of the Commandments applies to your relationships with God and others?

Primary Sources

The Ten Commandments

Review this list of the Ten Commandments from the *Catechism of the Catholic Church*. Then read the fuller account of the Ten Commandments that appears in the Book of Exodus (20:2–17). What new insights does the Exodus account give you?

1. I am the LORD your God: you shall not have strange Gods before me.
2. You shall not take the name of the LORD your God in vain.
3. Remember to keep holy the LORD's Day.
4. Honor your father and your mother.
5. You shall not kill.
6. You shall not commit adultery.
7. You shall not steal.
8. You shall not bear false witness against your neighbor.
9. You shall not covet your neighbor's wife.
10. You shall not covet your neighbor's goods.

(Pages 496–497)

covenant. At their heart are reverence and love for God and love of neighbor. When the Israelites received the Ten Commandments from God at Mount Sinai, their identity as the People of God was sealed.

> **How do rules help us to develop identities and form relationships? Why are they necessary in our relationship with God?**

Article 42: The Old Law and the New Law

The Old Law given to Moses was a preparation for the Gospel, the New Law, revealed through Jesus Christ. Jesus Christ came to fulfill the Old Covenant and Law. He affirmed the Old Law received by Moses (see Matthew 5:17) and brought it to perfection. Like Moses, Jesus delivered the law from a mountain in the Sermon on the Mount. Like the Old Law, the New Law is based in love of

Did You Know?

© mammuth / iStockphoto.com

Jesus Christ: The New Paschal Lamb and Bread of Life

We find many parallels between the Exodus story and Jesus Christ. For example, God, sustainer of all life, sent manna, a bread of life, from Heaven to feed the Israelites in the desert. During his earthly life, Jesus fed people not only with food but also with his presence and words. At a Passover meal, Jesus instituted the Sacrament of the Eucharist so that people of all times and places would be fed by his presence and Word. Jesus is our Bread of Life.

Jesus is also the new Paschal (or Passover) Lamb. At the Last Supper, Jesus broke the bread and said, "Take and eat; this is my body" (Matthew 26:26). He then took the cup and said, "Drink from it, all of you" (26:27). The sacrifice of the original Passover lamb saved the Israelites from physical death, but Jesus' sacrifice saves us from eternal death and gives us eternal life with God.

God and love of our neighbor. It is a law of grace because the Holy Spirit gives us the strength to live it out through faith and the Sacraments. And it is a law of freedom because, although it is guided by guidelines and rituals, it also calls us to freely share God's love in acts of charity and justice.

> **How do the Sacraments, especially the Sacrament of the Eucharist, support you in loving God and loving your neighbor?**

Chapter Review

1. What caused the enslavement of the Israelites?

2. How did God respond to the enslavement of his people?

3. Why did the tenth plague convince Pharaoh to release the Israelites?

4. What was the attitude of the people of Israel toward God while they were in the midst of the desert? Why did they feel like this?

5. What is manna? What is it a sign of?

6. What is at the heart of the Ten Commandments?

Chapter 9

The Historical Books

Introduction

Chapters 7 and 8 introduced you to the first two books of the Bible: Genesis and Exodus, which are also the first two books of law. As you learned in chapter 6, a second major category of Old Testament books is the historical books. The historical books recount the history of the Chosen People from around 1250 to 100 BC—but they are not like the history textbooks you read in school. The authors of the historical books were less concerned with recording historical data. Instead they intended to write a sacred history that reveals God's plan of salvation. The historical books focus on the settlement of the Promised Land and the unification of the kingdom under David. They discuss the eventual division of the united kingdom into northern and southern kingdoms. They also portray the eventual destruction of the two kingdoms and the rebuilding of a nation after exile. This chapter introduces you to the historical books by focusing on the first two events: settlement and unification.

Joshua, the judges, and the first three kings of Israel—Saul, David, and Solomon—are major figures in the historical books. God called each of them for a special mission grounded in his holy will. Do you think he called them because they were perfect? Not at all—they were flawed and sinful human beings through whom God performed amazing acts of love and mercy. The historical books place God at the center of our human experience, giving meaning to the struggles of everyday life. These unique books lift up people who were blessed when they lived in right relationship with God.

Article 43: The Book of Joshua: God Is on Our Side

Have you ever been on a long, difficult trip, only to face new challenges at the end of your journey? If so, you might have glimpsed what the Israelites faced after their Exodus from Egypt and their forty years in the desert. At long last, the Israelites finally reached Canaan, the Promised Land. But after the death of Moses, they once again needed a strong leader to guide them into the Promised Land. God commissioned the heroic and faithful Joshua, who had served Moses as a trusted leader: "So now, you and the whole people with you, prepare to cross the Jordan to the land that I will give the Israelites. Every place where you set foot I have given you, as I promised Moses" (Joshua 1:2–3).

polytheistic
Belief in many gods and goddesses.

Baal . . . Asherah
Two Canaanite gods of earth and fertility that the Israelites worshipped when they fell away from the one true God.

Joshua's and Moses' stories are similar. Both men experienced God in miraculous ways, both parted a body of water, and both heard trumpets when they accomplished God's covenant plan. Most important, both heeded God's call, saying yes with their entire beings to participate in the history of salvation.

© REUTERS

Pope Saint John Paul II prays for peace at Mount Nebo, the traditional site where God showed Moses the Promised Land.

The Israelites Enter a Foreign Land

Under Joshua's leadership, the Israelites entered Canaan, the land God had long before promised to Abraham and his descendants. The Israelites found Canaan to be hostile because of the **polytheistic** beliefs of the Canaanites, including their worship of the god **Baal** and his consort, the goddess **Asherah**. It was also hostile because the native peoples refused to hand over their land.

Joshua and the Israelite army swiftly conquered the land of Canaan. One of the pivotal moments in their conquest was the fall of Jericho, a small town on the west bank of the River Jordan. The town was notable as the place where the Israelites met the prostitute Rahab and other outcasts from the unjust system of governance in Canaanite society. Rahab helped the Israelites in their conquest, both to save herself and to help create a Canaan based on equality and justice. To reward Rahab for her help, the Israelites spared her and her family during the destruction of Jericho.

In Rahab we find a symbol of oppressed individuals governed by the selfish laws of humanity, not by the Law of Moses, which protects the rights of all people under

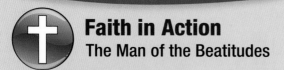

Faith in Action
The Man of the Beatitudes

© REUTERS / Daniel Munoz

Blessed Pier Giorgio (1901–1925) was born into the wealthy Frassati family of Turin, Italy. He seemed to know, from an early age, what life is all about. As a young boy, he received special permission to receive Holy Communion every day, a rare privilege at that time. Yet his spiritual life never simply centered on "Jesus and me." It was always "Jesus, my friends, and those who are poor, sick, or in need."

To serve Christ in others, especially those most in need, Pier Giorgio joined the Saint Vincent de Paul Society, which ministers to the poor, and other associations that promote Christian values through political activism. One year, instead of spending a vacation at his family's summer home, he decided to stay in the city, asking, "If everybody leaves Turin, who will take care of the poor?" He decided to become a mining engineer so that he could minister personally to the local miners.

Pier Giorgio was also a man of courage. At a Church-sponsored demonstration in Rome, he responded to a police attack by holding a banner high and fending off police blows with the banner's pole.

Just before he graduated with a degree in engineering, Pier Giorgio contracted polio, a contagious disease (now almost eradicated by vaccination) that can cause paralysis. He died in 1925, only twenty-four years old. On May 20, 1990, Pope Saint John Paul II beatified him, calling him The Man of the Eight Beatitudes. His tomb is now in the Cathedral of Turin. His feast day is the day of his death: July 4.

God's promise of peace and prosperity. This may be why Rahab is mentioned not only in the Book of Joshua but also in the New Testament. The Letter to the Hebrews says, "By faith Rahab the harlot did not perish with the disobedient" (11:31), and the Letter of James says, "Was not Rahab the harlot also justified by works when she welcomed the messengers and sent them out by a different route?" (2:25). The authors of the New Testament recognized Rahab as playing a role in God's plan. She is another example of how God can work through anyone, even those who seem most unlikely, to bring salvation to his people.

Joshua: Warrior and Faithful Leader

In its many accounts of battles and conquest, the Book of Joshua presents God as a warrior waging a holy war. How can a God of love wage such a savage war? Can you reconcile the image of a warrior with the image of a compassionate and merciful God? It is important to remember that the words in Sacred Scripture are conditioned by the language and culture of the Israelites. The Israelites believed God was on their side. Thinking of him as warrior provided the Israelites with a sense of security. Their warrior God had freed them from the clutches of Pharaoh and would lead them into battle for the Promised Land. For the Israelites, war was a holy act to fulfill the promise God had made to their fathers and mothers in faith by protecting them from the influences of cultures hostile to their religious beliefs and practices.

One important aspect of Joshua is easily overlooked among the stories of the battles: namely, his undying devotion to God. Joshua was a strong military leader for the Israelites, but he also modeled a true commitment to the covenant with God. Even when God provided seemingly odd directions, Joshua remained true to them. At the time of his death, Joshua said to the Israelites: "If it is displeasing to you to serve the LORD, choose today whom you will serve, the gods your ancestors served beyond the River or the gods of the Amorites in whose country you

judges
The eleven men and one woman who served the Hebrew people as tribal leaders, military commanders, arbiters of disputes, and enliveners of faith.

are dwelling. As for me and my household, we will serve the LORD" (Joshua 24:15). In remaining faithful to God, Joshua demonstrated to the Israelites that when they remain true to the covenant, God will abundantly bless them.

When we read the Book of Joshua today, we see that God, as both a just warrior and a loving covenant maker, does not seek brutality. Instead he longs for a world founded on the words he spoke to Abraham, the Law he gave Moses, and the truth he revealed in the heart of Joshua. We need to remember that God is always on the side of what is right and good. In the Book of Joshua, whose name means "salvation of God," we learn that God stands firm against the wicked ways of the world, challenges the people who lack trust, and fulfills the promise he made to Abraham.

> **In what ways does your family, your household, serve the Lord?**

Article 44: Judges: The Book of Deliverers

After the Israelites settled the Promised Land and began a time of peace, they had less need for strong leaders like Moses and Joshua. Over time, however, foreign invasions and the people's faithlessness to the covenant created the need for new leaders. Thus Israelite history from around 1200 to 1000 BC was marked by the leadership of twelve heroic yet flawed individuals known as the **judges**. Their role was different from that of our judges today. These leaders did settle disputes within their own tribe or between tribes, but the judges also led the military defense against outside invaders. Most important, they challenged Israel to remain faithful to God.

The Book of Judges does not attempt to give a chronological record of the time of the judges, between the settlement of Canaan and the rise of the monarchy. Rather it offers us short accounts of these human leaders who worked to accomplish God's will. We learn that after the death of Joshua, the Israelites fell into a cycle of sin. This cycle proceeded through sin, calamity, repentance, deliverance, and back to sin, over and over. The judges emerged when the Israelites began to fall away from their core religious identity by worshipping false gods, such as Baal and Asherah, two gods worshipped by the other peoples living in Canaan. Every time Israel forgot its covenant commitments, God's people became selfish and timid, which resulted in their being dominated by idol-worshipping neighbors. However, the Israelites eventually repented each time, and God introduced a hero, a judge, who led the people from destruction.

Given this history, you might expect that all the judges were faithful to the covenant. In fact, some were not. But even though the fidelity of some judges wavered, God's will was still accomplished. He transcended the frailty of the human condition so his plan could be fulfilled in the lives of the Chosen People. The judges were perhaps not as formidable as Moses and Joshua. But with all their strengths and weaknesses, the judges were key figures in God's fortifying plan of redemption and eternal happiness.

Deborah, Gideon, and Samson: Three Notable Judges

The twelve judges, as leaders of the Twelve Tribes of Israel, were important in their own ways, but three are worth discussing in greater detail: Deborah, Gideon, and Samson. Deborah, the fourth judge of Israel, was a strong, confident woman whom God commanded to launch a war against the Canaanites—including the Canaanite king, Jabin, and his general, Sisera—because they continued to attack and pillage Israel. After she led the Israelite army to victory, Deborah broke into song, praising God and his many servants: "So perish all your enemies, O Lord! / But may those who love you be like the sun rising in its might!" (Judges 5:31).

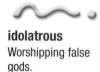

idolatrous
Worshipping false gods.

Gideon, another powerful judge, was an **idolatrous** man at first. But after he encountered a messenger of the Lord, he stopped worshipping foreign gods and pledged his loyalty to the one true God of Israel. Because of his conversion, Gideon made it his mission to destroy the altars of false gods. The account of Gideon demonstrates how one person's faith, or lack of it, can unite or divide a people. When Gideon's faith was strong, he brought the tribes together. When it was weak—practically nonexistent—he led them into idolatry.

© Mary Evans Picture Library/Everett Collection

It took an angel's appearance to cause the judge, Gideon, to be committed to the true God. Who is God using to help you in your relationship with him?

Samson was a strong, passionate man who, like Gideon, had trouble keeping his religious commitments. Samson accomplished amazing feats for God, including the legendary acts of tearing a lion apart with his bare hands and killing one thousand Philistines with the jawbone of an animal. His character flaws led him to be captured, mutilated, and imprisoned by the Philistines. However, because of a final act of trust in God, Samson was able to deliver Israel from the Philistines.

Deborah, Gideon, and Samson, along with the other nine judges, help us to recognize that Yahweh is the king of all people, deserving all our trust and reverence. The judges acted as a conscience for the Israelites, continually reminding them to be faithful to their covenant with God, for in God all things can be accomplished. Without him all action is meaningless and stands in the way of truth.

Who in your life acts as an external conscience, an outside voice reminding you to be faithful to God?

God blessed Samson with superhuman strength, but Samson also had many character flaws. His story teaches us that God works through imperfect people.

© JonnyJim / iStockphoto.com

Article 45: From Saul to Solomon: The Desire for Unity

The judges were important leaders of the Israelites during their early years in the Promised Land. Increasingly, however, the Israelites demanded a centralized form of leadership under a king, known as a **monarchy**. They were concerned about the growing divisions among the Twelve Tribes, as well as the increased power of other nations. Separated by tribal allegiance and lacking a consistent, central leader, the Israelites experienced the

Live It!
Priorities

Worshipping false gods may seem strange to you. Perhaps you are confident that the Trinity—Father, Son, and Holy Spirit—was, is, and will forever be the only God. However, idolatry really means letting something other than God take his place in your life. Idolatry can simply be the unconscious belief that you need something other than God to make you truly happy. Extravagant desires for money, sex, clothing, and popularity can all be forms of idolatry. A subtle form of idolatry led the judge Samson astray. His desire to be with Delilah, a Philistine spy, overtook his faith in God and led to his downfall.

Being aware of your priorities is essential. Write them down and evaluate them. Are your priorities consistent with all that Jesus taught and that the Church professes? Do any of your priorities indicate that deep down you feel the need for something besides God to be truly happy?

monarchy
A government or a state headed by a single person, such as a king or queen. As a biblical term, it refers to the period of time when the Israelites existed as an independent nation.

theocracy
A nation in which God is recognized as the head of the state and its divine ruler.

consequences of division and sin. We can find examples in the horrible accounts of violence against innocent people in the second half of the Book of Judges. The Israelites longed for someone to bring them together and to help them gather their many resources and talents to become a cohesive people, a powerful nation-state directed by God's holy will.

Samuel, a priest and prophet who was the last judge of Israel, resisted the calls for a monarchy because he feared that the Israelites wanted to replace the ruler of all creation, God, with the human authority of a king. Instead, Samuel wanted a **theocracy**, a nation ruled by God, not a monarchy ruled by a human being. Samuel repeatedly warned the people of the danger of kings. Nonetheless, God decided to honor the Israelites' request, and he directed Samuel: "Listen to them! Appoint a king to rule over them" (1 Samuel 8:22). This is how the monarchy of Israel was established. With the institution of the monarchy came the first three kings, wise yet flawed: Saul, David, and Solomon.

Saul, David, and Solomon: The First Kings

The Book of First Samuel recounts the life of Israel's first king, Saul (1020–1000 BC). This man from the Tribe of Benjamin was anointed king by Samuel. Saul committed his reign to freeing the Israelites from their enemies. However, after he was anointed king, he twice disobeyed God's Law. First, he offered his own prebattle sacrifice instead of waiting for Samuel to do so, even though only priests were allowed to offer sacrifices. Then following another battle, he captured the enemy king and livestock and kept them as spoils of war, rather than destroying them as God wanted.

Saul also faced a problem in the person of David, who eventually dethroned and replaced Saul as king. As David became popular, Saul became increasingly envious and eventually tried to kill him. Saul failed in his many attempts to form a centralized nation, and his reign as king ended tragically. Mortally injured in battle, he killed himself by falling on his sword.

You may already be familiar with David, because he appears in many picture books of Bible stories. King David (1000–961 BC) was a successful military leader, savvy politician, gifted musician, and lover of God. David struggled with his sinful nature, especially his lust for

Did You Know?

The First Temple

Solomon built the first Temple to honor David, his father. Solomon designed it according to God's instructions and funded it through taxes. The Temple, which took seven years to build, had cedar paneling, gold overlay, intricate carvings, and ivory-paneled doors. It symbolized the monarchy's political power as well as God's presence. Sadly, we cannot visit the first Temple, for it was completely destroyed by the Babylonian King Nebuchadnezzar (also known as Darius) in 586 BC.

The Israelites' worship at the Jerusalem Temple foreshadows our worship of Jesus Christ. The Israelites worshipped the glory of God in their Temple. Now we worship Jesus Christ in his resurrected glory. The Israelites worshipped God through animal sacrifice, and we worship Christ and his saving sacrifice, the fulfillment of the hopes of the Israelite people. Jesus even compared himself to the Temple (see John 2:19).

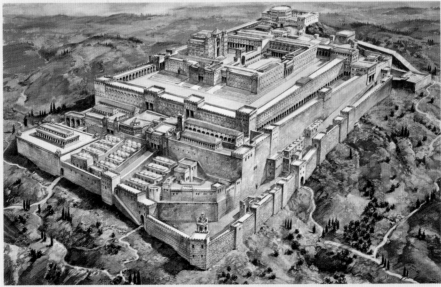

© Lebrecht Music & Arts / The Image Works

David wanted to follow God with his whole heart, and devoted much energy to praising and glorifying God for all that God did for him. We too can praise and glorify God in the good times and the bad.

power. But he accomplished whatever he set out to do when he followed the will of God. One well-known account describes an event that occurred before he was king: the young David's encounter with the dreaded Philistine giant, Goliath, when David managed to kill Goliath with a sling- shot. As king, David was both a visionary leader and a repentant sinner, remembered for uniting all Twelve Tribes of Israel under one ruler and for expanding the kingdom to include most of Palestine. You will read more about his important model of leadership later in this chapter.

Have you ever heard someone mention the wisdom of Solomon? In the Book of First Kings, we learn about Solomon (975–922 BC), the son of King David. Solomon was the third king of Israel. First Kings describes Solo- mon as an ambitious ruler who imposed steep taxes and forced labor on the Israelites to accomplish his plans. He is remembered for building the Temple of the Lord in honor of his father, for strengthening and modernizing the Israelite army, and for creating trade alliances with other nations. Solomon also constructed a magnificent palace and enlarged Jerusalem, by this time the capital city of Israel. Other stories of Solomon reveal that he was a man of great wisdom and judgment. You might have heard how Solomon resolved a dispute between two women who both claimed to be the mother of the same child. He suggested splitting the child in two—knowing that the woman who gave in to spare the child's life was the true mother.

Solomon was said to have had seven hundred wives and three hundred concubines—symbolic numbers indicating a great and perfect number of wives and concubines. Unfortunately, he allowed his foreign wives to practice their idolatrous ways. He eventually took up these practices himself. In response to his idolatry, God told Solomon, "Since this is what you want, and you have not kept my covenant and the statutes which I enjoined on you, I will surely tear the kingdom away from you and give it to your servant" (1 Kings 11:11).

All three kings show us why it is important to live in right relationship with God. When each man remained true to God's plan, he was able to accomplish great things and create a unifying bond among the Chosen People. When each was lured away from God by his own ego and self-interest, he stood in the way of what was good and holy. Whether or not human beings and their leaders remained faithful to God's covenant, God was always there. From Saul to David to Solomon, God built a glorious kingdom rich in mercy that only faltered because of the weakness and sin of human beings.

How have you found your way back to God when ego or self-interest led you away from him?

Article 46: David: Recognizing a Servant

Repentant heart, vengeful spirit, faithful companion, lover of God, lustful ruler, skilled musician, handsome hunk, jealous ego, military leader, passionate dancer, and visionary king—these characteristics all describe the great monarch King David, who united the northern and southern tribes. David is an intriguing figure in the Old Testament. It seems like his life was full of contradictions. One moment he committed his entire being to establishing God's covenant on earth. The next moment an adulterous affair ensnared him, leading him to commit murder. The example of David in the historical books shows us what it means to be caught in the tension between a life enamored with the world's empty promises and a life committed solely to the will of God. David fell prey to the ways of sin but always returned to the Lord with a repentant heart.

Deep Friendship

One of the lesser-known stories about David describes his friendship with Jonathan, son of King Saul. David and Jonathan loved each other with undying loyalty. Their relationship was volatile at times, but they were willing to do anything for each other, as demonstrated by Jonathan's willingness to risk his life to protect David from Saul. Reconciliation and sacrifice marked David and Jonathan's deep bond. When Jonathan died, David experienced an immense sense of loss. This relationship is significant because it reveals the tender, compassionate side of David—a man of enormous depth who was called by God to build life-giving relationships, leading us to a fuller understanding of God's covenant with his people.

Pray It!

Temptation, Sin, and Repentance

In our personal struggles with sin, we are no different from David, who committed grave sins against our Lord. One well-known account tells us how he committed adultery with Bathsheba while her husband, Uriah, was away. When Bathsheba became pregnant, David arranged for Uriah to be killed in battle. But David repented and asked God for forgiveness. Psalm 51 is his plea to God for mercy. It reminds us that if we are truly repentant, God will forgive us. Pray this passage any time you face temptation or sin:

Turn away your face from my sins;
    blot out all my iniquities.
A clean heart create for me, God;
    renew within me a steadfast spirit.
Do not drive me from before your face,
    nor take from me your holy spirit.
Restore to me the gladness of your salvation;

. . . .

My sacrifice, O God, is a contrite spirit;
    a contrite, humbled heart, O God, you will not scorn.
                          (Psalm 51:11–14,19)

A Servant of God

Another memorable account of David centers on his free-spirited celebration of the arrival in Jerusalem of the **Ark of the Covenant**, the sacred chest that housed the original tablets of the Ten Commandments. For the Israelites the Ark was an ancient symbol of God's presence and holy protection. Upon its arrival, we read, "David came dancing before the LORD with abandon, girt with a linen ephod [vestment]" (2 Samuel 6:14). David leaped, danced, and offered burnt sacrifices because God's presence was in the people's midst.

However, when David decided to build a house for the Lord, the prophet Nathan told David not to do so. God had another plan. God would instead build a house for David, but this house was not to be a building. It was to be a royal dynasty, a line of descendants that would endure forever. God's promise to David is known as the Davidic Covenant. We see this promise fulfilled with the birth of Jesus Christ, who descended from David through his foster father, Joseph.

A Servant Leader

Although David accomplished much for God, he allowed his human desires to blind him to God's saving action.

Ark of the Covenant
A sacred chest that housed the tablets of the Ten Commandments, placed within the sanctuary where God would come and dwell.

David and the Israelites worshipped the presence of God in the Ark of the Covenant. We adore God's presence in the Body and Blood of Jesus Christ.

© Finsiel / Alinari / Art Resource, NY

servant leadership
A type of leadership based on humble service to all God's people.

From his lust for women, especially his future wife Bathsheba, to his longing for power and fame, David's sinful ways sometimes prevented him from seeing or promoting the will of God.

What makes David a role model for us then? We learn that despite his sins, he always returned to the Lord, begging for mercy and promising to change. He recognized his need for God's strength if he was to serve the Chosen People and the unfolding covenant. In this way, David modeled **servant leadership**. Despite all his sins and faults, he asked God to raise him from the abyss of despair so he might rule with a just heart and serving hand. Servant leaders recognize their need for forgiveness and reconciliation. In return, they can extend mercy and compassion to all in need. Even in all his brokenness, King David journeyed through life serving the teachings of the covenant, leading the Israelites toward the horizon of eternal peace, and heralding the hope of a king yet unborn.

Primary Sources

Saint Augustine on God's Promise to David

How do we know Solomon, David's son, was not the promised king in God's covenant to establish an eternal kingdom in the line of David? Let's look at Saint Augustine's answer:

> He who thinks this grand promise was fulfilled in Solomon greatly errs; for he attends to the saying, "He shall build me [a] house," but he does not attend to the saying, "His house shall be faithful, and his kingdom for evermore before me." Let him therefore . . . behold the house of Solomon full of strange women worshipping false gods, and the king himself . . . cast down into the same idolatry: and let him not dare to think that God either promised this falsely, or was unable to foreknow that Solomon and his house would become what they did. But we ought not to be in doubt here, or to see the fulfillment of these things save in Christ our Lord, who was made of the seed of David.

(*The City of God*, book 17, chapter 8)

Another King, Yet Unborn

Who was the promised king to come? "I will raise up your offspring after you, sprung from your loins, and I will establish his kingdom. He it is who shall build a house for my name, and I will establish his royal throne forever" (2 Samuel 7:12–13). With these words to David, the Lord laid the foundation for the Jewish expectation of a Messiah, a descendant of David. This prophecy was fulfilled in Jesus Christ, the King of Glory. The genealogies at the beginning of the Gospels of Matthew and Luke trace Jesus' ancestry through David. Yet many people of Jesus' time did not acknowledge him as the fulfillment of this Old Testament prophecy, because he did not fit the traditional image of a king. He denounced the trappings of royal leadership and wealth by taking on the humility of a man, eventually resulting in his Death on a cross.

How can you follow Christ's example and simplify your life, letting go of material things to cultivate humility?

Chapter Review

1. Who was Moses' successor? What was to be his task?

2. List the similarities between Moses and his successor.

3. What important function did the judges serve in the lives of the Israelites?

4. Who were Deborah, Gideon, and Samson, and what were their accomplishments?

5. Why did the Israelites want a king?

6. What were the accomplishments of Saul, David, and Solomon? What were their personal weaknesses?

7. How is David a model of servant leadership?

Chapter 10

The Prophetic Books

Introduction

Like the historical books, the prophetic books of the Old Testament cover hundreds of years of Israelite history. You have already learned that the Israelite kingdom was unified under the reigns of Saul, David, and Solomon. After Solomon died, Israel split into two kingdoms: the northern kingdom, still called Israel, and the southern kingdom, called Judah. Each kingdom was ruled by different kings.

As they did in the time of the judges, the people in Israel and Judah continued to turn away from God and his holy Commandments. From the eighth to the fourth centuries BC, God called prophets to speak to the people on his behalf. When the people were unfaithful to God and unjust to one another, the prophets reminded them that God would hold them accountable for their sinful practices, as he had during the time of the judges and kings. But when the people were in crisis, the prophets reminded them of God's saving love. The prophetic books contain the words of the prophets, summarized in this threefold message: act justly toward one another, return to God with faithful hearts, and maintain hope in God's deliverance. Hope in God's deliverance would culminate in the expectation of a messiah.

Article 47: The Prophets: A Radical Redemption

Salvation history is a journey through many peaks and valleys, highs and lows. At the high points of this journey, according to the Old Testament accounts, a unified, holy people lived in right relationship with God and revealed the promise of the covenant through their words and actions. The low points happened because human beings are weak and forgetful. Time and again we see that God's people lost sight of their covenant relationship with God. They became absorbed in the sinful ways of the world.

Whenever the Israelites lost their way, they needed someone to call them back to God, the source of all life and hope. They needed a prophet. A prophet—in Hebrew, *nabi,* probably meaning "spokesperson" or "one who is called"—is a person chosen by God to communicate a message of salvation on his behalf. This message, or **prophecy**, usually offers divine direction or consolation.

The words and lives of many prophets, are recorded throughout the Old Testament. But the prophetic books, the subject of this chapter, focus on the speeches and deeds of specific prophets.

prophecy
A message communicated by prophets on behalf of God, usually a message of divine direction or consolation for the prophet's own time. Because some prophetic messages include divine direction, their fulfillment may be in the future.

Major and Minor Prophets

Can you name any of the prophets of the Old Testament? Perhaps you recall Isaiah, who prophesied about the coming of a messiah born of a virgin. Maybe you remember how God instructed Ezekiel to eat a scroll so he could prophesy to Israel. As a child, you might have read a picture book that retold the story of Jonah and the whale.

Sacred Scripture is filled with these and many other accounts of the lives of prophets, their prophecies, and their roles in salvation history. Seventeen Old Testament books are named for prophets, so we call these prophets the writing, or canonical, prophets. These writing prophets are divided into two groups: the major prophets and the minor prophets. These classifications don't refer to how important the prophets and their messages were.

Babylonian Exile
The period in Israelite history during which the Israelites of the ancient kingdom of Judah were held in captivity as slaves in Babylon. The period began with the Babylonians' destruction of the Temple and the city of Jerusalem in 587 BC and lasted until 539 BC.

herald
One who proclaims or announces a saving message. As a verb, the word means to proclaim or announce a saving message.

Rather, the terms *major* and *minor* reflect the length of the writings. Two additional books in the prophets section of the Old Testament are not collections of prophetic speeches, but they are related to the prophets: Lamentations and Baruch.

Major Prophets	Isaiah	Ezekiel
	Jeremiah	Daniel
Minor Prophets	Hosea	Micah
	Joel	Nahum
	Amos	Habakkuk
	Obadiah	Zephaniah
	Jonah	Haggai
Writings Related to the Prophets	Lamentations	Baruch

In addition to classifying the seventeen prophetic books based on their length, we also categorize the prophets into two groups based on when they lived in relation to the **Babylonian Exile** of the Israelites. The first group of prophets lived before and during the Babylonian Exile. They generally delivered messages of warning. The second group of prophets lived during and after the Babylonian Exile (which ended in 539 BC). They generally delivered messages of comfort and hope.

Awake, O Sleeper, the Time Is at Hand

"Wake up! Are you aware of what is going on around you? Why do you sleep when there is so much pain and division? When will you return to the Lord?"

Many of the prophets who wrote or spoke before the Babylonian Exile directed words like these to people whose lives and hearts were moving away from God. As **heralds** of God's salvation, the prophets acted as the conscience of a people who had been lulled into complacency and sinfulness. The prophets assured the people that God had not abandoned them and that they needed only to repent of their sins to find joy again. In this way, the prophets sought to open the Israelites' eyes to the many obstacles standing in the way of a meaningful relationship with God and others.

Through the prophets God reminded the Israelites "to do justice and to love goodness, / and to walk humbly" with him (Micah 6:8). The prophets challenged people to look at their individual lives, but the prophets also called the entire People of God to reflect on the unjust practices of the world and to respond in a spirit of hope. At other times the prophets provided solace and comfort to a hurting and oppressed people. But whether they called for a change of heart or offered hope to a distressed people, the prophets' messages were often not received well, because they challenged the existing way of life. As a result, prophets were <u>ostracized</u>, silenced, and sometimes killed for their messages of warning, reformation, and consolation.

Faith in Action
A Modern Prophet of Hope and Justice

© Bettmann / Corbis / AP Images

Archbishop Oscar Romero (1917–1980) was a man of great conviction and an avid defender of human rights. As archbishop of El Salvador, Romero witnessed the severe persecution and oppression of the poor by the Salvadoran political and social regime. In El Salvador numerous priests, brothers, nuns, and lay missionaries were being assassinated for providing educational opportunities for the poor and speaking out against the unjust ways of the government. Romero advocated for the rights of the marginalized and oppressed, and he spoke out forcefully against the assassinations and other injustices of the oppressive regime in power at the time.

While Romero celebrated Mass on March 24, 1980, he was assassinated by a political group opposed to his teachings. In one of his last interviews, he reportedly said: "If God accepts the sacrifice of my life, may my death be for the freedom of my people. . . . A bishop will die, but the Church of God, which is the people, will never perish." Because he spoke out against injustice and for the rights of the poor, even when it made him unpopular, some consider Romero a modern-day prophet.

A Universal Call and Message

The vocation to prophecy never dies. Every generation—even our own—needs men and women to challenge it to remain faithful to God in good times and bad. Sin, injustice, and despair affect every time and place. That is why a saving message of love must be proclaimed to all people everywhere. Beginning with the biblical prophets and continuing to our world today and beyond, God raises up holy prophets to "proclaim a radical redemption of the People of God, purification from all their infidelities, a salvation which will include all the nations²" (CCC, 64). When we hear and heed the messages of the prophets, we are no longer enslaved to the darkness of infidelity and sin. We become free to revel in the redeeming love of God.

> **What might a prophet say to the world today? How would you respond?**

Article 48: Ezekiel: Challenging Idolatry and Injustice

"Son of man, eat what you find here; eat this scroll, then go, speak to the house of Israel" (Ezekiel 3:1). God's way of calling Ezekiel to be a prophet was certainly unusual. By commanding him to eat the scroll, God was inviting him to feed on his holy word, his righteous law. When Ezekiel tasted the truth of God, the prophet proclaimed it to be "as sweet as honey" (3:3). Ezekiel began his prophetic ministry in 593 BC in Babylon and concluded it in 573 BC. He was among the first group of Israelites who were forced to relocate during the Babylonian Exile.

God called Ezekiel to speak on his behalf to a divided people. Some were still in Jerusalem, while others were taken to Babylon in captivity—but God was punishing all of them for their sinful ways. The Israelites were not only unfaithful and idolatrous but also unjust toward the poor and lowly in society. They had become comfortable with treating one other badly and with promoting dehumanizing attitudes toward those in need.

Ezekiel, more than any other biblical prophet, used symbolic actions to enhance his prophetic messages. Some actions included lying on his left side for 390 days and on his right side for 40 days (see Ezekiel 4:1–6), shaving his head and using his hair to deliver a message (see chapter 5), and packing his bags to act out an escape from captivity (see 12:1–16). After each symbolic act, God told Ezekiel how to explain its meaning to the Israelites.

A Call to Those Led Astray

Some of Ezekiel's major themes included the presence of the Lord in the Temple, the awesomeness of God, personal responsibility for one's life and faith, and oracles against the enemies of Israel. Ezekiel delivered particularly hard warnings to the leaders of Israel. He compared

Pray It!

Praying for Holy Words

God commanded Ezekiel to eat a scroll containing his holy words, so that Ezekiel would know how to prophesy to God's people. You too can offer prophetic witness to God's love for all of us every day, just by watching how you talk and what you talk about. Pray this prayer to ask Jesus Christ to give you his holy words:

Merciful Jesus:
It is very easy for me to join my friends
when someone is being talked about,
when the conversation is about
something inappropriate,
or when the language becomes coarse.
Give me the right words when the wrong words are being used.
May my words be only those that will bless others,
not hurt or offend them,
so I may witness to your divine love.
Amen.

(*The Catholic Youth Prayer Book,* page 25)

them to shepherds who have failed to lead their sheep on the path of righteousness. Because the Israelite leaders were too busy taking care of themselves, Ezekiel said, they "did not strengthen the weak nor heal the sick nor bind up the injured" (Ezekiel 34:4). Consumed by their selfish wants and misplaced loyalty, these shepherds allowed their sheep to scatter, wander, and fall prey to the wild beasts, according to Ezekiel. The wild beasts symbolized the foolish and idolatrous beliefs of the surrounding cultures. Because the leaders did not lead with the justice and fairness of good shepherds, Ezekiel held them personally responsible for the eventual destruction of the people.

Ezekiel was a powerful voice crying out against the abuses of the Israelite leaders and their followers. Once again the Israelites had forgotten the covenant and turned to idolatrous practices. The Israelites also failed to remember the dignity and worth of each human. By not caring for the needs of one another and especially of the vulnerable, they disrespected God's plan of loving goodness.

Did You Know?

The Cardinal Virtues

What do you think it means to be virtuous? A virtue is a habit that creates in us a kind of inner readiness or attraction to move toward or accomplish moral good. The four Cardinal Virtues are the key virtues on which the other virtues depend. They are intimately connected to the messages of the prophets. The Cardinal Virtues are justice, prudence, temperance, and fortitude.

- **justice** The fair and equitable distribution of life's necessities. The biblical idea of justice is based on the truth that all humans have innate dignity and worth as children of God.
- **prudence** An approach to problems and situations using a degree of caution and a discerning heart.
- **temperance** A balanced life characterized by moderation and self-control.
- **fortitude** Individual strength and courage to overcome obstacles to a moral life.

A Vision of Dry Bones

A well-known, seemingly bizarre prophecy in the Book of Ezekiel centers on dry bones. Ezekiel had a vision of a valley filled with bones. God directed him: "Prophesy over these bones, and say to them: Dry bones, hear the word of the LORD!" (37:4). God was really talking about the senseless, unjust lives of the Israelites. He commanded Ezekiel to herald a time when God would breathe new life into their dead faith. Even though the Israelites had chosen the ways of the wicked, God promised to transform them into a new people, cleansing them from all their iniquities. Ezekiel reminded them that God is a God of justice and faithfulness. He was not going to let their bones—that is, their hearts—remain dry and lifeless. Nothing would stand in the way of his promise of salvation. God is an awesome God, drawing life from the most unlikely places.

fidelity
Faithfulness to obligation, duty, or commitment.

© Flirt / Alamy

Ezekiel was a guardian of the covenant, protector of the truth, and prophet of justice. It is fitting that Ezekiel's name means "God will strengthen," because his prophecies proclaimed the might and power of God to turn a pile of dry bones into a "vast army" (Ezekiel 37:10) of the covenant. Ezekiel announced the establishment of a new House of Israel, built on **fidelity** to God, respect for the dignity of all God's children, and true worship in a new Temple. Can you see how this prophecy was fulfilled in Jesus Christ? Christ came so that we would not remain lifeless but might have abundant life (see John 10:10). Jesus Christ is the Word of God who prepares the way and brings about our resurrection from death to new life.

Ezekiel's vision of dry bones coming to life is a wonderful metaphor for how God can work in our lives. God's power can bring new life to our relationships, our work, and our spirituality.

How can you build your life of faith on fidelity to God, respect for human dignity, and true worship?

Article 49: Jeremiah: Success in the Lord

> Before I formed you in the womb I knew you,
> before you were born I dedicated you,
> a prophet to the nations I appointed you.
> (Jeremiah 1:5)

How would you feel if you heard these words from God? Would you be comforted? Would you be cautious, maybe even frightened? With these powerful words, God called Jeremiah, a reluctant but courageous prophet. Jeremiah was born to a priestly family in 645 BC. As a priest and prophet of the southern kingdom of Judah, Jeremiah struggled at times with God and his call to be a prophet. Nonetheless Jeremiah remained true to his prophetic mission, even when he was plagued with doubt and fear. Covering the time period of 626–583 BC, the writings and prophecies of the Book of Jeremiah are situated in the events leading up to, and occurring during, the Babylonian Exile. A central theme of Jeremiah's prophecies was the need for the unfaithful Israelites to repent and return to the Lord.

After reading about Jeremiah's life and prophecies, think about what emotion the artist is trying to capture in this statue.

A Call to Faithfulness

The Book of Jeremiah describes how the Israelites had once more fallen into the idolatrous practices of the surrounding nations and failed to live up to the terms of the covenant. Jeremiah warned the Israelites that their idolatrous customs were "stupid and senseless" (Jeremiah 10:8). Using vivid words like *desolation, destruction, sorrow, corruption,* and *horror,* Jeremiah prophesied that if the people did not repent of their sinful ways, punishment was inevitable. He pleaded for the Israelites' fidelity. He attempted to describe the destruction they would experience if they did not denounce their false and lying prophets. Jeremiah

© Hemis / Alamy

drew on the familiar analogy of a potter and clay (see 18:2–6). He compared God to a potter and Israel to the clay object a potter molds. God was disgruntled because the object he was making (Israel) was not turning out well. Jeremiah said that God, like the potter, would crush it to create something new and more beautiful. However, Jeremiah proclaimed, God would not crush the people if they repented and became a renewed people bound by the covenant.

Jeremiah confronted a people so distracted by the empty promises of the world that they did not seem to fear punishment. He described the punishment from God as a cup of judgment from which "they shall drink, and retch, and go mad" (Jeremiah 25:16). Although his message seems harsh and vengeful to us, we have to remember that Jeremiah was trying to motivate a stubbornly disloyal people to change. He suffered greatly for his prophetic ministry. He was imprisoned, beaten, and thrown into a well to die. Despite all this, Jeremiah continued to be faithful to his call. Sadly, he saw many of his prophecies come true when he witnessed the destruction of Jerusalem and the Temple at the hands of the Babylonians.

Following the destruction of Jerusalem, however, Jeremiah's prophecies became hopeful. He prophesied

Primary Sources

What Is a Prophet?

Abraham Joseph Heschel (1907–1972) was a Jewish rabbi and Scripture scholar. He studied the prophets and, through his writings, helped to make the prophetic word meaningful to contemporary readers of the Old Testament. This is his answer to the question: What is a prophet?

> Prophecy is the voice that God has lent to the silent agony, a voice to the plundered poor. God is raging in the prophet's words. In speaking, the prophet reveals God. . . . Divine power bursts in his words. The authority of the prophet is in the Presence his words reveal. . . . The prophet is a witness, and his words a testimony, to *His* power and judgment, to *His* justice and mercy.

> (*Essential Writings*, pages 62 and 64)

remnant
A prophetic term for the small portion of people who will be saved because of their faithfulness to God.

that the enemies of Israel would be destroyed and that a **remnant**, a smaller group of individuals who had remained faithful to God, would be safe from God's wrath. Jeremiah referred to this portion of faithful believers as "good figs" (Jeremiah 24:5). He promised the remnant that when the Israelites were delivered from exile, God would make a New Covenant with them, a law that would be written on their hearts. This prophecy has been fulfilled in Jesus Christ, the New Covenant. Through the power of the Holy Spirit, the separation caused by Original Sin has been erased, and Christ lives in our hearts. Through him salvation extends beyond the people of Israel to include all people.

Jeremiah's entire message was one of faithfulness. Saint Teresa of Calcutta (1910–1997), a nun and servant of the poor, once said, "I do not pray for success, I ask for faithfulness." But unlike Saint Mother Teresa, the Israelites lost sight of what was important. They were no longer a faithful and trustworthy people. Jeremiah called them back to the source of absolute truth and steadfast love: God. Jeremiah heralded a success that could be measured not by the standards of the world but only by fidelity to God's plan of salvation.

Why is faithfulness more important than success?

Article 50: Isaiah: Herald of the Messiah

We refer to Isaiah as if he were one prophet, but scholars believe that the name refers to the original prophet Isaiah as well as at least two later disciples over a 242-year period. That is, the Book of Isaiah appears to cover three different periods during the years 742 to 500 BC: before the Babylonian Exile, during the Exile, and after the Exile. In each period the voice of a prophet bearing the name Isaiah arose to speak about specific issues facing the people.

In the eighth century, during the events leading up to the Babylonian Exile, the original Isaiah, sometimes called First Isaiah, challenged the Israelites in Jerusalem to place their trust in God alone and to eliminate the unjust treatment of the poor by the rich. First Isaiah also foretold the arrival of a messiah, Emmanuel. *Emmanuel* comes from a Hebrew word meaning "God is with us." First Isaiah delivered a message of impending disaster at the hands of Babylon, but he also offered the hope of a kingdom where God's justice and peace reign supreme.

Second Isaiah, who prophesied during the Babylonian Exile, offered words of hope and encouragement to an exiled and captive people. Chapters 40–55 in the Book of Isaiah recount his prophecies. Second Isaiah foretold the fall of Babylon and the eventual liberation of the Israelites. He also gave us the "suffering servant" poems, which became the foundation for the people's **messianic hope**. In these poems we find some amazing parallels to the Passion of Christ (see Isaiah 42:1–4, 50:4–9, 52:13–53:12). The poems portray a servant of God who encounters great suffering but ends in glory. This prophecy was fulfilled in Jesus Christ, who suffered his Passion and Death but was glorified in the Resurrection and Ascension.

After the Exile, Third Isaiah (chapters 56–66) cried out against the Israelites' return to unjust and idolatrous practices. He demanded that they become a respectful community of equals. Third Isaiah challenged the people to work for justice as they rebuilt their lives after the Exile. He told the people that if they learned the ways of justice, God would lift up Israel as a glorious nation.

Emmanuel, God with Us

The Book of Isaiah sings of messianic hope. This hope is summarized in Isaiah 7:14: "The young woman, pregnant and about to bear a son, shall name him Emmanuel." Christians came to see that the promise of Emmanuel was fulfilled in Jesus Christ. Christ is with us in the struggles of everyday life, conquering all that enslaves and divides

Emmanuel
A Hebrew word meaning "God is with us."

messianic hope
The Jewish belief and expectation that a messiah would come to protect, unite, and lead Israel to freedom.

stump of Jesse
A phrase taken from Isaiah 11:1 that traces Jesus' lineage to Jesse's son, King David.

the family of God. In Isaiah's words, this Emmanuel, the Promised One, would be known as "Wonder-Counselor, God-Hero, / Father-Forever, Prince of Peace" (9:5). These titles revealed to Israel that the promised Messiah would be wisdom incarnate, a defender of his people, a faithful parent, and an agent of peace.

Isaiah prophesied that Emmanuel would inaugurate a peaceful kingdom where even "the wolf shall be a guest of the lamb, / and the leopard shall lie down with the young goat" (Isaiah 11:6). With the arrival of the Promised One, all things would change under the heavens and on the earth. A new king would come from the **stump of Jesse**, the throne of David, and he would judge with righteousness. The old order of infidelity and injustice would be replaced with a new order of trust, reconciliation, and equity. The long-awaited Messiah would be a "Morning Star, son of the dawn" (14:12), shining the light of his knowledge into the darkest corners of the earth. The earth and the heavens would no longer be ruled by the wicked and sinful ways of humanity. They would instead be ruled by a Savior who lifts up the lowly and sends the rich away empty.

Live It!
Called to Be a Prophet

We all are called to be prophets who speak the Word of God with both our words and actions. No special skills are needed. All God needs is an open heart willing to do his work. Even so, life as a prophet can be difficult. Prophets point out wrongdoing. They call people to respect God and one another.

Like many biblical prophets God called to do his work, you might feel inadequate for the task. Or you might be afraid of being made fun of, as many prophets were. Take courage by learning about more recent prophets, such as Saint Teresa of Calcutta, Saint Marianne Cope, Blessed Saint Pope John XXIII, or Saint Maximilian Kolbe.

How will you live out your role as a prophet? Pray and ask God to help you discern how you are called to witness to your faith as an athlete, student, or worker. God is calling you. Take a moment to be quiet and listen to his gentle voice.

Isaiah invited the people of the covenant to prepare their hearts and lives for the dawn of a new day when all creation would bow before Emmanuel, "God is with us." With the coming of Emmanuel, the heavens and earth would be made new. They would become a place where all can draw water joyfully "from the fountains of salvation" (Isaiah 12:3). The prophecy of Isaiah embodied the hopes and aspirations of a people longing for the moment when a savior would set them free. The Book of Isaiah heralded an event that changed the course of salvation: the arrival of the Word of God Made Flesh.

> **How do you think the prophets felt when the people ignored their cries for repentance? Why do you think they did not just give up?**

Chapter Review

1. What role did prophets play in salvation history?

2. What was the general message of the prophets before the Babylonian Exile? How did that message change after the Exile?

3. What is the difference between major and minor prophets?

4. Why is Ezekiel called a prophet of justice?

5. What were some of Ezekiel's symbolic actions, and why did he perform them?

6. How did Jeremiah respond to the idolatrous practices of the Israelites?

7. What message was Jeremiah preaching with his analogy of God the Potter?

8. What was the major theme of Jeremiah's message?

9. What is messianic hope, and how is it related to the prophecies of Isaiah?

Chapter 11

Wisdom Literature

Introduction

Many inspirational biblical quotations you may encounter come from a group of books known as wisdom literature. Wisdom literature is distinct from other categories of books in the Old Testament. The wisdom books express minimal interest in the history of Israel and rarely refer to the Law. Instead they focus on everyday life. Through poetry and other literary forms, the wisdom books draw universal truth and meaning from the mysteries of life. By exploring suffering and death, the fate of the righteous and foolish, and the splendor of love, these books offer advice on finding balance and harmony. They support our quest to glean wisdom from human emotion and struggle. God, the source of wisdom, is at the center of all our human experience.

For the most part, the authors of the wisdom books are unknown. Much of their content, however, is attributed to great leaders like Solomon and David. Attributing the writings to the kings served as a way to convey the authority of what these books teach. The following books make up wisdom literature: Job, Psalms, Ecclesiastes, Song of Songs (or Song of Solomon), Wisdom (or Wisdom of Solomon), Proverbs, and Sirach (or Ecclesiasticus).

Article 51: Job: Understanding Suffering

Why do good people suffer? Most of us ask this question at some point in life, because it is natural to look for meaning in undeserved suffering and pain. The Book of Job tells of a "blameless and upright" man (1:8) by the name of Job, who endures the tragic loss of family, land, home, and health. Written sometime between the seventh and fifth centuries BC, the book recounts one human being's struggle to make sense out of what seems to be unnecessary and undeserved suffering. Job's experience appears to contradict the core belief of his time: that God rewards the righteous and punishes the unjust. The Book of Job asks a question we still ponder today: Why do good people suffer and wicked people prosper? The author of Job wrestled with that question and wrote this poetic debate involving a virtuous and successful man named Job who loses everything. Despite his losses, Job's trust and faith in God never waver.

It's not fair! Job debated with his friends, maintaining that his suffering was not the result of any personal sin. Where have you witnessed people suffering unfairly?

God Does Not Cause Suffering

From the start the Book of Job makes clear that God has allowed Satan to test Job through a series of losses, but God has not directly caused his suffering. The presence of Satan in the Book of Job shows us that God never initiates human suffering. God allows the suffering, knowing that Job can withstand any trial because of his deep and abiding faith. But

© duncan1890 / iStockphoto.com

unlike Satan, God does not question the goodness of Job. God is on Job's side.

Even though Job's friends insist he is being punished for his actions, Job maintains his innocence and turns to God for answers. Job never blames God for his misfortunes. He does seek an audience with God to gain insight into his situation. God appears before Job and overwhelms him with questions he cannot answer. Then Job realizes a profound truth: God is so great and complex that the human mind can never fully grasp his ways. Bowing in humility and trust before the awesomeness of God, Job states:

> I know that you can do all things,
>   and that no purpose of yours can be hindered.
>
> ·
>
> I have spoken but did not understand;
>   things too wonderful for me, which I did not know.
>   (Job 42:2,3)

Job's suffering ultimately strengthens his faith.

Lessons Learned from Job

From the account of Job, we can glean many lessons about suffering, righteous anger, patience, and the glory of God. First, we learn that suffering is not always the result of personal sin and should not be viewed as a punishment from God. Although we human beings are limited in our understanding of suffering, suffering can also strengthen our faith, because we can either blame God or turn to God. Second, the Book of Job reassures us that God does not want his people to suffer. When we cry out in distress, God hears our cries. A third lesson is that the life of faith takes root in a patient heart. Patience in our sufferings and struggles is essential if we want to grow in our relationship with God. Our fourth and final lesson is that God deserves our love and respect even when life takes a turn for the worse. Though we may question God, we are called to realize that his ways are too immense and wondrous for the human mind to grasp.

Saint John Vianney said that the sufferings we encounter "on the road to heaven are like a fine stone bridge on which you can cross a river. Christians who don't suffer cross this river on a shaky bridge that's always in danger of giving way under their feet." Like Job we have to navigate suffering with faith and trust, so that our bridge to Heaven is firm.

Have you ever experienced hardship and wondered, "Why me?" What answers did you find?

Pray It!

Prayer of Serenity

Have you ever faced a situation that seemed unbearable? Like Job we will face obstacles and challenges throughout our lives. When this happens we must remember that God is always with us and that we can ask him for the acceptance, courage, and wisdom to overcome these challenges. The next time you feel overwhelmed by life or are facing a particular challenge, pray the Prayer of Serenity and ask God for help.

God, grant me the serenity
to accept the things I cannot change,
courage to change the things I can,
and wisdom to know the difference.
Living one day at a time,
enjoying one moment at a time,
accepting hardship as a pathway to peace,
taking, as Jesus did,
this sinful world as it is,
not as I would have it,
trusting that You will make all things right
if I surrender to Your will,
so that I may be reasonably happy in this life
and supremely happy in the next.
Amen.

(Reinhold Niebuhr)

hymns
Poetic song lyrics
written to honor
God.

lament
A cry for God's
intervention in
difficult situations.
Many of the Psalms
are laments.

Article 52: The Psalms: Learning to Pray

Have you ever found that a song or poem perfectly expresses how you feel? The historical and prophetic books give us important insights into the people and events that were part of God's plan for our salvation. But the poetry and music we find in the Book of Psalms reflect Israel's deeper experiences of both the joys and sorrows of the journey of faith.

In Hebrew the Psalms are called the *Tehillim*, meaning "praises" or "hymns of praise to God." When translated from the Greek word *psalmos*, the word *psalms* refers to songs accompanied by stringed instruments. The Book of Psalms was written by different authors spanning many generations. The authors of most of the Psalms are unknown, although many Psalms are attributed to King David because of his reputation as a gifted writer and musician. One thing is certain: the 150 Psalms sing to us about Israel's relationship with God.

Types of Psalms

We classify the Psalms according to three types of **hymns**: lament, thanksgiving, and praise.

Lament

A **lament** is a cry for God's intervention in difficult situations. People wrote hymns of lament when they felt disconnected from God or when they felt an absence of God during the harsh realities of life. Underlying this experience of absence was their confidence in God's ability to draw life from the darkest circumstances. Here is one example of a lament in the Psalms:

> Listen, God, to my prayer;
> > do not hide from my pleading;
> > hear me and give answer.
> I rock with grief; I groan
> > at the uproar of the enemy,
> > the clamor of the wicked.
> > > (55:2–4)

Thanksgiving

People composed hymns of thanksgiving to thank God for his amazing action in their lives. Hymns of thanksgiving are usually responses to amazing acts of vindication or deliverance on the part of God for his Chosen People. Read on for an example of a Psalm of thanksgiving:

> I love the LORD, who listened
> > to my voice in supplication,
> Who turned an ear to me
> > on the day I called.
>
> . . . .
>
> I will offer a sacrifice of praise
> > and call on the name of the LORD.
> I will pay my vows to the LORD
> > in the presence of all his people.
> > > (116:1,17–18)

Praise

Finally, hymns of praise extol God as Creator of the earth and author of history. This type of hymn sings of the majestic, faithful, and saving name of God. Here is an example of praise in the Psalms:

> The heavens declare the glory of God;
> > the firmament proclaims the works of his hands.
> Day unto day pours forth speech;
> > night unto night whispers knowledge.
> > > (19:2–3)

Mirror of the Soul

Saint Athanasius of Alexandria, a Church Father and defender of the faith, said: "It seems to me that these words of the Psalms become like a mirror to the person singing them, so that he might see himself and the emotions of his soul." The emotions contained in the Psalms mirror the experience of a particular people in time, but they also reflect the whole history of salvation. The Psalms were central to the teachings and prayers of Jesus. On the cross Jesus invoked the poetic words of Psalm 22:2: "My God, my God, why have you abandoned me?" (see Mark 15:34). At his Death he said, "Into your hands I commend my spirit" (Psalm 31:6; see Luke 23:46).

Qoheleth
A Hebrew word for *Ecclesiastes,* meaning "preacher" or "one who convokes an assembly."

The early Church Fathers wrote extensively about the meaning of the Psalms. Many saints have proclaimed their importance in learning how to pray. The Church continues to incorporate them into her sacramental and liturgical practices.

For the People of God, the Psalms are a voice of hope in despair, truth amid misunderstanding, and interconnection in the face of isolation. In Psalm 130:1 we read: "Out of the depths I call to you, LORD." The Psalms rise from the depths of the human heart to ground people in the past, give direction to the present, and point to a future beyond human imagination. The Psalms are filled with wisdom that empowers us to express our inner longing for God, so that we too can be a people of prayer.

> **How do the Psalms and other well-known prayers help to ground us in the past? Why is it important to recall our past when we pray?**

Article 53: Ecclesiastes: The Ongoing Search for Meaning

"For in much wisdom there is much sorrow; / whoever increases knowledge increases grief" (Ecclesiastes 1:18). This statement summarizes the overall perspective of the author of the Book of Ecclesiastes. At first this statement may sound pessimistic and discouraging, but it actually is grounded in a sense of realism. Like many of us, the author, known as the Teacher or **Qoheleth**, is perplexed by the mystery of God's ways. Having acquired great wisdom, the Teacher realizes there is much more he does not understand about life and God. Life is one big riddle. At the heart of the riddle is a God who transcends human intellect. Because our understanding of God is always changing, we have no easy answers to the difficult questions of life. The Book of Ecclesiastes, written in the third or fourth century BC, challenges us to see things in a different light by providing practical advice about the journey of faith.

A Time for Everything

Ecclesiastes shares with us the heart of true wisdom: an acknowledgment God's plans might not always agree with our own:

> There is an appointed time for everything,
>> and a time for every affair under the heavens.
> A time to give birth, and a time to die;
>> a time to plant, and a time to uproot the plant.
> A time to kill, and a time to heal;
>> a time to tear down, and a time to build.
> A time to weep, and a time to laugh;
>> a time to mourn, and a time to dance.
> A time to scatter stones, and a time to gather them;
>> a time to embrace, and a time to be far from embraces.
> A time to seek, and a time to lose;
>> a time to keep, and a time to cast away.
> A time to rend, and a time to sew;
>> a time to be silent, and a time to speak.
> A time to love, and a time to hate;
>> a time of war, and a time of peace.
>
> (Ecclesiastes 3:1–8)

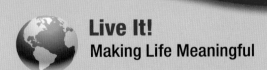

Live It!
Making Life Meaningful

What is the meaning of life? This question is often asked when someone is troubled about something. Perhaps the person has experienced a death in the family or is puzzled by all of the injustice and suffering in the world. The Book of Ecclesiastes addresses matters like these, but it does not provide easy answers. Many of the answers to questions about life, death, pain, and suffering are mysteries known by God only.

However, consider a similar question: How can *you* make life meaningful? We are all called to love and serve one another as Christ did, but we are given unique gifts and talents to carry it out in our own particular way. No two people are the same. You will find many ways to make life meaningful, and these ways will change as you grow older. Think about ways you can help to make your life and the lives of those around you meaningful right now, and follow through with action.

From life to death, tears to laughter, love to hate, we must bow before the infinite wisdom of God. "From beginning to end" (Ecclesiastes 3:11), God is author of all that is, was, and will ever be. The Teacher proclaims that God's ways are not our ways, nor is his time line ours. Therefore the wise heart embraces the unknown, realizing that "whatever God does will endure forever; there is no adding to it, or taking from it" (3:14). The closer we come to God, the more we become willing to trust in his care. Letting go of the need to control and know everything paves the way for God's plan of salvation.

Carpe Diem: Seize the Day

The author of Ecclesiastes exclaims that "all things are vanity!" (1:2). This means that life lacks permanence, and we don't know its meaning. This is not intended to put a damper on our living. The author advises us to respond to the vanity of life by making the most of all God's gifts. The author encourages us to eat, drink, and enjoy the fruits of our labors, all of which are gifts from God. Living every day with great energy and joy does not mean we stop seeking wisdom. Our wisdom may be limited, but it guides our searching hearts toward God. We are told, "Words from the mouth of the wise win favor, / but the lips of fools consume them" (Ecclesiastes 10:12).

Ecclesiastes helps human beings to find meaning in the chaos and ambiguity of life. It supports believers in the quest for wisdom, even a limited human wisdom that can never fully grasp God's ways. According to Saint Clare of Assisi, to find answers to the riddles of human existence, we need to "place [our] mind before the mirror of eternity, . . . place [our] soul in the brilliance of glory." God is the mirror of eternity and brilliance of glory. To find meaning, we must chase after wisdom, always living according to God's time line, seizing every opportunity to experience beauty, and recognizing the limits of our human understanding.

How does your own search for meaning match what the author of Ecclesiastes recommends?

Article 54: Song of Songs: The Beauty of Love

Take a moment to think about what makes a good love song. Did you immediately think of a popular song by a favorite artist today? You might be surprised to learn that the biblical book called Song of Songs (also the Song of Solomon) is considered to be one of the most passionate love songs ever written. Song of Songs may have been originally attributed to Solomon because his name conveyed authority, but King Solomon did not write the book. Scholars believe it was composed by an unknown author sometime after the Jews' return from the Babylonian Exile in 539 BC.

Although it is short, Song of Songs is composed of rich poetry with vivid imagery describing the beauty of love. Taken at face value (the literal sense), it is a collection of love poems that affirm the goodness of human sexuality and love. It lifts up the sanctity of human love and passion as gifts from God. Interpreted from an allegorical perspective (one of the spiritual senses), the relationship between the lover and beloved in Song of Songs symbolizes the relationship between God and Israel—or between Jesus and the Church.

Ideal Human Love

What is love? According to Saint Bernard of Clairvaux, "Love is an affection of the soul. . . . It is spontaneous in its origin and impulse; and true love is its own satisfaction." As much as we long to find true love and affection, authentic love cannot be forced, nor should it be self-seeking. Ideal human love flows from the depths of our soul. Because it is spontaneous, it finds joy in mutuality, honesty, trust, and sacrifice.

Love is powerful. In Song of Songs we learn, "You have ravished my heart, my sister, my bride; / you have

© Andrew Duany / Shutterstock.com

The faithful love between a husband and wife is an allegory of God's love for the Israelites and also of Christ's love for the Church. How would you describe an ideal marriage?

ravished my heart with one glance of your eyes" (4:9). Later we are told, "Deep waters cannot quench love, / nor rivers sweep it away" (8:7). These lines attest to the intensity and strength of the love between a lover and beloved. Through the use of bridal imagery, the author of Song of Songs demonstrates the beauty and splendor of love.

Love between Creator and Creature

As an allegory for God's relationship with the Israelites, Song of Songs paints us a picture of God as a faithful lover of his beloved People. God has called his Chosen People, his bride, to a spiritual union of perfect love. As the *Catechism* explains, we can also read Song of Songs as an allegory for Christ's relationship with the Church. In this allegory the Church is "the spotless spouse of the

Primary Sources

Learn about Love in Song of Songs

What does the word *love* mean to you? Is love more about you, or about the one you love? In his 2005 encyclical *Deus Caritas Est* (*God Is Love*), Pope Benedict XVI shows us how the understanding of love develops in Song of Songs:

> In the course of the book two different Hebrew words are used to indicate "love." First there is the word *dodim*, a plural form suggesting a love that is still insecure, indeterminate and searching. This comes to be replaced by the word *ahabà*, which . . . expresses the experience of a love which involves a real discovery of the other, moving beyond the selfish character that prevailed earlier. Love now becomes concern and care for the other. No longer is it self-seeking, a sinking in the intoxication of happiness; instead it seeks the good of the beloved: it becomes renunciation and it is ready, and even willing, for sacrifice. (6)

spotless lamb. It is she whom Christ 'loved and for whom he delivered himself that he might sanctify her'³" (CCC, 757). Like the bridegroom in Song of Songs, Christ has formed an unbreakable union with his beloved bride, the Church, whom he nourishes and sustains with saving love.

Taking this interpretation a step further, Saint Bernard of Clairvaux examined Song of Songs as an allegory for the relationship between God and the individual: "Of all the movements, sensations and feelings of the soul, love is the only one in which the creature can respond to the Creator and make some sort of return however unequal though it be." That is, no matter how imperfect our love may be, God desires the affection and love of each of his beloved children.

Are you surprised to find such a passionate book in the Bible? If so, you are not alone. Song of Songs is a

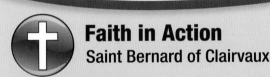

Faith in Action
Saint Bernard of Clairvaux

© Galleria degli Uffizi, Florence, Italy / Bridgeman Images

From a young age, Saint Bernard of Clairvaux had great wisdom, a profound love for Jesus Christ, and a special devotion to the Virgin Mary. Longing to serve the Lord as a monk, he entered the Cistercian order at the Abbey of Cîteaux in 1112 because of the Cistercians' simple and austere lifestyle. Early in his vocation to the monastic life, Bernard founded a new abbey in Clairvaux, French for the "valley of light." The monastery eventually grew into a community of several hundred monks, guided by Bernard as abbot of the monastery. During his thirty-eight years as abbot, Bernard helped to establish sixty-five Cistercian monasteries. Because of his wisdom, he was a trusted confidant and advisor to several popes and rulers, including King Louis VI of France. Along with his charismatic leadership, Bernard was known for his sound theological writings and sermons on Song of Songs and the role of Mary in God's plan for the salvation of humans. He was canonized a saint in 1174 and was declared a Doctor of the Church in 1830.

personification
A literary technique that uses human characteristics to describe nonhuman realities.

hidden treasure in the Old Testament. Many people are unaware of its existence, and those who have heard of it do not realize its great worth and significance. Whether we consider its literal or allegorical sense, Song of Songs emphasizes the central importance of ideal love in our quest for God.

> Why are mutuality, honesty, trust, and sacrifice all important parts of authentic love?

Article 55: Wisdom: Seeking Truth

During the first century BC, generations after the Babylonian Exile, Jewish leaders became concerned about preserving the Jewish heritage and faith. As the Jewish People settled in new lands and were removed from their homeland of Judah, their leaders feared they were losing sight of their ancestors' accomplishments. One of these leaders, whose name remains unknown, wrote the Book of Wisdom to encourage the Jews to remain faithful to the wisdom revealed in their history and tradition. The Book of Wisdom proclaims that authentic wisdom has guided the Jewish People since the beginning of time.

There are three main divisions of the Book of Wisdom. The first addresses the reward of justice, the second praises wisdom, and the third reflects on the Exodus events. We must remember and incorporate the wisdom of the past into the present. The same wisdom that guided the ancestors of the Chosen People passes "into holy souls from age to age," producing "friends of God and prophets" (Wisdom 7:27).

Wisdom Personified

One of the notable characteristics of the Book of Wisdom is its use of **personification**. This literary technique uses human characteristics to describe something that is non-human and often abstract. Wisdom, also called *Sophia* in Greek and *Sapientia* in Latin, is God's wisdom. In the

Book of Wisdom, wisdom is personified as a female. The use of the pronouns *she* and *her* emphasizes a feminine nature of wisdom. The book tells us:

> She is a breath of the might of God
> > and a pure emanation of the glory of the Almighty;
>
> ·
>
> For she is the reflection of eternal light,
> > the spotless mirror of the power of God.
> > > (Wisdom 7:25,26)

Christians understand that the ultimate embodiment of God the Father's wisdom is realized in Jesus Christ, the only Son of God. In First Corinthians, Paul calls Jesus the Wisdom of God (see 1:24).

Teacher, Counselor, and Preserver

The Book of Wisdom presents wisdom as a manifestation of the creative spirit of God. We must seek wisdom if we want to know and understand God. Wisdom instructs us in the ways of God (see 8:4). If we are willing to learn, wisdom will teach us about moderation, prudence, justice, and fortitude. For the author of the Book of Wisdom, wisdom is the ancient knowledge of the past and the awareness of what lies ahead. As a counselor, wisdom speaks to the inner heart, the inner soul. She

Did You Know?

© Jorisvo / iStockphoto.com

Our Lady, Seat of Wisdom

One of the devotional titles given to the Blessed Virgin Mary is Our Lady, Seat of Wisdom. This title connects Mary with Solomon's throne, the seat from which Solomon handed down his wisdom. "Seat of Wisdom" is a translation of *Sedes sapientiae*, the Latin title that the medieval Church first used to acknowledge Mary's role as the one who carried Jesus Christ, the Wisdom of God, when he became incarnate. Just as Solomon's throne was the seat of his wisdom, Mary was the throne, or seat, of the Wisdom of God, Jesus Christ.

directs the heart toward right judgment. When all is well, she counsels the heart in ways of righteousness. In times of grief, she infuses the soul with the healing knowledge of God.

In the Book of Wisdom, wisdom preserves the history of salvation by reminding the Jewish community of both God's creation of the world and his salvation of Israel in the Exodus. Wisdom reminds the people that God is both Creator and rescuer. Wisdom acts throughout salvation history by lifting up the sinner, giving courage to the fearful, delivering the enslaved, sheltering the lost, and opening "the mouths of the mute" (Wisdom 10:21). She continues dancing in the hearts of God's people. From the beginning of creation to its culmination, wisdom connects human beings to the stories of the past, unifies the family of today, and sings of things that have not yet been spoken.

How do these descriptions of wisdom and its effects compare with how you would define wisdom?

Article 56: Two More Voices on Wisdom

Finally, the Wisdom literature includes two other important books in the Old Testament: the Book of Proverbs and the Wisdom of Ben Sira. Each contributes to our human understanding of wisdom. The Book of Proverbs

Why do you think the Wisdom books of the Bible personify God's wisdom as a woman?

© Vicki Shuck / Saint Mary's Press

collects poems and wise sayings representing the wisdom from generations of Israelite history. Like the Book of Wisdom, Proverbs personifies God's wisdom as a woman and tells us where to find wisdom: the streets, the marketplace, and the city. The Wisdom of Ben Sira, also known as Ecclesiasticus, was written around 180 BC by Jesus Ben Sira. It is organized around one central theme: "All wisdom is from the Lord / and remains with him forever" (1:1). In support of this theme, Ben Sira praises the wisdom revealed in the heroes of Jewish faith.

Where can we turn for wisdom today?

Chapter Review

1. What is recounted in the Book of Job?

2. What lessons can we learn from Job's suffering?

3. Describe the three types of hymns found in the Book of Psalms.

4. How are the Psalms important for the People of God, the Church?

5. What are some of the main themes in the Book of Ecclesiastes?

6. What is the main literary genre found in the Song of Songs?

7. How is the Song of Songs an allegory?

8. Why is wisdom important according to the Book of Wisdom?

9. How is wisdom personified in the Book of Wisdom?

Revelation in the New Testament

God's saving work did not end with the prophets. The covenants, the Law, and the prophets of old prepared the way for the most important event in salvation history: the Incarnation. The Divine Son of God became man for the sake of our salvation. The New Testament announces the Good News of Jesus Christ, the only Son of God, who is true God and true man.

As heralds of the Good News, the Gospels deserve our special attention, beginning with why they were written and for whom. The Gospels of Matthew, Mark, and Luke are called the synoptic Gospels. We study them as a group because of their similar accounts of Jesus' life and teachings, his miracles and parables, and his Passion, Death, Resurrection, and Ascension. The Gospel of John merits separate attention because of its emphasis on Jesus' divinity, manifested through the signs (miracles) he performed, his discourses and "I am" statements, and the Paschal Mystery.

The rest of the New Testament gives us a glimpse into the early Church. In the Acts of the Apostles, we read about Peter, Paul, and other followers who spread the Good News to Jews and Gentiles alike. The letters of Saint Paul advised the communities he evangelized on his missionary journeys, whereas the catholic (non-Pauline) letters were written by other followers for larger audiences. Finally, the symbolism in the Book of Revelation was intended to reassure Christians who were being persecuted by the Roman Empire.

The enduring understandings and essential questions represent core concepts and questions that are explored throughout this unit. By studying the content of each chapter, you will gain a more complete understanding of the following:

Enduring Understandings

1. The Gospels present Jesus' life and teachings from four unique perspectives.

2. The Gospels of Matthew, Mark, and Luke have some differences in their portrayal of Jesus, but they also share many similarities.

3. The Gospel of John expresses the identity of Jesus largely through symbolism, imagery, and poetry.

4. The Acts of the Apostles, the Letters, and the Book of Revelation provide insight into the spread of Christianity and the challenges the early Christians faced.

Essential Questions

1. Why are the Gospels considered the heart of Scripture?

2. How are the Gospels of Matthew, Mark, and Luke similar?

3. In what ways is the Gospel of John distinct from the other Gospels?

4. How can the other New Testament books support us in faith?

Chapter

12 The Gospels

Introduction

The four Gospels are the very heart of Scripture. The Gospels according to Matthew, Mark, Luke, and John herald the Good News that God came to earth to fulfill the promises he made to our ancestors, to form a covenant with all people, and to overcome the slavery of sin and the darkness of death. The four Gospels are our primary source for all that our Savior and Messiah revealed in his life and teachings.

In chapter 4, you learned that the books of the Bible began with a human experience. That experience was then shared through storytelling and conversation before someone finally wrote it down. The Gospels were no different. Eyewitnesses to the life and teachings of Jesus handed on what they learned through oral tradition, and the four Gospel writers—guided by the Holy Spirit—synthesized these oral accounts into a written record to preserve the Good News for all generations. That said, the Gospels are not identical, for each presents Jesus' life and teachings in a different way to meet the needs of a particular community. Yet in harmony and without error, they announce the truth that Jesus is the one and only way to the Father. All who believe "will not walk in darkness, but will have the light of life" (John 8:12).

Article 57: The Central Place of the Gospels

People are sometimes surprised to learn that the Gospels were not the first books in the New Testament to be written down. For example, Saint Paul wrote his earliest letters years before Mark the **Evangelist** wrote the first Gospel. So why are the Gospels the first books we find in the New Testament? All of Sacred Scripture is essential for understanding God's saving plan, but the four **Gospels** teach us about God's most definitive and perfect

Evangelists
From a Greek word meaning "messenger of good news," the title given to the authors of the Gospels of Matthew, Mark, Luke, and John.

Faith in Action
The Gospel Message and Modern Communication

© Bill Wittman / www.wpwittman.com

In 1858, a young priest in New York named Isaac Hecker (1819–1888), a convert from a Protestant church, decided to preach the Gospel in a different way. He began to offer what he called "missions" to Catholic parishes, and he also found ways to reach out to Protestant Christians. To continue and expand evangelization of both Catholics and Protestants, he formed a new community named after Saint Paul, the great biblical preacher. The Congregation of Saint Paul, based in the United States, came to be known as Paulists. In addition to preaching, the Paulists used the media of their time—primarily books, pamphlets, and newspapers—to interest people in the Good News of Jesus Christ.

Gradually the Paulist Fathers have become active in campus ministry and have also opened bookstores and information centers in larger cities, welcoming inquirers to the Catholic faith. They have made videos to explain the Gospel and the Catholic faith to wide audiences. In recent years, they have expanded their evangelization efforts to the Internet, launching a Catholic site for young people as well as anyone seeking spiritual truth and meaning. Today the mission of the Paulists includes preaching the Gospel to the unchurched (that is, those who have no commitment to a particular faith), reconciling with Catholics who have left the Church, and promoting ecumenical and interfaith dialogue. They are truly modern-day "missionaries to North America."

Gospel
Translated from a Greek a word meaning "good news," referring to the four books attributed to Matthew, Mark, Luke, and John. The Gospels are the principal source for accounts of Jesus Christ's life and teaching and work of salvation.

venerate
Treat with deep reverence and devotion.

Revelation: his Son, Jesus Christ, who is true God and true man.

As the *Catechism of the Catholic Church (CCC)* states: "The *Gospels* are the heart of all the Scriptures 'because they are our principal source for the life and teaching of the Incarnate Word, our Savior'[1]" 125). The word *Gospel* literally means "good news." The Gospels of Matthew, Mark, Luke, and John tell the Good News that God sent his only Son to save his people from sin. In the Gospels we find accounts of Jesus' teachings, his actions, and the events of the Paschal Mystery: his Passion, Death, Resurrection, and Ascension. No other story or text could ever compare to the revelatory truth contained in the Gospels.

In other words, the Gospels are at the heart of all of Scripture because Jesus Christ is at the heart of the Gospels. We can think of salvation history as a circle with Jesus as its axis, or center point. Our primary sources for information about Jesus Christ, the axis of salvation history, are the Gospels. Because they recount Jesus' life and teachings, they reveal to us the amazing, miraculous action of God. Building on themes from the Old Testament, the four Gospels point to Jesus as the New Covenant. They contain the redeeming truth of the long-awaited fulfillment of God's promises.

It would be a mistake for us to read the Gospels as strictly accurate biographies of the life of Jesus. Yet all four Gospels do tell us about real historical events that occurred in the life and mission of Jesus Christ. Though the four Gospels differ from one another, together they announce the Good News of Jesus Christ in harmony and without error. Therefore we must read them, **venerate** them, and study them.

An Invitation to Faith

"But these [accounts] are written that you may [come to] believe that Jesus is the Messiah, the Son of God, and that through this belief you may have life in his name" (John 20:31). This statement from the Gospel of John summarizes the overall intent of the Gospel writers. The Gospels foster our faith in Jesus Christ as the Divine Son of God, who assumed a human nature to save us from sin and death. The healings, exorcisms, and miracles we find in the Gospels point to Jesus' divinity. Jesus' perfect obedience to his Father, his sinlessness, his sacrificial Death, and his glorious Resurrection and Ascension revealed his saving work. Realizing that generations of people would not be able to hear Jesus' words and witness his works firsthand, the Gospel writers wrote everything down so people would have abundant faith.

The Gospels call us into the light of God's truth revealed in and through the Incarnation. They invite us to accept Jesus into our hearts and be baptized, becoming a part of the Body of Christ, the Church. They call us to participate in the sacramental life of the Church. The Gospels challenge us to follow Jesus and to apply his teachings to our everyday lives. Your own choice to follow Jesus Christ means deciding to become a person

Pray It!

We Are Called to Be Disciples

The Old Testament tells us about person after person who responded to God's call: to prophesy, to lead, to follow, to trust. The New Testament offers many more accounts of people who followed God's call, from Mary to the Apostles to the countless other followers. How is God calling you to follow him? Pray this prayer, and ask God to help you hear, trust, and respond.

Lord,
You have chosen me
and humbly I respond to your invitation.
Help me to reach out to those most in need,
to have compassion for the poor,
and to live a just life.
You have taught me to turn the other cheek;
may I show mercy through forgiveness,
and pray for those who have harmed me.
Thank you for the gift of salvation
and the freedom, joy, and inner peace it brings me.
Amen.

of just action. Matthew, Mark, Luke, and John express the clear conviction that faith in Jesus requires a response—a change in attitude and habit. As our primary source of God's Word Made Flesh, the Gospels invite all people to know and understand the Lord.

> **Do you think the Gospel writers succeeded in help-ing later generations have faith in Jesus? Why or why not?**

Article 58: Three Stages in Gospel Formation

To begin our study of the Gospels, we must first consider how they developed. Like all the books in the canon of Sacred Scripture, the Gospels resulted from an experi-ence that was passed on by word of mouth and eventually was preserved in writing. Specifically, we can identify three stages in the formation of the Gospels: the life and teachings of Jesus, oral tradition, and the written Gospels (see CCC, 126).

The Life and Teachings of Jesus

Like every one of us, the Incarnate Son of God lived in a particular time and place. Because he became man and lived, died, rose, and ascended to Heaven within a historical context, our ancestors in faith had the amazing opportunity to witness God in the flesh. They were able to touch him, hear his holy Word, and witness his saving actions. They heard him teach, and they witnessed his miracles and signs that pointed to him as the true Son of God. In Jesus' Passion, Death, Resurrection, and Ascen-sion, human beings saw the Divine Word of Life. The awaited Messiah dwelled among them.

Oral Tradition

"What we have seen and heard / we proclaim now to you, / so that you too may have fellowship with us" (1 John 1:3). After the Ascension and the outpouring of the Holy Spirit at Pentecost, the teachings and actions of Jesus and the events of the Paschal Mystery were transmitted by word of mouth. Aided by the Holy Spirit, the Apostles and early disciples shared the Good News that God came to earth to save his People and inaugurate his holy Reign. Oral proclamation helped to spread the vitally important message of salvation offered to all through Jesus Christ. This message is known as the **kerygma**. The recounting of Jesus' Good News and all he did for the sake of our salvation fostered faith and converted hearts.

The Written Gospels

After some time the early Church became concerned about preserving authentic records and testimonies about Jesus. There was a growing fear that the Good News of Christ's saving work could be distorted or interpreted incorrectly if the Church did not preserve it more formally. This effort may have become especially necessary because many eyewitnesses to Jesus' life were elderly and dying—or worse yet, being martyred. This is why the oral accounts were written down for various communities of believers. Guided by the Holy Spirit, the Gospel writers synthesized into writing what the original witnesses had

kerygma
A Greek word meaning "proclamation" or "preaching," referring to the announcement of the Gospel or the Good News of divine salvation offered to all through Jesus Christ. *Kerygma* has two senses. It is both an event of proclamation and a message proclaimed.

Did You Know?

An Itinerant Preacher

An itinerant preacher is a person who travels from place to place preaching the Word of God. Jesus was an itinerant preacher, as were the Apostles and other missionaries in the early Church. They traveled throughout the Roman Empire and neighboring lands to spread the message of salvation. Following their example, some Catholic religious orders began as communities of traveling preachers and continue this mission today. One of those orders is the Dominicans, founded in the Middle Ages by Saint Dominic. This order is also known as the Order of Preachers, which is why the abbreviation that appears after the name of members of the Dominican order is OP.

© Massimo Merlini / iStockphoto.com

told their followers in person. The goal was to preserve and hand on the Good News, unchanged, for all future generations.

How do you think the Evangelists might share their Gospels today, given the technology available to us?

Article 59: Why Four Gospels?

Just as people today differ not only in race and gender but also in affiliations, loyalties, and experiences, so did people of the early Christian communities. Although they were unified by their belief in Jesus Christ, the Incarnate Son of God, the early Christian communities were separated by different concerns and challenges. To respond to the specific needs of their audiences, the Evangelists—the Gospel writers Matthew, Mark, Luke, and John—composed four accounts of Jesus' life and

Primary Sources

So That We Might Know the Truth

How and why did the four Evangelists write their Gospels? Vatican Council II gives us a general overview of the formation of the Gospels in its *Dogmatic Constitution on Divine Revelation* (*Dei Verbum*, 1965):

> The sacred authors wrote the four Gospels, selecting some things from the many which had been handed on by word of mouth or in writing, reducing some of them to a synthesis, explaining some things in view of the situation of their churches and preserving the form of proclamation but always in such fashion that they told us the honest truth about Jesus. For their intention in writing was that either from their own memory and recollections, or from the witness of those who "themselves from the beginning were eyewitnesses and ministers of the Word" we might know "the truth" concerning those matters about which we have been instructed (see Luke 1:2–4). (19)

teachings. The four Evangelists proclaimed the Paschal Mystery in unique and varied ways to the communities to which they belonged.

Different Portraits of Faith

The Gospels are a unique literary form, or genre. You might think of them as religious or theological biographies of Jesus Christ. They are based in the actual teachings of Christ and the historical events of his life. Inspired by the Holy Spirit, the Evangelists focused on aspects of Jesus' life and teachings that were most meaningful to their Christian communities. What one community valued or needed to learn may not have been the same as what another community valued or needed to learn. The Evangelists could tell the same story in slightly different ways to emphasize the religious truth their communities needed.

The Gospels of Matthew, Mark, and Luke are called the **synoptic Gospels** (from a Greek word meaning "seeing the whole together"). These Gospels are similar in style and share much of the same content. We think this is because Luke and Matthew probably compiled their Gospels using the Gospel of Mark, as well as another source called the **Quelle**, or Q, Source. Even though they are similar in style and content, the three synoptic Gospels present slightly different images of Jesus that were meaningful to the members of their intended communities. The Gospel of John was written much later than the synoptic Gospels. It uses more symbolic language to express the true identity of Jesus as the Son of God and Incarnate Word.

Four Images of Jesus

Woven throughout each Gospel is a prevailing image or portrait of Jesus. Each image reveals an aspect of Jesus' role in salvation history.

synoptic Gospels
From the Greek for "seeing the whole together," the name given to the Gospels of Matthew, Mark, and Luke, because they are similar in style and content.

Quelle
Also called the Q Source, a theoretical collection of ancient documents of the teachings of Jesus shared among the early followers of Christianity; believed by Scripture scholars to be a source for the Gospels of Matthew and Luke.

Paschal Lamb
In the Old Testament, the sacrificial lamb shared at the Seder meal of the Passover on the night the Israelites escaped from Egypt; in the New Testament, the Paschal Lamb is Jesus, the Incarnate Son of God who dies on a cross to take away "the sin of the world" (John 1:29).

- **Gospel of Matthew** *Teacher and Prophet:* Jesus taught and proclaimed the radical redemption of God.
- **Gospel of Mark** *The Suffering Servant of God:* Jesus is the **Paschal Lamb**, who redeemed the human family by his self-sacrifice on the cross.
- **Gospel of Luke** *Compassionate Healer:* Jesus restored humanity to right relationship with God.
- **Gospel of John** *Incarnate Word of God:* Jesus was the Word of God Made Flesh, present since the beginning of time, "who takes away the sin of the world" (John 1:29).

These unique images complement the names and titles of Jesus Christ that are common to all the Gospels: Jesus (literally meaning "God saves"), Christ or Messiah (meaning "Anointed One"), Lord, and Son of God.

The Same Truth

Four Gospels, four portraits of the same Jesus. What do they all mean? All four Gospels form the very heart of all Sacred Scripture, because they are necessary for us to comprehend God's saving love revealed in his Incarnate Son. As our primary source for all that was revealed in

Live It!
Images of Jesus

The Gospels provide us with many different images of Jesus. You can find Jesus telling about the Father's love and mercy, but you will also find him warning people of the consequences of sin. He washes the feet of his disciples, but he also drives the money changers out of the Temple area with a whip. He loves sinners unconditionally, but he also challenges them to live in accordance with God's Law.

Which images of Jesus speak to you and your life today? Compile a list of Gospel passages that speak to your life right now. Be sure to choose passages that inspire you and also challenge you to change yourself to be more Christ-like. Keep the list handy and refer to it regularly in prayer.

the life and teachings of our Savior and Messiah, the Gospels reflect the mystery of Christ. The Holy Spirit guided the Gospel writers to foster and enliven the faith of human beings who come from different backgrounds and have varying needs. The Gospels may diverge in some details, but they never contradict one another in meaning. The Gospels point to the one and absolute truth—Jesus Christ is the Divine Son of God and the Lord of all creation.

How can the Gospels have different details but the same meaning?

© Netfalls - Remy Musser / Shutterstock.com

Chapter Review

1. Why are the Gospels the heart of all Scripture?

2. How were the Gospels developed?

3. What prevailing image or portrait of Jesus does each Gospel present? What is the meaning of each?

4. What is the primary difference between the synoptic Gospels and the Gospel of John?

5. What is the overall message of the Gospels?

Jesus is the Teacher and Prophet, Suffering Servant, Compassionate Healer, and Incarnate Word of God. Each of these images reveals an essential truth about who Jesus is and what he does for us.

Chapter 13

Revelation in and through Jesus in the Synoptic Gospels

Introduction

Synoptic means "allowing a view of the whole." When we look closely at the Gospels of Matthew, Mark, and Luke, we can see why they are known as the synoptic Gospels. Their structures and narrative styles follow a similar pattern, and their accounts present similar views of the life and work of Jesus. However, the shared accounts contain some differing details. The synoptic Evangelists, especially Matthew, point to Jesus as the Son of the Father and as the perfect teacher of God's saving message because he is God's Son. They announce Jesus' role as the compassionate Savior who had special concern for the sick, the poor, and others generally considered unimportant by the people of his time. This role is especially visible in the Gospel of Luke. All three synoptic Gospels emphasize the Paschal Mystery, asserting that Jesus was the Suffering Servant who had to die to ransom all humanity from sin and death.

Article 60: The Gospel of Matthew

The Gospel according to Matthew is the first Gospel in
the New Testament. Although the Gospel of Mark was
written first, this placement of the Gospel of Matthew
indicates the high esteem the Gospel held in the early
Church. Composed by AD 85, the Gospel of Matthew
addresses a mixed community of Jewish Christians and

Did You Know?

Symbols of the Gospels

Have you ever noticed stained glass images or icons in your church, each
depicting one of the following four figures: a human, a lion, an ox, and an
eagle? These colorful images, taken from Ezekiel 1:1–14, symbolize the four
Gospels, alluding to the unity of the Old and New Testaments.

The human figure signifies the Gospel of Matthew, because his Gospel
opens with a genealogy of Jesus' ancestors. Represented by a lion, Mark's
Gospel begins with John the Baptist, the voice of one roaring in the desert.
Beginning with Zechariah's offering sacrifice in the Temple, the Gospel of Luke
is symbolized by an ox, a sacrificial animal. John's Gospel speaks of Christ
coming from Heaven. As a result an eagle was selected to represent John,
because of its ability to soar through the clouds, the heavenly dome.

© Chartres Cathedral, Chartres, France / Bridgeman Images

Gentiles
Non-Jewish
people.

Matthean
Related to the
author of the Gospel of Matthew.

The Gospel of Matthew connects the Jewish faith and Scriptures with the words and life of Jesus Christ.

Gentiles (non-Jewish people). The community included diverse social groups, ethnic identities, and economic classes. The **Matthean** community probably experienced rejection and even some persecution by Jewish leaders as a result of its belief in Jesus. Many Jews did not accept the truth of Jesus. He did not fit their image of the expected Messiah. They were expecting a royal king who rules from a throne and abides by the laws of the past.

Matthew's community was caught in the tension between the old and the new. They strongly desired to remain true to their Jewish roots, but they ardently believed that Jesus was the long-awaited Messiah. Because of this tension, and because many Jews did not accept the divinity of Jesus, the Gospel of Matthew highlights Jesus as the fulfillment of many Old Testament hopes and prophecies. Matthew wanted his Jewish Christian readers to know that believing in Jesus was not a break with their tradition; he wanted them to see it as a continuation of their tradition. The Gospel of Matthew begins, therefore, by listing Jesus' genealogy. The genealogy connects Jesus to Abraham, the father of Judaism, and to David, Israel's greatest king. By showing an ancestral connection between Jesus and these two great leaders of faith, Matthew proclaimed continuity between the history of Israel and God's new, full Revelation in Jesus Christ. Matthew validated the community's link to the covenant promises of their cultural past. At the same time, he justified these Christians' new devotion to Christ and his mission.

© Bibliotheque Municipale, Epernay, France / Bridgeman Images

Jesus, the Supreme Teacher

In the Gospel of Matthew, we learn how Jesus frequently conflicted with Jewish leaders. He especially disagreed with the Pharisees and **scribes**. The conflicts centered on the proper interpretation of the Law. The Pharisees and the scribes believed that Jesus was doing away with the Law as presented by Moses. But Jesus clarified that he did not come to get rid of the Law of Moses—he came to fulfill it (see Matthew 5:17). He challenged certain Jewish beliefs that were too narrowly interpreted and criticized the Jewish leaders for being overly concerned with the letter of the Law, rather than its spirit. In the Sermon on the Mount (see 5:1–7:29), Jesus gave a new interpretation of the Law.

To further emphasize the role of Jesus as teacher, Matthew's Gospel is structured around five major discourses, or speeches. In these discourses Jesus radically redefined Jewish Law and proclaimed the saving love of God. The Law given to Moses in the Old Testament found its fulfillment in the life and teachings of Jesus Christ.

Jesus, Savior of All

The Gospel of Matthew includes several titles for Jesus, including Son of God, Son of David, and Son of Man. These titles emphasize the true identity of Jesus. Each title points to Jesus as the teacher and Savior of all people, including non-Jews. Indeed in the Gospel of Matthew we encounter amazing people of faith who were not Jews: the **Magi** (see 2:1–12), a Roman centurion (see 8:5–13), and a Canaanite woman (see 15:21–28). Matthew portrays Jesus as the master teacher, or **rabbi**, who redefined the Chosen People to include all who hear and accept the Good News of salvation.

> **How would you explain to a friend what it means to truly accept the Good News?**

scribes
Jewish legal scholars or teachers of Jewish Law. In the New Testament, they are associated with the Pharisees and the High Priests as opponents of Jesus.

Magi
From the Greek for "priest" or "learned one," refers to the wise men from the East who visited the newborn Jesus in Bethlehem.

rabbi
An honored teacher in the Jewish tradition.

Article 61: The Gospel of Mark

The Gospel of Mark is the shortest of the four Gospels. But its length does not determine its value. In sixteen chapters Mark manages to capture the essence of who Jesus is and what it means to be a disciple. The identity of the original author of this Gospel is uncertain. One

© Bibliotheque Municipale, Epernay, France / Bridgeman Images

The Gospel of Mark emphasizes Jesus' humanity and his suffering for our salvation.

tradition suggests that the author was John Mark, a companion of Saint Peter who is mentioned in the Acts of the Apostles 12:12. Whomever the author was, he was most likely a Gentile Christian, who may have been a disciple of Peter. Mark was the first Gospel written, approximately between AD 65 and 70. It seems to be directed at a community of non-Jewish Christians experiencing persecution, possibly at the hands of the Roman emperor Nero. Mark constructed a narrative of Jesus' life to help his community make sense of their suffering and persecution.

Mark's Portrayal of Jesus

The Gospel of Mark casts an aura of secrecy around the identity of Jesus. This atmosphere is known as the **messianic secret**. More than any Gospel, Mark emphasizes the humanity of Jesus. Mark's Jesus experiences the full range of human emotions, including anguish and pain. Central to Mark's Christology is the image of Jesus as the Suffering Servant. In contrast to some Jews' expectation of a victorious messianic king, Mark presents a messiah who suffered in doing the will of God his Father. Jesus' **Passion** and Death were necessary for God's saving plan to be realized.

Adding to Mark's portrayal of Jesus' humanity, the Gospel almost never portrays Jesus as referring to himself as the Messiah or by any synonymous titles, such as Son of God, Savior, or Son of David. We find only one exception in Mark's Gospel: when the high priest asked Jesus if he was the Messiah, Jesus responded, "I am" (14:62). Other people in the Gospel of Mark, however, did identify Jesus as the Messiah. In Mark 8:29 we learn that Jesus asked his disciples, "Who do you say that I am?" Peter replied, "You are the Messiah." In another encounter a blind man named Bartimaeus identified Jesus as the Son of David (see Mark 10:46–52). The only others whom the Gospel consistently portrays as naming the true identity of Jesus are the demons he cast out (see, for example, Mark 1:23–27).

True Discipleship

From the start Mark's Gospel lifts up the disciples as models of faith. They were the ones who left everything behind to follow Jesus. As the Gospel continues, Mark sometimes portrays the disciples unfavorably. For example, he depicts the disciples as lacking trust and faith. They were unable to comprehend Jesus' teachings and were disloyal in Jesus' darkest hour. Unique to Mark is the favorable representation of less-known people. We learn about a poor widow who gave all she had to the Temple treasury (see Mark 13:41–44). We journey with a **Syrophoenician** woman who humbled herself before Jesus for the sake of her daughter's health (see 7:24–30). We are introduced to Simon the Cyrenian, who carried Jesus' cross on the road to **Golgotha** (see 15:21). Through the shortcomings of the disciples, contrasted with the strong faith of these minor figures, Mark's Gospel teaches us that true discipleship must imitate Jesus in both his ministry and his suffering. Our call to be disciples requires us to remain faithful to Jesus' message even in times of great difficulty and persecution.

What do you think it means to be a disciple? What Gospel passages reflect your understanding?

messianic secret
A theme in the Gospel of Mark that portrays the disciples and others as recognizing Jesus' identity as the Messiah. However, Jesus directed them not to tell anyone else.

Passion
The suffering of Jesus during the final days of his life: his agony in the garden at Gethsemane, his trial, and his Crucifixion.

Syrophoenician
A person from the Phoenician cities of Tyre and Sidon. Jews considered Syrophoenicians "outsiders" because of their idolatrous practices.

Golgotha
A Hebrew word meaning "place of the skull," referring to the place where Jesus was crucified.

anawim
A Hebrew word
for the poor and
marginalized.

Article 62: The Gospel of Luke

The author of the Gospel of Luke seems to have been a Gentile convert to Christianity. One tradition suggests the author may have been Luke, "the beloved physician" (Colossians 4:14), a companion of Saint Paul. But whomever he was, the author wrote not only the Gospel of Luke but also another book in the New Testament: the Acts of the Apostles (or simply Acts). The Gospel of Luke and the Acts of the Apostles form a two-volume work on the life and mission of Christ and the life and growth of the early Church. They are best understood when read together and interpreted as a whole.

© Bibliotheque Municipale, Epernay, France / Bridgeman Images

Luke writes of Jesus as, among other things, a friend to the outcast. How does Luke's portrayal of Jesus enhance the picture begun by Matthew and Mark?

Luke had to rely on information from eyewitnesses to Jesus' life and ministry because he did not personally know Jesus. Biblical scholars believe the Gospel of Luke was written by AD 80–90. The audience of both the Gospel of Luke and the Acts of the Apostles is identified by the title Theophilus: "I too have decided, after investigating everything accurately anew, to write it down in an orderly sequence for you, most excellent Theophilus, so that you may realize the certainty of the teachings you have received" (Luke 1:3–4). The name Theophilus means "lover of God." Although Luke sounds like he is writing a letter to a personal friend, "Theophilus" likely refers to a group of Gentile Christians in either Antioch in Syria or Achaia in Greece. Luke's Gospel is structured around the question, Who is welcome in the Kingdom of God?

Who's "In" and Who's "Out"?

Luke makes clear that Jesus is the compassionate Savior who welcomes all. He emphasizes that Jesus was a friend to those who were poor. Much of Jesus' ministry and preaching was directed toward the plight of the **anawim**.

Anawim is the Hebrew word for the poor and marginalized. We find another example in Luke's **Canticle** of Mary, also called the ***Magnificat*** (a Latin term that means "it [my soul] praises"). In the canticle Mary sings of a God who lifts up the lowly, fills the hungry with "good things," and sends the rich away empty (see Luke 1:46–55). And the Parable of the Rich Man and Lazarus (see 16:19–31) points to a future when the poor will dine in the Kingdom of Heaven, and the rich will be shut out if they have neglected the poor.

Luke also portrays Jesus as a friend to those who were rejected by society. In describing the faith of a Gentile centurion (see 7:1–10) and of a **Samaritan** (see 10:25–37), Luke demonstrates that both the Gentiles and Jews were part of God's saving plan.

Luke's Gospel also emphasizes the presence of women in the ministry of Jesus. The Gospel of Luke includes many accounts about women, including Mary's visit to her cousin Elizabeth before the births of their sons, Jesus and John the Baptist (see Luke 1:39–66). The accounts of others—like the widow's son (see 7:11–17), the sinful woman (see 7:36–50), and Mary and Martha (see 10:38–42)—highlight the significance of women in the Reign of God.

Other groups given special attention in the Gospel of Luke are the sick and sinners. During Jesus' time, sickness was thought to be a sign of evil or a punishment from God for a sinful life. Dispelling this myth, Jesus traveled throughout Galilee, healing people possessed by demons, those with leprosy, and those who were paralyzed. He offered forgiveness to sinners.

The Gospel of Luke emphasizes that Jesus came as a Savior to all. His message of salvation was not confined to a particular religious or social group. Rather, it is for all people of all times who willingly hear and heed the Good News. Jesus fulfilled the hopes of ancient Israel. At the same time, Jesus demonstrated God's fidelity to all humanity, including the lowly and marginalized. Jesus is

canticle
From the Latin *canticum,* meaning "song." It usually refers to biblical hymns (other than the Psalms), such as those found in the Song of Solomon in the Old Testament and the hymns of Mary (see Luke 1:46–55) and Zechariah (see 1:68–79) in the New Testament. By extension, *canticle* is sometimes used to describe other hymns in the liturgy.

Magnificat
This is the first Latin word (from *magnus,* meaning "great," and *facere,* meaning "to make") and the title of the prayer of Mary in response to the Annunciation of the birth of Jesus in the Gospel of Luke (see Luke 1:46–55).

Samaritan
An inhabitant of Samaria, in the central hill country of Palestine. The Samaritans rejected the Jerusalem Temple and worshipped instead at Mount Gerizim. The New Testament mentions the Jewish rejection of Samaritans in both the Parable of the Good Samaritan (see Luke 10:29–37) and the account of Jesus' speaking with the Samaritan woman at the well (see John 4:1–42).

Infancy Narratives
The accounts of Jesus' birth and early childhood.

Annunciation
The event in which the Archangel Gabriel visits the Virgin Mary to announce that she is to be the Mother of the Savior.

the universal Savior, healing, redeeming, and reconciling all creation.

> **As a follower of Christ, what can you do today to be a friend to someone who is marginalized in your school or community?**

Article 63: Central Accounts in the Synoptic Gospels

The synoptic Gospels contain similar accounts of several defining moments in Jesus' life and public ministry. Among these moments are the birth of Jesus, the Baptism of Jesus, the temptation of Jesus, the multiplication of the loaves, and the Sermon on the Mount (or the Sermon on the Plain, in the Gospel of Luke). By reading and studying how each Gospel describes these key events, we are led further into the truth of God's saving plan as manifested in his most definitive Revelation, the Incarnate Word.

The Birth of a Savior

The Gospels of Matthew and Luke provide accounts of Jesus' birth, called the **Infancy Narratives**. These narratives have many similarities but also major differences. For example, Matthew tells us that an annunciation of Jesus' birth took place with Joseph. The angel of the Lord told Joseph not to be fearful of taking Mary into his home. The angel also let Joseph know that Mary would conceive through the Holy Spirit. In the Gospel of Luke, however, we read that the **Annunciation** of Jesus' birth took place with Mary. The Archangel Gabriel told Mary that the Holy Spirit would descend upon her, and that she would conceive a child while remaining a virgin (see the Did You Know? sidebar in article 13 for more about Mary). The angel also told her that her child would be called "Son of the Most High" (Luke 1:32). In God's divine time line, the Holy Spirit completed in Mary all the preparations for Christ's coming. By the action of the Holy Spirit, the Father gave the world his Son as foretold by the prophet Isaiah: "the young woman, pregnant and about to bear a son, shall name him Emmanuel" (Isaiah 7:14).

By the power of the Holy Spirit, Mary conceived Jesus, the Divine Son of God and the Second Person of the Trinity. She remained a virgin in conceiving him and giving him birth—and for all eternity. Because she is the mother of the Son of God, who is also God himself, we call Mary the Mother of God. By accepting God's will at the Annunciation and agreeing to her role in the Incarnation, Mary was already collaborating in the work Jesus was to accomplish.

By studying Matthew's and Luke's accounts, we come to understand the focus of each synoptic Gospel. Matthew and Luke each use the Infancy Narratives as a prologue to help their readers see their central themes. Both Evangelists place the conception and birth of Jesus, the Incarnation, in the context of a humble family. We see that salvation comes in the form of an ordinary child. The Messiah did not take on the trappings of power and wealth; instead he was clothed in humility and service. The Christmas mystery proclaims that we too must become humble and little if we want to enter the Reign of God. The Infancy Narratives also show us that particular groups of people, like the shepherds and the Magi, recognized Jesus as the Messiah, whereas others, such as Jewish leaders like King Herod, did not.

© Isabella Stewart Gardner Museum, Boston, MA, USA / Bridgeman Images

Jesus' lowly birth was not how most people expected the long-awaited Savior to arrive. How is our faith shaped by the humble life of Jesus?

The Baptism of Jesus

"I am baptizing you with water, for repentance, but the one who is coming after me is mightier than I. I am not worthy to carry his sandals. He will baptize you with the holy Spirit and fire. . . . He will clear his threshing floor and gather his wheat into his barn, but the chaff he will burn with unquenchable fire." (Matthew 3:11–12)

© Keith McIntyre / shutterstock.com

Jesus did not have to be baptized to be cleansed of sin, as we do. But he chose to be baptized in order to completely identify with the human condition, to become the perfect offering to save us from sin.

Do you know which important figure in the Gospels spoke these words to alert the Jews to the coming of Christ? If the mention of Baptism made you think of John the Baptist, you're right. John, who was also Jesus' cousin, prepared the way for the Messiah through his ministry. In fact, Jesus went to John the Baptist to be baptized at the beginning of his own public ministry.

The Baptism of Jesus manifested his identity as the long-awaited Messiah of Israel and as the Son of God. The Holy Spirit came upon Jesus in the form of a dove, and the Father's voice declared that Jesus is his Beloved Son. Jesus' Baptism inaugurated his mission and ministry in the world. Jesus began a new chapter in salvation history by obeying the will of his Father to proclaim the Reign of God. He said yes to the whole of God's plan, which culminated in his Death on a cross to save us from sin and death. Just as Jesus anticipated his own Death and Resurrection in the waters of Baptism, we do likewise in our own Baptism. We are dipped into the waters of Baptism to rise with Jesus, reborn of the Spirit so we "live in newness of life" (Romans 6:4).

The Temptation of Jesus

Scripture tells us that Jesus was led by the Holy Spirit into the desert, where he encountered temptation. Mirroring the temptation of Adam in the Garden of Eden and of the Israelites in the wilderness during the Exodus, Satan tempted Jesus in the desert. Unlike Adam and the Israelites, however, Jesus remained faithful and totally obedient to his Father's will. Jesus is the New Adam, who conquers sin and evil. In the words of the *Catechism*, "Jesus' victory over the tempter in the desert anticipates victory at the Passion" (539).

The Multiplication of the Loaves

One miracle that appears in all three synoptic Gospels as well as the Gospel of John is the multiplication of the loaves. In this miracle Jesus blessed a few loaves of bread that miraculously became enough to feed thousands of people. The multiplication of the loaves reminds us of the miracle of the manna in the Book of Exodus. The account of the multiplication of loaves also carries Eucharistic significance. Later, when he instituted the Eucharist at the Last Supper, Jesus took bread, lifted it, blessed it, and gave it to those around him. He satisfies our spiritual hunger with his own flesh and blood.

The Beatitudes

In the Gospels we learn that Jesus proclaimed a New Law: the grace of the Holy Spirit, which we receive through faith in Christ and the Sacraments. The New Law finds its clearest expression in Matthew's Sermon on the Mount and Luke's Sermon on the Plain, both of which contain the Beatitudes. The **Beatitudes** (see Matthew 5:3–10 and Luke 6:20–26) capture the heart of the New Law. These blessings fulfill the divine promises of the Old Law by orienting us toward their true meaning and goal: the establishment of the Kingdom of Heaven.

    The difference between Matthew's and Luke's proclamations of the Beatitudes is that Matthew focuses more on spiritual reality ("Blessed are the poor in spirit" [5:3]),

Beatitudes
The teachings of Jesus that begin the Sermon on the Mount and that summarize the New Law of Christ. The Beatitudes describe the actions and attitudes by which one can discover genuine happiness, and they teach us the final end to which God calls us: full communion with him in the Kingdom of Heaven.

© David Barnet / Illustration Works / Corbis

All four Gospels tell of the multiplication of the loaves and fish, signifying the importance of this event. How would you describe the meaning of this miracle to someone who is unfamiliar with it?

whereas Luke focuses more on material reality ("Blessed are you who are poor" [6:20]). Despite these slight differences, however, both versions of the Beatitudes send us the same message.

Namely, the Beatitudes tell us our goal. They show us the end to which God is calling us: communion with him in the Kingdom of Heaven, where we will see him face-to-face. There we will find our rest in him and live eternally. The Beatitudes call for a reversal of the world's value system and a total conversion of the heart. The Beatitudes respond to our innermost desires for happiness because they fulfill God's promises to Abraham and direct our lives toward Heaven. The Beatitudes also send us the message that

Live It!
Turning It All Upside Down

"Blessed are the poor in spirit . . . they who mourn . . . the meek" (Matthew 5:3–5). These don't really seem like blessings in our culture, do they? Too often we hear the message that to be happy, we must satisfy every desire—right now! The Jewish People and Roman citizens of Jesus' day also thought of someone who was prosperous, happy, and healthy as being "blessed."

In the Beatitudes, Jesus turned it all upside down. He taught us that living for others is the way to the Kingdom of Heaven. Being meek and merciful peacemakers means putting others first, just as Jesus did. Mourning or poverty can prepare us for the Kingdom of Heaven, because both can prompt us to reach out to God. When have you cried out to God? Do you call to him in good times, or only when you are in need? Have you asked him to help you to be humble? How can the Beatitudes turn your own thinking upside down?

God is calling each one of us to enter his Kingdom. The Reign of God belongs to all who accept it with humble hearts.

> **What faith-filled events or moments define your life up to this point? Why?**

parables
Short stories that use everyday images to communicate religious messages. Jesus used parables frequently in his teaching as a way of presenting the Good News of salvation.

Article 64: The Parables and Miracles in the Synoptic Gospels

During his public ministry, Jesus was always on the move. He traveled all over the land of Galilee, preaching and teaching about the Reign of God. He proclaimed the saving message of God in both word and deed. In presenting the Good News of salvation, Jesus taught in **parables**. They are short stories that use everyday images to communicate "mysteries of the kingdom of heaven" (Matthew 13:11). Coupled with Jesus' use of parables were "mighty deeds, wonders, and signs" (Acts of the Apostles 2:22) known as **miracles**. These were marvelous and unexpected events that manifested the presence and power of God.

miracles
Signs or wonders, such as healing or the control of nature, that can only be attributed to divine power.

Parables

The word *parable* comes from a Greek word meaning "comparison." Parables often present a story in the form of a simile, a literary device in which two different things are compared to illustrate a point. The words *like* or *as* often connect the two things being compared. For example, Jesus often said, "The Kingdom of Heaven is like . . ." or "The Reign of God is like . . ." Then he made comparisons to a mustard seed, a wedding feast, ten virgins, a pearl of great price, and so on.

Jesus' parables had five characteristic features:

1. Jesus usually told parables in response to questions or situations. To understand a parable's message, it helps to know whom or what Jesus was responding to.

2. The parables are based on everyday life at the time of Jesus. Just as priests today deliver homilies that use familiar examples and images to relay the truths of Scripture to us, Jesus' parables grew out of the common life and cultural experiences of his audience: family, farming, shepherding, trades, crafts, and religious practices.

3. The parables are often filled with surprises. Jesus captured the attention of his listeners by adding a surprising twist or ending to a story.

4. The parables teach timeless spiritual and ethical truths. Each parable gives deeper insight into the true meaning of the Reign of God.

5. One must have the eyes of faith to understand a parable's truth. Nonbelievers are confused and perplexed by the story and its larger meaning.

Let's look at the Parable of the Prodigal Son as an example of these characteristics (see Luke 15:11–32). The Pharisees and scribes were complaining that Jesus was eating with sinners (characteristic 1). In response, Jesus told a story about a younger son who leaves home and squanders his entire inheritance, while the older son remains loyal to his father and fulfills his duties as a son. At the younger son's return home, his father does not greet him with anger, nor does he reject him, as the culture of his time might have expected (characteristic 2). Instead the father welcomes the prodigal son with open arms and throws a party (characteristic 3). He was illustrating the boundless and forgiving love of God even when we make mistakes (characteristic 4). Do you think it's likely that the grumbling Jewish leaders understood or agreed with the larger meaning of this parable (characteristic 5)?

Parables challenge listeners to implement the Word of God in their everyday lives. Individuals must respond to the message revealed.

Miracles

When Jesus performed miracles, he revealed himself to be the embodiment of the Kingdom, the Messiah promised by the prophets. The miracles provided credibility to his words and teachings by concretely demonstrating his power over sin and evil. They revealed the Reign of God as a place where all are welcome, including the outcasts, and where suffering and evil are banished. Jesus performed four types of miracles: healings, exorcisms, control over nature, and restoration of life.

Healing Miracles

In miracles of healing, Jesus cured people with leprosy (see Matthew 8:1–4, Mark 1:40–45, Luke 5:12–16), fever, blindness, deafness, and paralysis (see Matthew 9:1–8, Mark 2:1–12, Luke 5:17–26).

Exorcisms

In his miracles of exorcism, Jesus drove evil spirits (see Matthew 8:16, Mark 1:32–34, Luke 4:40–41) or demons (see Matthew 17:14–21, Mark 9:14–29, Luke 9:37–43) out of people. For example:

Primary Sources

How Do the Parables Make You Feel?

Sometimes Jesus' parables strike a nerve, don't they? Theologian Megan McKenna explains that the parables are supposed to affect us. They make us look at who we are and who we want to be:

Often parables make us angry. There may be anger about others' behavior and attitudes. But, at root, we are angry at ourselves. The parable tells us the truth in some way about ourselves. Parables and the whole of scripture are truth-tellers. The text exposes us before ourselves and others.

. . . [The] parables and the gospels always say that we are all sinners, we are all in the same boat, and we have to look at this together because we either go down together or rise together. The parables of Jesus make us angry, sad, glad, nervous, because they tell us the truth about what we claim to be, even though the truth may not be apparent from our behavior, attitudes and alliances.

(Parables: The Arrows of God, page 28)

Nature Miracles

Nature miracles demonstrated Jesus' control over the forces of nature, including his calming a storm (see Matthew 8:23–27, Mark 4:35–41, Luke 8:22–25) and walking on water (see Matthew 14:22–33, Mark 6:45–52).

Restoration of Life

The miracles in which Jesus restored life pointed to his power over life and death. He raised the daughter of Jairus (see Matthew 9:18–19,23–26; Mark 5:21–24,35–43; Luke 8:40–42,49–56) and the widow's son (see Luke 7:11–17).

> **Which of Jesus' parables and miracles do you find most memorable? What do they tell you about Jesus?**

Article 65: The Paschal Mystery in the Synoptic Gospels

The Gospels are the heart of Sacred Scripture, and the Paschal Mystery is the heart of the Gospels. That is, God's plan for our salvation centers on our redemption through Christ's Passion, Death, Resurrection, and Ascension into glory. God's glorious love was revealed in the Death of his Son. Jesus willingly handed over his life for the ransom of many—paying the debt for our sins to save us.

The synoptic Gospel writers begin to draw us into the Paschal Mystery in their accounts of the Last Supper. During this event Jesus instituted the Holy Eucharist. The night before Jesus suffered and died on the cross, he gathered the Twelve Apostles to celebrate the Feast of Passover, the Jewish feast to remember the Exodus from Egypt. During this meal Jesus identified himself as the new Paschal Lamb. He was ready to lay down his life to liberate humanity from sin. At the Last Supper, Jesus took ordinary bread and wine and consecrated them. Through Consecration they became his Body and Blood, the Holy Eucharist. He stated: "Take and eat; this is my body. . . . This is my blood of the covenant, which will be shed on behalf of many for the forgiveness of sins" (Matthew 26:26,27).

From Passion to Death

The Passion of Christ refers to all that Jesus suffered during his final days in this life: his agony in the **garden at Gethsemane**, his trial and scourging, and his Crucifixion. In these accounts we encounter the very human side of Jesus. We journey with him as he experiences feelings of fear, betrayal, and abandonment.

In the garden Jesus said, "My Father, if it is possible, let this cup pass from me" (Matthew 26:39). He was mocked and ridiculed during his trial. He was cruelly whipped before his journey to Golgotha. On the road to Golgotha, Jesus experienced pain and exhaustion. On the cross he cried out, "My God, my God, why have you forsaken me?" (Matthew 27:46). Even though Jesus experienced these real human emotions, he remained obedient to his Father's will throughout his entire Passion.

Jesus' Death on the cross was the most selfless act of love human beings have ever witnessed or ever will witness. Crucifixion is one of the cruelest and most painful methods of execution, and the Romans reserved it for the lower classes and those who rebelled against Roman authority. By obediently accepting suffering and Death on a cross, "Jesus atoned for our faults and made satisfaction for our sins to the Father[2]" (CCC, 615). It was his love for us to the end that gave his sacrifice its redemptive value. His Death opened the gates of Heaven for all.

By accepting suffering and death for our salvation, Jesus modeled for us the path of true discipleship. We come to understand that the faithful disciple willingly accepts suffering for the greater glory of God. As Saint Rose of Lima said so eloquently, "Apart from the cross there is no other ladder by which we may get to heaven[3]" (quoted in CCC, 618).

garden at Gethsemane
An olive grove near the Mount of Olives, where Jesus gathered with the Apostles to pray before his Crucifixion on Calvary.

corruption
Decomposition or decay.

From Resurrection to Ascension

Only through the Resurrection can we understand the ultimate message of the Cross: God loves us so much that he offered his Son as the Paschal Lamb to make up for our disobedience. Jesus finally and definitively redeemed all humankind. The synoptic Gospels clearly describe the Resurrection, through their accounts of an empty tomb as well as Jesus' post-Resurrection appearances around Galilee. The empty tomb and linens signified that "by God's power Christ's body had escaped the bonds of death and **corruption**" (CCC, 657). The Resurrection affirmed the truth of Jesus' teachings. It heralded that

Faith in Action
The Land Where Jesus Walked

For centuries the Franciscan order has been entrusted with pre-serving and maintaining the places in the Holy Land (comprising the state of Israel and the territory of Palestine) where Jesus lived, walked, died, and rose from the dead. The Franciscans also minister to the people who still live where Jesus lived.

The order has created the Franciscan Foundation for the Holy Land to help them in their work. Why is such a foundation needed?

1. It is difficult and expensive to maintain and preserve the ancient holy sites.
2. The Holy Land has long been marked by political upheaval. The state of Israel and the territory of Palestine have not agreed on stable and workable borders. The friction among the people who make their homes in the Holy Land (Jews, Muslims, and Christians) can erupt in violence. One unfortunate consequence of this difficult situation is that Christians have been leaving the Holy Land for other places.
3. The Foundation promotes our awareness of the needs of the people in the Holy Land and of the ancient sites that are a legacy for the entire world.

On Good Friday, every Catholic parish in the world takes up a special collection for the Holy Land. This collection helps the Franciscans in their work to preserve the sacred places of the Holy Land and their ministry to people of all faiths there. The Holy Land is our land too. We owe a debt of support and gratitude to the Franciscans who help to preserve and protect the people and the land where Jesus walked.

Jesus was and is the Savior of all humanity. Jesus was not just an extraordinary man; he is also the Messiah who offered us new life through his Resurrection. Christ's Resurrection points to our own future resurrection.

The final event in the Paschal Mystery was the Ascension, during which Christ was taken up into Heaven to be seated at the right hand of the Father. Through their accounts of the Ascension, the Evangelists wanted to emphasize that Jesus passed totally into the presence of God and, in doing so, moved beyond our experience of space and time. This may seem confusing, but it actually means that Jesus entered into the Father's presence in Heaven while still keeping his human nature. Just as important, Jesus wasn't taken away from us—he is still in our midst. His Ascension allows him to be any-where at any time. He is the Head of the Church, and he ensures that the Holy Spirit continuously pours out on all God's people. As the Church prays:

Pray It!

Centering Our Prayer

One way to pray is to choose a word or a phrase and then meditate on it by reciting it over and over. You can do this with the great prayers of the Liturgy. For example, at the Easter Vigil the ancient hymn known as the Exsultet is proclaimed. It recounts the history of our salvation. This hymn fills us with great joy and exultation as we gain a deeper awareness of Christ's loving sacrifice. To make this prayer part of your personal prayer life, choose a portion of the text of the Exsultet and meditate on it. Here are some phrases that you might use for this purpose:

O wonder of your humble care for us!

O love, O charity beyond all telling,

to ransom a slave you gave away your Son!

(Roman Missal)

Take time to sit in prayer and repeat these words of the Exsultet in your mind and in your heart. Let them fill you with hope and joy.

For by his birth he brought renewal to humanity's fallen state, and by his suffering, canceled out our sins; by his rising from the dead he has opened the way to eternal life, and by ascending to you, O Father, he has unlocked the gates of heaven. (*Roman Missal*)

Commemorating the Paschal Mystery

We commemorate the events of the Paschal Mystery every year as part of the Church's liturgical calendar. The Easter Triduum is the three-day period when we remember the Last Supper, the Crucifixion, and the Resurrection of Jesus Christ. The Easter Triduum begins on the evening of Holy Thursday, with a celebration of the Last Supper. It continues on Good Friday with a memorial of the Crucifixion. On Holy Saturday evening, at the Easter Vigil, the Triduum reaches a high point by celebrating the Resurrection. The Triduum ends with evening prayer on Easter Sunday.

The Easter Vigil, held sometime between sunset on Holy Saturday and sunrise on Easter Sunday, is the first Easter celebration of the Resurrection of Christ. This first celebration of the Resurrection opens the door to the liturgical season of Easter. After forty days of rejoicing comes the celebration of the Ascension. The Easter season ends on the fiftieth day with the celebration of Pentecost. We commemorate the Paschal Mystery because it is Christ's work of redemption that grants us salvation.

The Service of Light at the beginning of the Easter Vigil reminds us that Christ is the Light of the World. At this liturgy we celebrate Christ's crossing over from death to life and opening the gates of Heaven.

How does the Resurrection of Christ offer us new life?

Chapter Review

1. What was the tension that existed in the community Matthew's Gospel addresses? How did this affect the manner in which Matthew wrote about Jesus?

2. What is unique about the way Mark presents Jesus in his Gospel?

3. What image of Jesus is prominent in the Gospel of Luke?

4. What is a central question about the Kingdom of God that the Gospel of Luke answers?

5. What three important accounts about Jesus' life are found in all three synoptic Gospels?

6. What role do the parables play in the message of Jesus?

7. How do Jesus' miracles manifest the Father's saving plan?

8. How does Jesus accomplish the redemption of humanity?

9. Describe the central events of the Paschal Mystery.

Chapter 14

Revelation in and through Jesus in the Gospel of John

Introduction

The Gospel of John, like the synoptic Gospels, proclaims that Jesus is the Messiah, the true path to salvation. The Evangelist John uses dialogues filled with symbolic language and rich theology. The dialogues present Jesus as the Incarnate Word of God.

However, whereas the synoptic Gospels describe Jesus' life and ministry to illustrate his humanity, the Gospel of John emphasizes the divinity of Jesus. John's Gospel makes use of signs and allegorical statements to reveal the true identity of Jesus as the Eternal Son of God. Lengthy speeches, or discourses, provide the framework for Jesus to teach about his body and Word as bread for the soul and to teach about the intimate connection between discipleship and service. John also contains the most developed teaching on the Holy Spirit, the third Divine Person of the Trinity. Particular to this Gospel is its distinctive presentation of the Paschal Mystery as a glorious manifestation of God's self-giving love.

Article 66: The Gospel of John: God Incarnate

If you find the Gospel of John difficult to read, you're not alone. We can read the synoptic Gospels more easily because they emphasize Christ's humanity through stories about his life and ministry. But many find it difficult to understand the heavily symbolic imagery, poetry, and mystery in John's Gospel, written between AD 90 and 100.

Some believe John the Evangelist was one of the disciples—"the one whom Jesus loved" (John 13:23). However, the actual author is unknown, but scholars believe the author was a member of a Christian community founded by the **Beloved Disciple**. Because John's Gospel seems to have undergone at least three stages of development, its tradition and teachings likely represent the whole **Johannine** community rather than just one individual.

That said, the Gospel appears to have been written for two main purposes. First, it was composed to evangelize both Gentiles and Jews. Second, the author wanted to strengthen the faith of his local Christian community, as well as the faith of Christians everywhere.

John's Gospel is divided into two major sections: the Book of Signs (1:19–12:50) and the Book of Glory (13:1–20:31). The Book of Signs focuses on seven miraculous **signs** Jesus performed. Unlike the synoptic Gospels, the Gospel of John describes Jesus as teaching primarily through signs, not parables. These signs reveal the identity of Jesus as the one sent from the Father in Heaven. Also in the Book of Signs, John gives special attention to our relationships with God and with one another.

The second section, the Book of Glory, centers on the Paschal Mystery. It is called the Book of Glory because John describes the Passion, Death, Resurrection, and Ascension as a glorification of Jesus according to the Father's plan. Throughout the Book of Glory, John emphasizes the importance of the Holy Spirit in the life of the Church after Jesus' Death.

Beloved Disciple
A faithful disciple in the Gospel of John who is present at critical times in Jesus' ministry. The Beloved Disciple may have been the founder of the Johannine community.

Johannine
Related to the Apostle John or the New Testament books attributed to him.

sign
The Johannine name for a miracle of Jesus.

Logos
A Greek word meaning "Word." *Logos* is a title of Jesus Christ found in the Gospel of John that illuminates the relationship between the three Divine Persons of the Holy Trinity. (See John 1:1,14.)

John's Christology

The synoptic Gospels emphasize the humanity of Jesus. The Gospel of John stresses his divinity. In his prologue, John describes Jesus as the preexistent **Logos** (Word), who is God and was with God at the beginning of Creation and became man to dwell among us. John proclaims that Jesus, the Incarnate Word, is "the light of the human race" (John 1:4). Jesus is the Light that overcomes the darkness and gives direction to our lives. The themes of light and darkness appear frequently in John. For John light comes from above, and darkness comes from below. In declaring Jesus to be the Light, the Evangelist asserts the divinity of Jesus. John concludes his prologue by describing Jesus as the fulfillment of the Old Law. He reminds us that "no one has ever seen God" (1:18), so the only way we can see and know God the Father is through his only Son, Jesus Christ.

How would you define *glory*? Why is it an appropriate word to describe the Paschal Mystery?

Live It!
Giving Flesh to Your Faith

The word *incarnate* literally means "to become flesh." Because the Father loves us, he sent his Son to redeem us. Notice that the Father did not send his only begotten *idea* to us. He sent his Son in the flesh, who taught, fed, healed, and loved both his friends and his enemies.

Jesus does not walk the earth today in the same way he did two thousand years ago. We are called to be part of the Body of Christ to continue his mission, with the help of the Holy Spirit. We are called to give flesh to our faith. Faith is not simply a thought or a belief. It must be lived.

Have you given enough time to praying to discover God's will in your life? In what particular ways is God calling you to live out your faith? What concrete actions can you begin taking now to flesh out his will in your life? Take some time to reflect on these questions. You may be surprised by what you discover.

Article 67: Signs and Miracles in John's Gospel

The use of the word *sign* in place of *miracle* is unique to the Gospel of John. What is a sign? You might immediately think of signs around your school, or perhaps street signs that tell drivers to stop, yield, or merge. But in John's Gospel, a sign points to (or signifies) a deeper reality and meaning.

In calling Jesus' miracles "signs," the Evangelist conveys that these momentous actions and wonders point to a larger truth. They move us beyond what was witnessed to reach a deeper level of mystery and understanding. Specifically, these signs reveal the divinity of Jesus, the only Son of God and the Incarnate Word. They confirm that the Father sent Jesus to chart a new course of salvation. The Evangelist tells his readers that the signs were "written [so] that you may [come to] believe that Jesus is the Messiah, the Son of God, and that through this belief you may have life in his name" (John 20:31).

The Seven Signs

John's Gospel contains seven signs, or miracles—far fewer than we find in the synoptic Gospels. This Gospel focuses on presenting a smaller number of profound miracles in greater detail and depth.

- **First Sign:** Jesus changed water into wine at Cana (see 2:1–11).
- **Second Sign:** Jesus restored the health of an official's son (see 4:46–54).
- **Third Sign:** Jesus healed a paralytic (see 5:2–18).
- **Fourth Sign:** Jesus multiplied loaves and fish to feed the five thousand (see 6:1–15).
- **Fifth Sign:** Jesus walked on water (see 6:16–21).
- **Sixth Sign:** Jesus restored sight to a man born blind (see 9:1–7).
- **Seventh Sign:** Jesus raised Lazarus to life (see 11:1–44).

Three of these seven miracles appear in the synoptic Gospels as well. But we encounter four of these miracles only in John's Gospel: changing water to wine at Cana (the first sign), curing the paralytic (the third sign), healing the man born blind (the sixth sign), and raising Lazarus from the dead (the seventh sign).

The signs are moments of teaching. In the synoptic Gospels, we learn that Jesus often taught through parables. In the Gospel of John, we find Jesus teaching through signs and allegories. John includes no parables in his Gospel, probably to emphasize the meaning behind

At his mother Mary's urging, Jesus performed the miracle of changing water into wine at a wedding. What do you think this first sign indicates about Jesus and his ministry?

© Scrovegni (Arena) Chapel, Padua, Italy / Bridgeman Images

Primary Sources

God Multiplies Our Small Acts of Love

All four Gospels tell us how Jesus multiplied loaves and fish to feed the multitudes. But John's account includes a detail not found in the synoptic Gospels: the loaves and fish came from one boy. As Pope Benedict XVI explains, this tiny detail points to an important teaching:

> A boy's presence is also mentioned in the scene of the multiplication [in the Gospel of John]. On perceiving the problem of feeding so many hungry people, he shared the little he had brought with him: five loaves and two fish (cf. Jn 6:9). The miracle was not worked from nothing, but from a first modest sharing of what a simple lad had brought with him. Jesus does not ask us for what we do not have. Rather, he makes us see that if each person offers the little he has the miracle can always be repeated: God is capable of multiplying our small acts of love and making us share in his gift. (*Angelus*, July 29, 2012)

the seven signs. The signs reveal that Jesus, the Wonder Worker, is God himself and the fullness of Revelation. Some biblical scholars have also drawn a parallel between the seven signs in John and the seven days of Creation. Just as God miraculously created the world in seven days, so too God, in the person of Jesus, miraculously performed seven acts of wonder to bring about a new world order.

Symbolic Meanings

John's accounts of Jesus' miracles focus on symbolic meaning rather than on the concrete action itself. The physical miracles—signs—symbolize a deeper truth and reality: Christ's glory and divinity. Specifically, when Jesus changes water into wine (see John 2:1–11), John foreshadows that Jesus will be the Blood (wine) of the New Covenant. When Jesus heals the official's son (see 4:46–54), we learn that faith in Jesus leads to wholeness and health. Jesus also heals a paralyzed man at the pool in Jerusalem (see 5:1--18), signifying that Jesus' Word gives a new and lasting life that the cures of this world cannot offer. The feeding of the five thousand (see 6:1–15) alludes to Jesus' satisfying of our spiritual hungers. The story of Jesus' walking on water (see 6:16–21) demonstrates that Jesus has the power to calm our every fear and rid our hearts of all anxiety. The restoration of sight to the blind man (see 9:1–7) symbolizes spiritual insight into the real identity of Jesus: the blind man had eyes of faith to see the one and only Light, Jesus Christ. Finally, the account of Lazarus's resurrection from the dead (see 11:1–44) heralds Christ's power over life and death and shows that Jesus is the path to eternal life. It foreshadows the Death and Resurrection of Jesus.

> **Why is the symbolic meaning of each sign more important than the specific action Jesus took?**

Article 68: The "I Am" Statements

Time and again the Gospel of John challenges us to recognize Jesus as the Messiah. In addition to his miraculous signs, Jesus declared his role in salvation history through a series of "I am" sayings. These sayings ask us to recall God's revelation of himself to Moses in the burning bush. In that encounter God revealed his name as "I am who I am" (Exodus 3:14). Similarly, through Jesus' "I am" sayings, John makes it clear that Jesus is God.

The "I am" statements use familiar images and symbols to establish Jesus' divinity. They also provide us with several ways of understanding Jesus' mission. Seven "I am" sayings appear in the Gospel of John:

- "I am the bread of life" (6:35).
- "I am the light of the world" (8:12).
- "I am the gate for the sheep" (10:7).
- "I am the good shepherd" (10:11).
- "I am the resurrection and the life" (11:25).
- "I am the way and the truth and the life" (14:6).
- "I am the vine, you are the branches" (15:5).

> **Choose one "I am" statement from the list. What does it help you to understand about Jesus Christ?**

Article 69: The "Bread of Life Discourse" and the "Last Supper Discourse"

A discourse is a long speech. Jesus gave discourses to teach about matters of faith and salvation. The heart of his discourses in the Gospel of John is the revelation that he is God and that his presence is the presence of God. To receive his words is to receive the Word of God. We find two important discourses in John's Gospel: the "Bread of Life Discourse" and the "Last Supper Discourse." In both of these discourses, Jesus taught about his true identity and reassured his followers of his continued presence. Those who don't believe or understand his message tended to demand signs to prove his identity as the Son of God. Those who did believe sought assurance that Jesus would always be with them.

The "Bread of Life Discourse"

In his "Bread of Life Discourse," Jesus declared, "I am the bread of life; whoever comes to me will never hunger, and whoever believes in me will never thirst" (John 6:35). Speaking to a group of people who were demanding signs of his identity, Jesus asserted that he is Bread of Heaven. He is not the perishable manna their ancestors ate in the desert—rather, he is the "true bread" (6:32) that "gives life to the world" (6:33). And unlike those ancestors who ate manna in the desert yet still died eventually, those who eat the Bread of Jesus will live forever. Jesus was teaching a group of people who were very familiar with the Old

Did You Know?

© Bill Wittman / www.wpwittman.com

The Necessity of Relationship

Jesus' teaching in the Gospel of John emphasizes two relationships: between Jesus and the Father, and between us and Jesus. For example, throughout the "Bread of Life Discourse" and the "Last Supper Discourse," Jesus constantly taught that he is the path to the Father. Jesus proclaimed, "The Father and I are one" (John 10:30). In Jesus' priestly prayer at the end of the "Last Supper Discourse," he interceded for us with his Father. Jesus prayed for the protection of the disciples and their continued mission to spread the Good News revealed in the Incarnation.

Indeed all four Gospels affirm the importance of the Kingdom of God and the need to be in right relationship with God and with one another. With the grace of the Holy Spirit, our faith in Christ restores our relationship with God, making the Kingdom present in our lives and helping us in our relationships with others.

Testament tradition, which depicts Wisdom as providing nourishment (see Sirach 24:21 and Isaiah 49:10). As the Bread of Life, Jesus is our sole source of nourishment. He perfects and fulfills the teachings of the Old Law and the Wisdom tradition.

In the Gospel of John, the Bread of Life refers to both Jesus' Body and his Word. We are to feast on his Body and Blood made present in the Eucharist, and we must also assimilate his life-giving Word into our lives. John foreshadows Jesus' Death by emphasizing that Jesus will give his "flesh for the life of the world" (John 6:51). His Body will be broken and his Blood will be poured out so all might have life abundantly.

The "Last Supper Discourse"

John's account of the Last Supper is different from the synoptic Gospels' accounts. In John it is not a Passover meal, nor does the account describe the preparations for the meal. Instead John points to Jesus as the Paschal Lamb who will be slaughtered for the salvation of all. A defining moment of John's Last Supper is Jesus' humble act of washing the feet of his disciples (an act we commemorate every year in the Mass of the Lord's Supper on Holy Thursday). Jesus demonstrated that the path of authentic discipleship is humility, service, and love—from the simple act of serving a meal to the washing of a person's feet, as a household servant in Jesus' time would have done.

"I am the bread of life; whoever comes to me will never hunger, and whoever believes in me will never thirst" (John 6:35).

This message was reinforced in the "Last Supper Discourse." Jesus directed us to give our lives in service to others, just as he gave himself in the breaking of bread and

the washing of feet. Our service must be rooted in a "new commandment: love one another" (John 13:34). As Jesus demonstrated throughout his teaching, service and love are the fruits of those who remain in him. Those who remain connected to Jesus—who is the vine—will be sustained, nourished, and bound by selfless service and love.

Another important aspect of the "Last Supper Discourse" is the way Jesus addressed the role of the Holy Spirit. The disciples sensed his impending departure, and they were afraid of what lay ahead. Jesus assured them they would not be left alone. They would receive the gift of the Holy Spirit, also called the **Paraclete**. The Holy Spirit, the Third Divine Person of the Trinity, acts as an advocate and counselor for all who believe in Jesus Christ.

> **What is one thing you can start doing today to serve others on the path of authentic discipleship?**

Paraclete
A term meaning "advocate" or "helper," used in the Gospel of John to describe the Holy Spirit, the Third Divine Person of the Trinity, whom Jesus promised to the disciples as an advocate and counselor.

Article 70: Jesus' Passion, Death, and Resurrection

In your literature studies, you may have learned to identify the climax of a book or story: that is, the turning point or peak of dramatic tension, after which the action resolves (for better or worse). The climax of the Gospel of John is Jesus' willingness to lay down his life for the salvation of all. This moment embodies the most selfless act of love we will ever witness.

Recall that John uses light and darkness to drive home his message. The betrayer of Jesus, Judas, came at night, representing the power of darkness. But Jesus, as the power of light, was fully aware and in charge of what was happening to him. Unlike the synoptic Gospels, the Gospel of John does not focus on the tragedy of the Paschal Mystery. Rather, it portrays every moment, from Jesus' betrayal to his Resurrection, as God's glorious power at work in Jesus. Jesus glorified his Father even when the forces of evil seemed to be winning.

Imminent Glory: From Passion to Death

The details of Jesus' Passion, Death, and Resurrection in the Gospel of John differ from their parallels in the synoptic Gospels. For example, John's Passion narrative does not include the account of the agony in the garden at Gethsemane. Instead John focuses on Jesus' declaration of his identity as "I AM" (John 18:5) to those who come to arrest him, at which point they fell to the ground. This moment echoes God's revelation of his name in the Old Testament, "I am who I am" (Exodus 3:14)—it points to Jesus as the Lord of all.

The chapters in John that tell of Jesus' Passion and Death are sometimes called the Book of Glory. Why do you think this is?

Upon being questioned by Pilate, Jesus responded, "You would have no power over me if it had not been given to you from above" (John 19:11). We also learn that Jesus was seated on the judge's bench after the inquisition by Pilate. This detail symbolizes that Jesus is the judge of the world. He controls his own fate, as well as the fate of those who surround him. John does not depict Jesus as crying out from the cross, as in the synoptic Gospels. He simply says that Jesus stated, "It is finished" (19:30).

© Prado, Madrid, Spain / Bridgeman Images

The Gospel of John describes another event in the Crucifixion of Jesus that does not appear in the synoptic Gospels: a soldier pierced Jesus' side on the cross, "and immediately blood and water flowed out" (John 19:34). The blood and water that flowed from the side of Jesus are signs of the salvation he won for us by his Death and Resurrection. The blood and water point to the Sacraments of the Eucharist and Baptism. Through his Death Jesus offered his body for the salvation of the world and poured out his

Spirit on his followers. His blood freed the human heart from the powers of sin and evil. Through his life-giving water, we are reborn as children of God. Jesus' Death was not an end but a beginning. John's Crucifixion account illustrates Jesus' triumph even at the moment of his Death. Jesus' Death was glorious because he shattered the power of sin and death and revealed God's love to all creation.

Triumphant Glory: Beyond Death to Resurrection

Five significant Resurrection appearance accounts appear in the Gospel of John. In two separate instances, we learn that Simon Peter and the Beloved Disciple found the tomb empty and believed Jesus had risen. Then, even though the tomb was empty, Mary Magdalene did not believe until she encountered the Risen Christ in the garden. Later, the disciples recognized the Risen Christ by the wounds in his hands and feet. Finally, upon touching Jesus' wounds, the Apostle Thomas exclaimed, "My Lord and my God!" (John 20:28). Each of these Resurrection appearances heralds the triumphant love of God. His powerful light burns away all darkness. No one can extinguish the light of his saving love.

Pray It!

Reflecting on the Passion of Jesus

A traditional Catholic prayer is the "Prayer before Jesus Christ Crucified." Take time to reflect on the sacrificial, loving action of Christ using this prayer:

> My good and dear Jesus, I kneel before you, asking you most earnestly to engrave upon my heart a deep and lively faith, hope, and charity, with true repentance for my sins, and a firm resolve to make amends. As I reflect upon your five wounds, and dwell upon them with deep compassion and grief, I recall, good Jesus, the words the prophet David spoke long ago concerning yourself: "They have pierced my hands and my feet; / I can count all my bones!" (Psalm 22:17–18).

One Message of Salvation

Though the Gospel of John differs from the synoptic Gospels in significant ways, all four Gospels together announce the same Good News. Jesus Christ, the only Son of God, became man; and through his Passion, Death, Resurrection, and Ascension, he made it possible for us to share in the divine life of the Trinity.

Faith in Action
Great Men of Faith

John Baptist de La Salle, Pierre Leger, 1794
(Brothers of the Christian Schools, Generalate Museum)

The name John comes from the Hebrew name Yochanan, meaning "Yahweh is gracious." John is a popular name because of two New Testament saints: John the Baptist and the Apostle John. Throughout Church history more than two hundred holy men have borne the name John, including these notable figures:

- **Saint John Chrysostom** was an early Church Father known for his wonderful preaching, contributions to the development of liturgical theology, and avid denunciation of political and Church abuse.

- **Saint John Fisher** was a Catholic bishop in England during the Protestant Reformation. Along with Saint Thomas More, he was executed by King Henry VIII for refusing to accept the king as the head of the Church of England.

- **Saint John Houghton** was a Carthusian who refused to accept King Henry VIII as the head of the Church of England, which led to his martyrdom.

- **Saint John Baptist de La Salle** was a French priest who founded the Institute of the Brothers of the Christian Schools (or Christian Brothers) to develop educational methods that meet the needs of all young people.

- **Saint John Bosco** was an Italian priest and educator who dedicated his life to the education and salvation of poor and neglected children. Popularly known as Don Bosco, he founded the Salesian order of religious.

What does it mean to glorify God, our Father? What are some specific things you can do to glorify God?

Chapter Review

1. What were two main reasons the Gospel of John was written?

2. What does the Gospel of John emphasize about Christ? Give some examples.

3. Name four signs or miracles found in the Gospel of John but not in the synoptic Gospels.

4. What is the purpose of the seven signs or miracles in the Gospel of John?

5. What do we call the seven special statements that Jesus makes about himself in the Gospel of John? What do these statements indicate about Jesus?

6. How does John's account of the Last Supper differ from the accounts in the synoptic Gospels?

7. What is the emphasis in the Gospel of John's account of the Passion and Death of Jesus? Describe one event that occurs in the Gospel of John that does not occur in the synoptic Gospels.

Chapter

15

Acts and Letters

Introduction

The Gospels are the heart of the New Testament because they tell us about Jesus Christ, the Incarnate Word of God. The books in the rest of the New Testament give us insight into the spread of Christianity. These books also help us to recognize the challenges the first Christians faced. In the Acts of the Apostles, the Pentecost account tells about coming of the Holy Spirit upon the Apostles and the Church. The Holy Spirit empowered the Apostles to proclaim the Good News to all peoples. Later in Acts we learn about the spread of the Church through missionary journeys to take the Good News of Jesus Christ to the corners of the earth.

A key figure in the development of early Christianity was Saint Paul of Tarsus. Christian communities founded by Paul and other evangelizers needed wisdom and support to live out their faith. These communities faced internal strife and external persecution. The New Testament contains Paul's letters as well as the letters of other early Church leaders. All of these letters provided advice, pastoral encouragement, and support to the new Christian communities. The final book in the New Testament is the Book of Revelation. The Book of Revelation offered a message of hope to a people in crisis through highly symbolic language and vivid imagery.

Article 71: Acts of the Apostles

In chapter 13, you learned that the Acts of the Apostles is the second volume in the two-volume work that we sometimes call Luke-Acts. Written around AD 80 by the Evangelist Luke, the Acts of the Apostles picks up where the Gospel of Luke ends. Acts begins with the promise of the Spirit and the Ascension of Jesus. Then it recounts how the early Church grew under the guidance of the Holy Spirit. In Acts, the Church begins as a small group of disciples in Jerusalem and ends up spanning the Roman Empire, miraculously bridging the gap between the Jewish and Gentile worlds. Two significant events and movements form the backdrop of Acts: the coming of the Spirit at **Pentecost** and the evangelization and missionary efforts of early Christianity.

Pentecost
The fiftieth day following Easter, which commemorates the descent of the Holy Spirit on the early Apostles and disciples.

Tongues as of Fire

In the Jewish liturgical calendar, the Feast of Pentecost is an annual agricultural celebration. When the disciples celebrated this feast not long after Jesus' Ascension, the house where they gathered, with Mary in their midst, was filled with the Holy Spirit in the form of a "strong driving wind" that rested as "tongues as of fire" on each of them (Acts 2:2,3). This event marked the call of the disciples to go into the world, crossing borders and barriers, to spread the Good News of Christ. For Christians the Feast of Pentecost now celebrates the fulfillment of Jesus' promise to send the Holy Spirit to guide the Church as she proclaims the truth of salvation in Jerusalem and beyond. We commemorate Pentecost fifty days after Easter.

A Missionary Church

Three people stand out in the Acts of the Apostles as models of Christian faith: Saint Peter, Saint Stephen, and Saint Paul. These three men embodied the evangelization and missionary efforts of the early Church. The first, Saint Peter, preached a message of repentance and forgiveness. He called disbelieving Israelites to a conversion

martyrdom
Witness to the saving message of Christ through the sacrifice of one's life.

of heart so the Risen Messiah might wipe away their sins. Saint Stephen was filled with the power to do "great wonders and signs" (Acts 6:8), and he prophesied about how Jesus' life, especially his Death and Resurrection, fulfilled the Torah. His message met with great resistance, eventually leading to his **martyrdom**. Finally, after his dramatic conversion, Saint Paul (originally named Saul) embarked on three missionary journeys to bring the Light of Christ to all. Some embraced his message, but many rejected it. He was persecuted, encircled by riots, and imprisoned, finally being executed in Rome.

Peter's, Stephen's, and Paul's experiences of teaching, persecution, and suffering paralleled those in the life of Christ. Their stories remind us that true discipleship is missionary in nature and risks all for the greater glory of God.

The Holy Spirit was sent to empower and guide the Church from her humble beginning until she is perfected in the glory of Heaven. The Church is the means of God's plan. Through her the Good News is preached to all

Pray It!

Saint Augustine's Prayer to the Holy Spirit

Just as the early Church did, we must rely on the Holy Spirit for guidance in our lives. Saint Augustine of Hippo wrote this "Prayer to the Holy Spirit." Pray it often to ask the Holy Spirit for guidance in your life.

Breathe in me, O Holy Spirit,
    that my thoughts may all be holy,
Act in me, O Holy Spirit, that
    my work, too, may be holy.
Draw my heart, O Holy Spirit,
    that I love but what is holy.
Strengthen me, O Holy Spirit, to
    defend all that is holy.
Guard me then, O Holy Spirit,
    that I always may be holy.
Amen.

people, and all are invited into the Body of Christ. But the Church is also the goal of God's plan. Through her we participate, however imperfectly, in the joy of communion with God, which we will experience in complete glory in Heaven.

If you were called to die for your faith, would you be frightened or joyful?

Article 72: The Pauline Letters

The conversion of Saint Paul is an exciting story. Saul (his Hebrew name) was a Roman citizen and Jewish leader who worked to destroy the early Church and imprison Jewish Christians. Then he encountered the Risen Christ on the road to Damascus, in Syria. Light flashed around him, and a voice called to him, "Saul, Saul, why are you persecuting me? . . . I am Jesus, whom you are persecuting" (Acts 9:4–5). Christ told him to head into Damascus, where someone would tell him what Christ

Did You Know?

Gifts and Fruits of the Holy Spirit

© tkachuk / Shutterstock.com

We learn a lot about the Holy Spirit in the New Testament, especially through the Acts of the Apostles and Saint Paul's letters. The Holy Spirit gives us special graces that support spiritual growth, happiness, and wisdom so we can build a more just world in this life and prepare for full communion with God in Heaven. These graces, called the Gifts of the Holy Spirit, are Wisdom, Understanding, Counsel (Right Judgment), Fortitude (Courage), Knowledge, Piety (Reverence), and Fear of the Lord (Wonder and Awe).

These Gifts of the Holy Spirit in turn help us to develop positive virtues, known as the fruits of the Holy Spirit. In his Letter to the Galatians, Saint Paul tells us that people who open their minds and lives to the Holy Spirit are blessed with nine fruits: "love, joy, peace, patience, kindness, generosity, faithfulness, gentleness, self-control" (5:22–23).

Pauline letters
Thirteen New Testament letters attributed to Saint Paul or to disciples who wrote in his name. The letters offer advice, pastoral encouragement, teaching, and community news to early Christian communities.

wanted him to do. Saul was baptized in Damascus, where he began to preach the Good News. Eventually he began to use the name Paul, his Latin name as a Roman citizen.

Paul embarked on three missionary journeys to found new Christian communities and spread the Good News of Christ. Once he established each community, he moved on. Sometimes he was forced to leave. He traveled to other cities to carry his mission further. To remain in contact with the communities he helped to form, Paul wrote letters to offer advice, pastoral encouragement, and teaching.

Some of Paul's letters were collected and shared with other Christian communities. In this way, they became part of the collection of sacred writings that later formed the canon of the New Testament. The thirteen letters in the New Testament that are attributed to Paul—or to disciples who wrote in his name—are called the **Pauline letters**: Romans, First and Second Corinthians, Galatians, Ephesians, Philippians, Colossians, First and Second Thessalonians, First and Second Timothy, Titus, and Philemon. You might notice that nine of these letters address communities, and four address individuals. The letters Paul wrote are the oldest Christian documents we have, even older than the four Gospels.

Some of the Pauline letters are grouped into two subcategories: the captivity letters and the pastoral letters. The captivity letters (Ephesians, Philippians, Colossians, and Philemon) are attributed to Paul writing from jail. The pastoral letters (First Timothy, Second Timothy, and Titus) are attributed to Paul and his companions writing while they were on missionary journeys. The Pauline letters differ from one another in content, but all follow a common pattern:

1. Each begins with a greeting from the sender to the receiver or receivers.
2. Following the greeting, the letter offers a prayer.
3. The body of the letter addresses a particular issue and offers advice.

4. Each letter closes with greetings and instructions to specific people, and a final blessing.

Most of Paul's letters also address some common themes. Two recurring themes are (1) Jesus the Christ is the path to salvation and (2) the Church is the Body of Christ.

Jesus Christ Is the Path to Salvation

Paul's letters present Jesus as the New Adam. Referring to the Fall of Adam and Eve, Paul asserts, "For just as through the disobedience of one person the many were made sinners, so through the obedience of one the many will be made righteous" (Romans 5:19). According to Paul, by accepting Death on a cross, Jesus modeled perfect obedience, unlike Adam and Eve. Jesus' obedience made salvation possible for all people.

Paul uses three Christological titles to highlight the Christ's role in God's plan of salvation. He uses the title "the Son" to point to Jesus as God's Divine Son, who has been with God from the beginning of time. The title "the Christ" shows that Jesus fulfilled the hope of Israel. The third title, "Lord," is how Paul refers to the Risen Christ's dominion over creation, won through his obedience and Death. This title "Lord" expresses Jesus' divinity. God

Paul journeyed tirelessly to spread the Good News. His letters encouraged communities in living the faith and corrected any misunderstandings that arose.

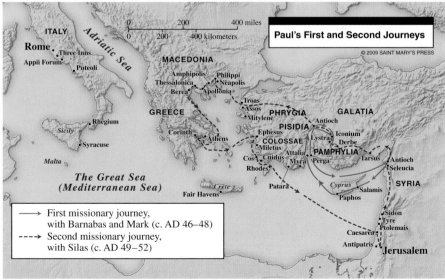

Paul's First and Second Journeys

© 2009 SAINT MARY'S PRESS

First missionary journey, with Barnabas and Mark (c. AD 46–48)

Second missionary journey, with Silas (c. AD 49–52)

The Great Sea (Mediterranean Sea)

© Saint Mary's Press, Thomas Nelson, and maps.com

raised up Jesus as the Lord of all creation, because Jesus emptied himself, "taking the form of a slave / . . . becoming obedient to death, even death on a cross" (Philippians 2:7–8).

The Church Is the Body of Christ

Paul's teaching that the Church is the Body of Christ rings loudly through most of his letters. Paul was writing to communities who were dealing with the struggles of everyday living, sometimes resulting in disunity and discord. His letters use an analogy of the human body to teach an important lesson. Paul says that all parts—the head, the hands, the heart, and the feet—are necessary for a body to fully function. If one part of the body is cut off, the rest of the body suffers. In the same way, all people, with their varied gifts and talents, are essential in the Body of Christ. The entire Body of Christ suffers when one of its parts, its people, is broken or cut off from the whole. Paul proclaims that Christians are one Body, the Church, of which Jesus is the Head. The Church is a visible sign of God's presence in the world. Therefore she must be joined and knitted together in Christ, building herself up in love (see Ephesians 4:16).

Just as the Holy Spirit guided and strengthened Paul and his companions as they preached the Gospel, the Holy Spirit guides us to share the Good News by our lives.

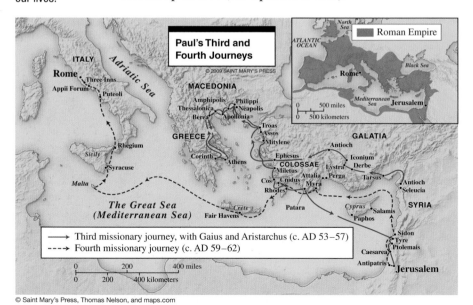

© Saint Mary's Press, Thomas Nelson, and maps.com

From his prolific writings to his lasting influence on early Christianity and beyond, Paul was one of the most important figures in the formation of the early Church. It is obvious from his writings and missionary journeys that Paul was profoundly affected by Jesus' message and mission and by all Jesus did for our salvation. The thirteen Pauline letters continue to plant the seeds of faith today, just as they planted faith beyond the limits of Judaism.

epistle
Another name for a New Testament letter.

> **Whom does our society tend to cast out or over-look? What advice might Paul give us about these outcasts?**

Article 73: The Catholic (Non-Pauline) Letters

In addition to the thirteen Pauline letters, the New Testament includes seven non-Pauline letters, or **epistles**: the letters of James; First and Second Peter; First, Second, and Third John; and Jude. Each is named for an Apostle

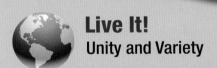

Live It!
Unity and Variety

High school can be difficult socially. It is a tough place to be weak or different. You can be shunned because of the clothes you wear, your inadequacies, your race, or for hanging around the "wrong" crowd. In high school, being different is usually not cool.

Some early Christians went through similar problems. In his First Letter to the Corinthians, Saint Paul tells the Corinthians that they are one body with different gifts and talents. He counsels them not to say to one another, "I do not need you" (12:21). He even says, "The parts of the body that seem to be weaker are all the more necessary" (12:22). Having everyone think, look, and act the same is not beneficial for a community. What differences among your classmates do you need to respect, perhaps by considering them in a different light? How might respecting and embracing differences help to unify your school?

or disciple of Jesus, but biblical scholars believe anonymous authors wrote these letters, using the pseudonym of one of Jesus' Apostles or disciples to convey authority and respect.

The seven letters attributed to the Apostles and disciples are known as the catholic letters. Here the word *catholic* means "universal" or "general." Unlike Paul's letters, which originally addressed particular faith communities (though now they address the universal Church), the catholic letters were originally intended for a general audience or unnamed individual. However, like Paul's letters, they offer advice, encouragement, and teaching about community life and faith in Jesus Christ. When we read the catholic letters, we must remember that they were written for new believers living in a world that did not necessarily accept the truth of Jesus Christ.

The importance of the catholic letters is often not recognized. Sometimes they are overlooked altogether. Yet the catholic letters, like the Pauline letters, are invaluable to our faith. Although short, the catholic letters complement Paul's letters by providing a unique perspective on how to be authentic witnesses to Christ in a divided and disbelieving world.

Primary Sources

Inspired Writing

Examining the historical contexts of the letters of the New Testament can give the impression that these are examples of ordinary, human correspondence. Not so! At all times, we must remember that Sacred Scripture, which includes the letters of the New Testament, is the revealed Word of God. The Catholic bishops of the United States remind us:

> The Church approaches Scripture as God's revealed Word. Its authors wrote under the guidance and inspiration of the Holy Spirit. The Bible is more than a human work; it is God's words put into human words. It will always be a fountain of faith for those who read it in a spirit of prayer.
> (*United States Catholic Catechism for Adults*, page 31)

Important Teachings

Numerous key teachings appear in the catholic letters. For example, the Letter of James emphasizes the importance of both faith and good works for salvation. The letter's author says, "A person is justified by works and not by faith alone" (2:24). According to this letter, true faith leads to good works, and good works are the fruit of faith in Christ.

In James 5:13–15 we also find the biblical basis for the Sacrament of Anointing of the Sick:

> Is anyone among you suffering? He should pray. Is anyone in good spirits? He should sing praise. Is anyone among you sick? He should summon the presbyters of the church, and they should pray over him and anoint [him] with oil in the name of the Lord, and the prayer of faith will save the sick person, and the Lord will raise him up. If he has committed any sins, he will be forgiven.

The First Letter of Peter encourages suffering Christians not to lose faith and to keep their hearts rooted in Christ. The author affirms that followers of Christ are "a chosen race, a royal priesthood, a holy nation" (1 Peter 2:9), called from darkness into the amazing light of God. The Second Letter of Peter preaches against false teachers who claim that Christ will not come again. The author reminds his readers to remain true to the teachings of Jesus, including the proclamation of his second coming.

The First and Second Letters of John address a new challenge: divisions among the Christian community due to **Gnosticism**. Both letters tell the community to beware of members who have fallen prey to the

Gnosticism
A group of heretical religious movements that claimed salvation comes from secret knowledge available only to the elite initiated in that religion.

The Letter of James gives directions for anointing and praying for the sick, providing the biblical basis for the Sacrament of Anointing of the Sick.

© Bill Wittman / www.wpwittman.com

antichrist
A pseudo-messianism whereby a human being puts himself or herself in the place of God or declares himself or herself to be a new messiah.

deceitful ways of the world. These letters warn against allowing deceivers to disrupt and destroy the community of Christ. First and Second John also speak of the **antichrist**, which can be defined as any human being who puts himself in the place of God or who declares herself to be a new messiah. Reinforcing the message of First and Second John, Third John warns against evil: "Whoever does what is good is of God; whoever does what is evil has never seen God" (verse 11).

Last but not least, the Letter of Jude challenges Christians to remain firm in their beliefs. It encourages us to show his mercy to those who oppose us.

> **Based on these brief introductions to the catholic letters, which are you most interested in reading from beginning to end? Why?**

Article 74: What about the Letter to the Hebrews?

There has been great debate over the origins of the Letter to the Hebrews (written about AD 80–90). In the past, Hebrews has been identified as a catholic letter. But many biblical scholars today do not include it among the catholic letters, for two reasons. First, it was originally circulated as a Pauline letter, although it differs from Paul's letters in certain ways. Second, Hebrews does not follow the literary form of a traditional letter. Instead it is written in the form of a homily and is much longer than the other catholic letters.

The author of the Letter to the Hebrews is thought to have been a Hellenistic Jewish Christian. That means he was influenced by Greek culture (including Greek philosophy), was extremely familiar with Jewish customs and beliefs, and wholeheartedly embraced Christianity. He was writing for the Hebrews: Jewish Christians who were suffering persecution, but not to the point of martyrdom. They were no longer meeting together, and the author feared that some were on the verge of becoming

apostates—that is, people who once believed but who have renounced their faith. These details point to an audience likely located in Jerusalem or Rome between AD 60 and 90.

Despite our unanswered questions about the Letter to the Hebrews, what is most important is its message. The author of Hebrews uses typical methods of Jewish argumentation to show that Jesus is the new and perfect High Priest and the perfect sacrifice, and that he thereby embodies the New Law. Hebrews emphasizes the divinity of Christ, as well as the redeeming power of his Death on the cross. The Letter to the Hebrews heralds the saving plan of God revealed in his Son.

> **Is it important to know whom the author of the Letter to the Hebrews really was? Why or why not?**

apostate
A person who was a believer but has abandoned his or her faith.

Asia Minor
An area corresponding roughly to modern-day Turkey.

Article 75: The Book of Revelation

What do you know about the Revelation to John, also called the Book of Revelation? Confusion often surrounds the Book of Revelation. Due to its highly symbolic language, and also its placement at the end of the New Testament, many people interpret the Book of Revelation as a collection of prophetic predictions and visions about the end of the world. Some even interpret these predictions quite literally.

However, we must place the Book of Revelation within its historical context before we can properly understand it. The historical context makes clear that the original author, rather than predicting the future, intended to respond to the plight of the Christian Churches in **Asia Minor** (modern-day Turkey). These churches were being intensely persecuted during the time of the Roman emperor Domitian (AD 81–96). Revelation was composed somewhere between AD 92 and 96. It was written by a Jewish-Christian prophet identified as John—not to be confused with the author of the Gospel of John.

apocalyptic literature
A literary form that uses dramatic events and highly symbolic language to offer hope to a people in crisis.

Visions and Voices, Numbers and Colors

The Book of Revelation—as well as parts of the Book of Daniel and Matthew's Gospel—takes a literary form called **apocalyptic literature**. Apocalyptic literature is often written during a time of crisis. This literary form describes cosmic battles between good and evil, with good always winning in the end. As is the case in Revelation, apocalyptic literature contains visions, voices, angelic messengers, and other extraordinary phenomena.

The Book of Revelation also includes symbolic numbers and colors. Many people mistakenly interpret the numbers and colors literally. However, the author symbolically uses them to communicate a message to his hearers. Here are some numbers and colors with brief descriptions of their meanings in Revelation.

Numbers

- 3: a limited amount of time
- 4: fullness, universality
- 7: perfection
- 10: sometimes denoting a limited number, at other times meaning oppressors
- 12: fullness, completeness
- 1,000: countless, innumerable
  (Adapted from *The Book of Revelation,* page 12)

Colors

- white: victory, triumph, conquest
- red: violence, conflict, bloodshed
- scarlet: royalty, bloodshed
- purple: sovereignty, royalty
- black: famine, plague
- pale green: death, the end
  (Adapted from *The Book of Revelation,* pages 12–13)

Does Revelation Predict the Future?

The language of apocalyptic literature tends to sound futuristic or future-oriented, especially in regard to the end of one time and the beginning of another. This can sometimes cloud our understanding of the purpose and intent of Revelation. Just because Revelation was written in this literary form does not mean its purpose is to predict the end of the world. Rather, the veiled language of apocalyptic literature provides a means of secret communication. In the case of Revelation, this literary form presented information in a way that Christians at the time could understand. It allowed the author to criticize the Roman authorities without putting his audience at risk of further persecution. It also allowed the author to communicate messages about the situation of his readers.

This painting portrays a symbolic battle between good and evil described in the Book of Revelation. Whom might the various figures in the image represent?

Like most apocalyptic literature, Revelation cannot be read as a continuous story with a beginning, middle, and end. Instead it describes a series of visions the author says he received. The author might introduce an idea or image in an early vision and build on it later. The temptation to read Revelation as a chronological story often leads us to distort its meaning.

© Bildarchiv Preussischer Kulturbesitz / Art Resource, NY

Hope for All Time

The Book of Revelation provides hope for a people in crisis. A renewed commitment to faith, a message of consolation, and a call to maintain hope are the three main themes of the prophecy in the Book of Revelation. This message of hope is revealed in both the present and future. Through the symbolic language of his visions, John assures the persecuted Christians of Asia Minor that God has not abandoned them in their suffering. God is always present to those who trust and are faithful. He

also encourages these Christians to renew their commitment to the life and teachings of Jesus Christ, even in
the face of the harsh reality of persecution. Focusing on
the future, Revelation proclaims the justice and sovereignty of God. The plight of those being persecuted will
be short, the author says, because God will triumph over
evil at the end of time. Christ will come again in glory.

Notice that the message of Revelation does not predict when or how the final coming will happen. Rather
it speaks of a time when God will "make all things new"
(Revelation 21:5). At the end of time, the Kingdom of
God will be fully realized. The faithful will live with

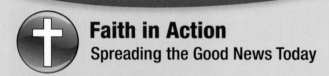

Faith in Action
Spreading the Good News Today

© i4lcocl2 / shutterstock.com

Most of the time we hear the Word of God
proclaimed in church. But who reaches
people who have not yet heard of Christ,
who do not go to church regularly, or who are
poor and homeless? Sometimes those are
the very people in great need of hearing the
Good News of the Gospel. LAMP Ministries
was formed to reach them.

LAMP stands for Lay Apostolic Ministries
with the Poor. Founded by Tom and Lyn
Scheuring, a married couple with doctorates in theology, LAMP Ministries goes
into the streets of New York City to focus on those who are poor. LAMP's aim
is to support those who are poor not only in material ways but also in spiritual
ways. Strengthened by the Eucharist, LAMP ministers reach out to those in
need. A canteen truck called the LAMPCafé distributes sandwiches every day,
along with pamphlets of Scripture readings, rosaries, and opportunities to pray
with LAMP ministers. LAMP ministers work with homeless families and also
with young women who are dealing with crisis pregnancies. A Prayer House for
the Poor is available for those who want a quiet place to pray. LAMP ministers
sometimes just sit on the steps of a parish church to share the Word of God
with anyone who wishes to speak with them.

Today we can often reach people around the world with the click of a
mouse. The work of LAMP Ministries reminds us that there is still a great
need—and a great opportunity—for each one of us to speak the Word of God
person to person, to someone in spiritual or material need.

Christ forever, glorified in body and soul, and all creation will be renewed. All tears will be wiped away, and death will no longer have the last word. The Book of Revelation also describes the torment of those who follow Satan and reject the love of God. We learn about the sad reality of hell, which is eternal separation from God and the Communion of Saints.

The message of the Book of Revelation is timeless. It was written in a particular time and place, but it declares a message of hope to all people of faith. God is with us in the trials and tribulations of life. All faithful members of the body of Christ—the persecuted, the suffering, and the martyrs—will be among God's elect in the end. God rewards the righteous and punishes the unjust.

> **Do you think the original audience found the message of Revelation comforting? Why or why not?**

Chapter Review

1. What two significant events and movements form the backdrop of the Acts of the Apostles? Why were these events important?

2. In what ways do the graces given by the Holy Spirit help us?

3. What purpose did the letters of Saint Paul serve among the early Christian communities?

4. Name and briefly describe two recurring themes in Paul's letters.

5. What important teaching is found in the Letter of James? in First Peter?

6. What literary form is the Book of Revelation? What are some of the characteristics of this literary form?

7. What are the three main themes of the Book of Revelation?

Unit 5

Sacred Scripture and the Life of Faith

We have studied the history and substance of Sacred Scripture as part of God's Revelation. But we must always remember that the Bible is not just another history textbook or work of literature. Sacred Scripture is central to our life of faith, as a Church and as individuals.

How do we encounter Sacred Scripture in the life of the Church? Perhaps the Mass and the Sacraments come to mind. Sacred Scripture is at the heart of the Liturgy of the Word and the Liturgy of the Eucharist during Mass, as well as other sacramental liturgies. Scripture readings and the Psalms are also at the heart of the Liturgy of the Hours: the official, public, daily prayer of the Church. The Lord's Prayer, the prayer Jesus taught us, springs directly from the Gospels. And the "Rules of Life" that govern religious communities often center on teachings found in the Bible.

How do you include Scripture in your own faith? On your own or in a group, you can study and pray with Sacred Scripture to help you face life's challenges and moral dilemmas. In the ancient practice of *lectio divina*, you can pray directly with Sacred Scripture to connect more closely with God's Revelation. The Stations of the Cross and the Rosary are two popular devotions with a strong scriptural basis.

Sacred Scripture is the living Word of God. This living Word nourishes the life of the Church every day. Let it nourish your own life too.

The enduring understandings and essential questions represent core concepts and questions that are explored throughout this unit. By studying the content of each chapter, you will gain a more complete understanding of the following:

Enduring Understandings

1. Sacred Scripture plays an essential role in the Church's sacramental and liturgical celebrations.

2. Sacred Scripture has nourished and inspired people of faith through many centuries.

3. Catholics view the Word of God as integral to an individual's life of faith as it offers support, guidance, and challenge.

Essential Questions

1. In what ways is Sacred Scripture central to the Church's communal prayer?

2. What impact has Sacred Scripture had on people of faith throughout salvation history?

3. How can the Word of God have an impact on the everyday lives of Catholics?

Chapter 16

Sacred Scripture and the Life of the Church

Introduction

Sacred Scripture is not a dusty old book about other times and places, with no relevance for our lives. No, it is the living Word of God, vital to the life of the Church. As followers of Christ, we are called to study the Bible so we can discover "the supreme good of knowing Christ Jesus" (Philippians 3:8). The Good News of the Gospel nourishes our sacramental and liturgical celebrations. We make holy our mornings, afternoons, evenings, and nights by praying the Psalms and reading Scripture in the Liturgy of the Hours. The basis for our understanding of perfect prayer is found in the Gospels of Matthew and Luke, with their similar accounts of Jesus' teaching the disciples the Lord's Prayer. Saints incorporate the teachings of the Bible into their spiritual writings. Sacred Scripture is also included in the religious rules for communities who are living the evangelical counsels. Any time the Church gathers, the living Word of God is present.

Article 76: The Study of Sacred Scripture

Perhaps you have heard our current time period referred to as the information age. More people have access to more information than at any other time in the world's history. The creation, ownership, and use of information play increasingly large roles in our lives and livelihoods. But when you look for answers to life's big questions, whom do you trust? Many people spend their lives pursuing the latest fads and looking to so-called "experts" in happiness. They overlook the true and inerrant compass God has provided to guide us: Sacred Scripture.

Sacred Scripture supports and strengthens the Church as she carries out her mission to announce the Good News of salvation. The divinely inspired words of Sacred Scripture provide "food of the soul, the pure and everlasting source of spiritual life" (*Dogmatic Constitution on Divine Revelation [Dei Verbum*, 1965], 21). At the heart of Sacred Scripture is the Revelation of God as Father, Son, and Holy Spirit—a communion of Divine Persons.

Did You Know?

© Joachim Hiltmann/ imag /
imageBROKER / SuperStock

Saint Jerome and the Vulgate

Saint Jerome was an early Christian apologist and Doctor of the Church. He was known for his intelligence, love of learning, and knowledge of Sacred Scripture. Saint Augustine is credited with saying, "If Jerome doesn't know, nobody does, or ever did." An exceptional scholar, Saint Jerome is well known for his translation of the entire Bible, known as the Vulgate. He translated the Old Testament from its original Hebrew into Latin. He also translated the New Testament from Greek into Latin. The Council of Trent promulgated the Vulgate as the official text of the Church, finding that Saint Jerome's translation was more faithful to the original Old Testament and New Testament languages than earlier translations. This is why the Vulgate remains important to the Church today.

Saint Jerome, the great biblical translator and scholar, emphasized the importance of studying Sacred Scripture. He believed that "ignorance of Scripture is ignorance of Christ" (*Commentary on Isaiah*). That is, we must know Sacred Scripture if we are to understand the saving action of God. Vatican Council II, in its constitution *Divine Revelation,* asserted that all the Christian faithful should have access to the life-giving words written in the pages of the Bible. Frequent study of the Old and New Testaments helps us to know Christ. We encounter the truth of Jesus' identity. We also see his mission in a profound and very real way. When we study Scripture, we embark on a journey of continual discovery of God's presence. Such study also enables us to see his action in human history. Each time we read the Bible, our human heart and soul are further enlightened and directed toward our Maker.

Divine Revelation states, "The Church has always venerated the divine Scriptures just as she venerated the body of the Lord" (21). Sacred Scripture informs every aspect of the Church. The Magisterium—minister and servant of the Word—is charged with the important responsibility of interpreting, teaching, and proclaiming the Word. Those entrusted with preaching are called to break open the Word of God in new and enlightening ways. As minister and interpreter of the Word, the Church especially and earnestly calls all Christians to be attentive to God's saving message manifested in his Son, the Incarnate Word.

> **When you look for answers to life's big questions, whom or what do you trust?**

Article 77: The Central Place of Sacred Scripture in the Mass and Other Liturgies

A common misconception about Catholics is that we do not regularly use or read the Bible. Nothing could be less true. Sacred Scripture is integral to the life of the Church.

Even though it contains accounts and teachings from particular moments in time, Scripture's message is timeless and universal. God continues to speak to us through Scripture. This is why the liturgies of the Church are founded on and sustained primarily by the Word of God. Indeed the heart of the Mass and all other sacramental celebrations is the living Word of God.

The Heart of the Mass

When we gather for the Mass, the Church's most important **liturgy**, we are nourished by "the bread of life, taken from the one table of God's Word and Christ's Body[1]" (*Catechism of the Catholic Church [CCC]*, 103). In other words, both the Sacred Scripture and the Eucharist feed us. Together they compose one celebration. The Word of God prepares and readies our hearts for participation in **Holy Communion**. During the Mass we are truly blessed to encounter Jesus Christ in both the Word and the Eucharist.

The two main parts of the Mass are the Liturgy of the Word and the Liturgy of the Eucharist. These two parts draw "their inspiration and their force" (*Constitution on the Sacred Liturgy [Sacrosanctum Concilium, 1963]*, 24) from Sacred Scripture. The Liturgy of the Word is integral to the celebration of the Eucharist. The words and actions present in the Liturgy of the Word nourish our faith. The Word of God expresses the deep meaning of the Eucharistic celebration, both in the proclamation of the priest and in the response of the faithful.

On most Sundays and solemnities, the Liturgy of the Word contains an Old Testament reading, a responsorial Psalm, a New Testament reading, and a passage on the life of Jesus taken from the Gospels. During the Easter Season, the first reading comes from the Acts of the Apostles. In daily Mass we hear one reading, a Psalm, and a reading from one of the Gospels. The reading from the Gospels is always the centerpiece of the Liturgy of the Word. The Liturgy of the Word also includes a **homily**, or brief sermon, given by a priest or deacon to explain the

liturgy
The Church's official, public, communal prayer. It is God's work, in which the People of God participate. The Church's most important liturgy is the Eucharist, or the Mass.

Holy Communion
Another name for the Sacrament of the Eucharist.

homily
A brief liturgical sermon that explains the Scripture readings, helps the People of God accept Sacred Scripture as the Word of God, and encourages them to put the teachings of Scripture into practice in their daily lives.

Eucharistic Prayer
The part of the Mass that includes the Consecration, beginning with the Preface and concluding with the Great Amen.

psalmody
From the Greek word *psalmos,* meaning "a song sung to a harp," and *aeidein,* meaning "to sing." The word has multiple meanings: the art of singing psalms, the arranging or composing of psalms for singing, or a collection of psalms for singing or reciting.

Gregorian chant
A monophonic, unaccompanied style of liturgical singing that takes its name from Pope Gregory the Great.

Scripture readings. The homily gives the priest an opportunity to encourage us to put the teachings of Scripture into practice. The Liturgy of the Word culminates in the profession of faith (often the Nicene Creed) and the prayers of the faithful.

Sacred Scripture is also present in the Liturgy of the Eucharist, which makes present Christ's saving work accomplished mainly through his Passion, Death, Resurrection, and Ascension. The Liturgy of the Eucharist includes the **Eucharistic Prayer**, which recalls saving events from Scripture, and the Communion Rite.

In the first part of the Mass, we "feast" on God's Holy Word, followed by the banquet of Jesus' Body and Blood. In the words of the Church, "the liturgy of the Word and liturgy of the Eucharist together form 'one single act of worship'[2]; the Eucharistic table set for us is the table both of the Word of God and of the Body of the Lord[3]" (CCC, 1346).

The Heart of All the Sacraments

Other sacramental and liturgical celebrations also draw their inspiration and strength from Scripture. From the Sacrament of Baptism to the Sacrament of Matrimony to the Sacrament of Penance and Reconciliation, Scripture is the focal point. When the Christian community gathers for liturgical celebrations in the name of Jesus, Sacred Scripture provides the foundation for the celebration. God—the Father, Son, and Holy Spirit—is the center of our celebration. Thus we must proclaim his Word.

The Heart of Liturgical Music

Sacred Scripture especially enhances the music that forms a vibrant part of all our liturgical celebrations. Some liturgical celebrations tap into the rich tradition of sacred music, including **psalmody** and **Gregorian chant**. Liturgical music is steeped in Sacred Scripture. Sacred music should mirror salvation history. Numerous Church documents, especially *Sacred Liturgy,* address the intimate connection between the Word of God and the writing and singing of sacred music. In fact, the music that is part of the Mass "should be drawn chiefly from holy scripture and from liturgical sources" (*Sacred Liturgy*, 121).

> **How does the place of Scripture in the liturgies of the Church model how you can use Scripture in your life?**

Liturgy of the Hours

Also known as the Divine Office, the official public, daily prayer of the Catholic Church. The Divine Office provides standard prayers, Scripture readings, and reflections at regular hours throughout the day.

Article 78: The Liturgy of the Hours: A Window into the Daily Rhythms of Life

Have you encountered the phrase "Pray without ceasing"? Do you know where it comes from? How is it possible to pray without interruption?

Saint Paul exhorted the early Christian community of Thessalonica to "pray without ceasing" and "in all circumstances give thanks" (1 Thessalonians 5:17,18). His message was meant not only for the Thessalonians but also for Christians everywhere. Drawing on the ancient Jewish practice of sanctifying days and hours by reciting the Psalms, the Church developed the **Liturgy of the Hours**, the prayer also known as the Divine Office. The Liturgy of the Hours is the official, public, daily prayer of the Catholic Church. Prayed at regular

Primary Sources

Praying the Liturgy of the Hours

The Liturgy of the Hours, the public prayer of the Church, is truly the prayer of Christ in us. Saint Augustine of Hippo explained this in his commentary on praying the Psalms:

> When we speak in prayer to the Father, we do not separate the Son from him and when the Son's Body prays it does not separate itself from its Head. It is the one Savior of his Body, the Lord Christ Jesus, who prays for us and in us and who is prayed to by us. He prays for us as our priest, in us as our Head; he is prayed to by us as our God. Recognize therefore our own voice in him and his voice in us.

hours throughout the day, it is composed of standard prayers, Scripture readings, and reflections. The Liturgy of the Hours makes holy the cycle of life with its many hours and days. Through this official prayer of the Church, the mystery of Christ fills and transfigures every hour of the day. When we stop at various times during the day to pray, we remember Christ's continual work of redemption in the ordinariness of life.

The Word of God at Each Hour

"Seven times a day I praise you," sings the psalmist (Psalm 119:164). Following this wise counsel, we can pray the Liturgy of the Hours seven times a day. The following table names each "hour," gives its traditional Latin name, and summarizes its customary theme:

Hour	Latin Name	Themes
Morning Prayer	*Lauds*	Christ's Resurrection, praise for creation, dedication, light, dawn
Midmorning Prayer	*Terce*	New life, beginnings
Midday Prayer	*Sext*	Renewed commitment to the mission of Christ
Midafternoon Prayer	(none)	Awareness of the end of life and time
Evening	*Vespers*	Gratitude for Christ, reflection of Christ's Passion and burial, thanksgiving for the day, repentance for sin
Night Prayer	*Compline*	Divine protection and peace, restful sleep and happy death
Office of Readings	*Matins*	Wisdom revealed in the words of Scripture, writings of the Church Fathers, and lives of the saints

Although the Liturgy of the Hours includes seven opportunities to pray, the primary hours, or "hinges," of each day are morning and evening prayer. The Liturgy of the Hours follows a four-week cycle. This cycle includes adjustments for the feasts and seasons of the liturgical year.

Sacred Scripture in the Divine Office

Central to the Divine Office is the Word of God, especially the recitation or singing of Psalms and the reading of Scripture. Although the Liturgy of the Hours has
undergone many transformations through the centuries,
the Psalms have remained the heart of the prayer. Reading the Psalms brings into harmony all that was revealed
to our ancestors, under the Old Covenant, with all that
was disclosed in Jesus Christ, the New Covenant. When
we meditate on the Psalms, we meditate on God's unified, saving action in human history. The Liturgy of
the Hours integrates the psalms into the prayer of the
Church. Scripture readings from both the Old and New
Testaments are likewise key aspects of the celebration of
the Liturgy of the Hours.

The Liturgy of the Hours includes two important
prayers in the life of the Church: the Canticle of Mary
(the *Magnificat*) and the Canticle of Zechariah (the *Bene-
dictus*). Both canticles come directly from the Gospel
of Luke. When we pray the *Magnificat,* we join Mary in
singing of God's salvation for all:

> My soul proclaims the greatness of the Lord;
>   my spirit rejoices in God my savior.
>
> . . . .
>
> He has thrown down the rulers from their thrones
>   but lifted up the lowly.
> The hungry he has filled with good things;
>   the rich he has sent away empty.
> He has helped Israel his servant,
>   remembering his mercy,
> according to his promise to our fathers,
>   to Abraham and to his descendants forever.
>   (Luke 1:46–47,52–55)

In the Canticle of Zechariah, we thank God for sending
a Savior from the line of David. Rejoicing in the birth
of his son, who would grow up to be John the Baptist,
Zechariah anticipated his son's role in preparing the way
for Christ:

breviary
A prayer book that contains the prayers for the Liturgy of the Hours.

opus dei
A Latin phrase meaning the "work of God."

You, child, will be called prophet of the Most High,
　　for you will go before the Lord to prepare his ways,
to give his people knowledge of salvation
　　through the forgiveness of their sins,
because of the tender mercy of our God
　　by which the daybreak from on high will visit us
to shine on those who sit in darkness and death's shadow,
　　to guide our feet into the path of peace.

(Luke 1:76–79)

In the Liturgy of the Hours, the Canticle of Zechariah is recited during morning prayer, and the Canticle of Mary is recited during evening prayer.

Reading Sacred Scripture at the principal hours of the day invites us to enter more deeply into relationship with our Triune God: Father, Son, and Holy Spirit. Praying the Liturgy of the Hours moves us into a deeper understanding of the Liturgy and Sacred Scripture.

© Bill Wittman / www.wpwittman.com

Seconds, minutes, hours, and days possess eternal significance when molded by the living Word of God. Along with the readings and canticles from Sacred Scripture, the Divine Office includes other key elements that originate in Scripture: antiphons (sung responses), a meditation (reflection on the Scriptures), and the Lord's Prayer. The prayers of the Liturgy of the Hours are found in the **breviary**.

The Liturgy of the Hours reminds us that prayer should be a daily practice. How do you make prayer a part of your daily routine?

The Liturgy of the Hours: The *Opus Dei*

The religious communities of the Benedictines follow the rule of Saint Benedict. They refer to the Liturgy of the Hours as the *opus dei*, Latin for "work of God." Saint Benedict believed that the primary work of his community was to pray the Divine Office. Vatican Council II acknowledged that priests and religious have a special calling to pray the Liturgy of the Hours, but the Council went further, calling the entire People of God to pray the

Liturgy of the Hours. The Divine Office is one way the Church continues Christ's priestly work. We must all participate in this wonderful work of God so his name may resound in every moment of every day.

> **How might hourly prayer help you to focus on God during the rest of your day?**

prayer
Lifting up of one's mind and heart to God or the requesting of good things from him. The five basic forms of prayer are blessing, praise, petition, thanksgiving, and intercession. In prayer we communicate with God in a relationship of love.

Article 79: The Lord's Prayer: The Prayer of the Church

Our Father who art in heaven,
hallowed be thy name.
Thy kingdom come.
Thy will be done on earth, as it is in heaven.
Give us this day our daily bread,
and forgive us our trespasses,
    as we forgive those who
trespass against us,
and lead us not into temptation,
but deliver us from evil.

God created us to be in communion with him. Even though Original Sin separates us from the full communion God intended, he continues to call us into relationship, and we continue to seek him. All salvation history reveals the importance of prayer as God calls to us and we search for him. **Prayer**, as communication and conversation with God, nourishes the seeds of faith.

Throughout the Gospels we find that Jesus modeled deep and meaningful prayer. Before almost every significant event in Jesus' life, according to the

© digitalskillet / iStockphoto.com

Gospel of Luke, Jesus prayed to his Father in Heaven. Realizing Jesus' true identity and affinity for prayer, one of the disciples said to him, "Lord, teach us to pray just as John [the Baptist] taught his disciples" (Luke 11:1). In response Jesus taught the disciples the Lord's Prayer, which we also call the Our Father. It is called the Lord's Prayer because the Lord Jesus gave it to us. Jesus also revealed to us who God is so that we too can call on God as Father. When we pray to the Father, we are in communion with him and with his Son, Jesus Christ. When we pray to our Father, we seek to develop the will to become like him.

The Church describes the Lord's Prayer as "'truly the summary of the whole gospel,'[4] the 'most perfect of prayers'[5]" (CCC, 2774). Christians highly esteem the Lord's Prayer because it came to us directly from Jesus and lays the foundation for all our desires in the

Pray It!

Hail Mary!

When he first greeted the world after his election, Pope Francis immediately invited the crowd to recite the Lord's Prayer and the Hail Mary. You know the Lord's Prayer comes straight from the Gospels, but did you know that the Hail Mary is also based in Scripture? This well-loved prayer combines two passages from the Gospel of Luke: the Angel Gabriel's salutation to Mary at the Annunciation, "Hail, favored one! The Lord is with you" (1:28); and Elizabeth's greeting at the Visitation, "Most blessed are you among women, and blessed is the fruit of your womb" (1:42). You probably know the Hail Mary by heart, but pray it now as a way to reflect on its scriptural origins:

Hail Mary, full of grace,
the Lord is with you!
Blessed are you among women,
and blessed is the fruit of your womb, Jesus.
Holy Mary, Mother of God,
pray for us sinners
now and at the hour of our death.
Amen.

Christian life. Along with the Psalms, the Lord's Prayer
is a biblical prayer all Christians share. As Catholics we
recognize the Lord's Prayer as the model prayer of the
Church. It is especially important in the Liturgy of the
Hours and in the Sacraments of Christian Initiation:
Baptism, Confirmation, and the Eucharist.

hallowed
Holy, sacred, or
revered.

Seven Petitions, Seven Requests

The Lord's Prayer unfolds for us as a model of prayer and
devotion to God. In the Church's liturgical tradition, we
use the Lord's Prayer as it appears in the Gospel of Matthew. The Lord's Prayer is made up of seven petitions.
A petition is a prayer that requests a grace or blessing
from God. In her spiritual memoirs, Saint Teresa of Ávila
wrote that asking great things of God is a compliment to
him.

The seven petitions in the Lord's Prayer are no ordinary requests but rather are models of Christian prayer.
In the first petition, "**Hallowed** be thy name," we ask that
our words and deeds radiate respect and reverence for
the name of God. When we say the second petition, "Thy
kingdom come," we pray for the fulfillment of the Reign
of God through the second coming of Christ, also called
the Parousia. As a Church we also pray for the strength to
be a visible sign and presence of the Reign of God in the
world. The third petition, "Thy will be done on earth, as
it is in heaven," asks for obedient and trusting hearts so
our desires may never stand in the way of God's plan of
salvation. Together these first three petitions focus on the
glory of God the Father.

"Give us this day our daily bread." In this fourth
petition, we pray for an even greater awareness of our
absolute and total dependence on God. In this petition,
we acknowledge God as the source of all we need. We
pray for not only our needs but for those of everyone in
the world. The fifth petition, "Forgive us our trespasses,
/ as we forgive those who trespass against us," centers on
the intimate connection between God's forgiveness and
our willingness to forgive others. To be forgiven for the

temptation
An invitation or enticement to commit an unwise or immoral act that often includes a promise of reward to make the immoral act seem more appealing.

Satan
The fallen angel or spirit of evil who is the enemy of God and a continuing instigator of temptation and sin in the world.

charism
A special gift or grace of the Holy Spirit given to an individual Christian or community, commonly for the benefit and building up of the entire Church.

harm we cause others, we must forgive those who harm us. In the sixth petition, we pray that God will not allow us to be led "into temptation." A **temptation** is an invitation or enticement to commit an unwise or immoral act. Our prayer asks for a wise and vigilant heart that is able to identify and resist temptation.

Continuing the theme of the sixth petition, the final petition asks God to "deliver us from evil." As individuals and as a collective whole, we petition God to deliver us from **Satan**, the evil one, the fallen angel who is the enemy of God and a continuing instigator of temptation and sin in the world. We pray with confidence that good will triumph over evil.

Which petition in the Lord's Prayer do you find difficult to understand? Who can you ask for help to understand it better?

Article 80: Sacred Scripture and the Rules of the Saints

Saint Augustine, Saint Benedict, and Saint Francis are three well-known saints who founded religious communities. The members of these communities publicly profess the evangelical counsels of poverty, chastity, and obedience. They also lead lives in common as a public witness to Christ. Each religious community has its own particular history, **charism**, and rules. Founders of religious communities write a "Rule of Life." The "Rule of Life" is a type of constitution that provides practical guidelines and rules for day-to-day life in community. Although rules can differ from one community to another, the heart of any rule is Sacred Scripture.

The Rule of Saint Augustine: Community

Saint Augustine of Hippo wrote one of the earliest and best-known religious rules. Throughout the ages numerous religious communities have adopted his rule. It has also influenced the extraordinary writings of the saints.

A strong theme in Augustine's rule is the importance of community. Drawing on the Acts of the Apostles, Augustine maintained that a community of religious men or women must be "of one heart and mind" (Acts 4:32) in God. The community must "live harmoniously in this house" ("The Rule of Our Holy Father Augustine," 3). The members of the community must have compassion and love for one another, as visible signs of Christ's love for humanity.

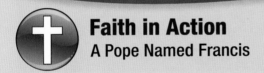

Faith in Action
A Pope Named Francis

© neneo / Shutterstock.com

In March 2013, the archbishop of Buenos Aires, Argentina, Cardinal Jorge Bergoglio, was elected Pope and took the name Francis, after the saint of the poor, Saint Francis of Assisi. In the following days, Pope Francis explained that his choice of name was significant. He chose the name Francis to signal to the Church and to the world that he would endeavor to bring an attitude of simplicity into his life as Pope and into the life of the Church. In his first homily as Pope, he reminded the Church and the world to care for and protect those who are poor.

As archbishop of Buenos Aires, Pope Francis had already embraced simple, ordinary ways to live every day. He chose to live in a small apartment instead of an elaborate mansion. Rather than employ a cook, he prepared his own meals. Rather than being chauffeured in a sleek limousine, he rode the city bus to his office. As Pope, he has continued this preference for simplicity by staying in a smaller apartment at the Vatican guest house rather than moving into the more elaborate papal apartment. On his first Holy Thursday as Pope, he celebrated the Mass of the Lord's Supper with young people at a juvenile detention center, breaking with the tradition of celebrating the Mass at Rome's ornate Basilica of Saint John Lateran.

In choosing the name Francis, Pope Francis is following the path of Jesus, living the simple life and loving those in need, as recorded in Scripture.

© Hemis / Alamy

Monks are not the only people who practice community, hospitality, and simplicity. How are these values part of your family life? your parish life?

The Rule of Saint Benedict: Hospitality

Saint Benedict of Nursia is considered the founder of Western monasticism. His rule was instrumental in the founding of many religious communities during the Middle Ages—from roughly the fifth century to the early fourteenth century. The rule of Saint Benedict lifts up the value of hospitality. Chapter 53 of the rule states, "Let all guests who arrive be received like Christ" ("The Order of Saint Benedict: The Rule of Saint Benedict," chapter 53). The Benedictine vision of hospitality is based on Matthew 25:35: "For I was hungry and you gave me food, I was thirsty and you gave me drink, a stranger and you welcomed me." Benedict wanted religious communities to be people of hospitality so all would know and heed the saving message of Christ.

The Rule of Saint Francis: Simplicity

After hearing a sermon on Matthew 10:9–10, in which Jesus tells the Twelve Apostles to leave everything behind to proclaim the Reign of God, Saint Francis of Assisi responded by founding a religious community dedicated to poverty and simplicity. His rule asserts that if someone wants to join the community, the person's life must be modeled on the poor and crucified Christ. People called to live the simple life "should go and sell all that is their own and strive to give it to the poor" ("The Rule of St. Francis—1223," chapter II). Francis wanted his fellow brothers to rid themselves of material wealth. By living more simply and removing the distractions from their lives, they could more easily know and proclaim the wealth of God's mercy.

How can community, hospitality, and simplicity become guiding principles of your life?

Live It!
Oblates and Third Orders

Some members of religious communities are not sisters, brothers, or priests. Sometimes called oblates or third orders, these Catholics promise to follow a community's rule in ways that their lives allow. For example, those who are married with children cannot live in a Benedictine community, but as lay oblates they can still follow the rule of Saint Benedict by feeding those who are hungry. Those with families to support might not be able to take on the poverty required of Franciscans, but they can still promise to live simply and care for the poor. Each community's rule guides its members to live as Christ did—something we all are called to do.

Research one of the rules described in this chapter. Then choose one requirement from that rule and follow it for a week. At the end of the week, reflect on what you learned. What would it be like to commit to that requirement for a lifetime?

Chapter Review

1. Why did Saint Jerome say Sacred Scripture was so important in the life of the Christian faithful?

2. What is a common misconception about Catholics and their relationship to Scripture? Why is this a misconception?

3. What are the two main parts of the Mass? How do we encounter Jesus Christ in each part?

4. In what ways does Sacred Scripture influence Catholic worship besides being actually read in the liturgy?

5. What is the Liturgy of the Hours? What is its purpose?

6. Why is the Lord's Prayer the model prayer of the Church?

7. What role does Scripture play in the rules of Saint Augustine, Saint Benedict, and Saint Francis?

Sacred Scripture and the Life of the Individual

Chapter 17

Introduction

People have pondered the words of Sacred Scripture ever since they were written, because they make the Word of God known to us. The Word of God can support us in difficult times, help us to rejoice when things are going well, guide us to make good moral decisions, and unite us as children of God. Spending personal time with Scripture also brings us closer to God, because he continues to speak to us through them. This is why the Church earnestly calls Christians to reflect on and pray with Scripture.

Through ancient traditions of prayer, specifically *lectio divina,* we awaken to God's Holy Word on a more personal level. Religious devotions like the Stations of the Cross and the Rosary arise from and point to the Word of God. Participating in Bible study groups and prayer groups at our parishes and schools invites us into deeper relationships with the Lord and one another. As Catholics we view the Word of God as integral to our everyday lives. Reading, studying, and praying Sacred Scripture can make the most ordinary moments of life extraordinary.

Article 81: Sacred Scripture and Morality

Taking time to consider our decisions in the light of God's Word can help us to hear God's guiding voice in our lives.

Every day we face tough choices between right and wrong. When we talk about right and wrong, we are talking about **morality**. Morality refers to the goodness or evil of human acts, attitudes, and values. Through our God-given capacity to reason, we are "capable of understanding the order of things established by the Creator" (CCC, 1704). Through our God-given free will, we can choose what is truly good for ourselves and for others. One way we direct ourselves to God's true good is through reflection and prayer with Sacred Scripture.

© Lincoln Rogers / shutterstock.com

Did You Know?

Harsh Words

" Anyone who curses father or mother shall be put to death" (Leviticus 20:9). After reading this you might be thinking: "Wow! That is harsh. I better watch what I say to my parents from now on!" Scripture is an excellent source of moral advice. But we must be careful not to take passages out of context.

For people in biblical times, cursing someone was more than just an outburst of anger. It expressed a desire for serious harm to come to the person. Such curses were taken very seriously. Parents were also to be treated with the utmost respect. So cursing your parents was almost the moral equivalent of physically attacking or killing them. Cursing your parents today is not good, but it certainly is not the same thing as cursing parents in ancient times. Reading and quoting the Bible requires a careful understanding of biblical cultures, as well as the overall message of the Bible.

God's Word Lights Our Path

How do you know what is right and what is wrong? Who or what has taught you the difference? Learning to do what is right is a lifelong task. It is a difficult task because the world is filled with conflicting voices about right and wrong. One voice we can turn to is the Word of God. God's Word lights our way and helps us learn to live moral lives.

morality
Refers to the goodness or evil of human acts. The morality of an act is determined by the nature of the action, the intention, and the circumstances.

To acquire this wisdom, we must read, study, and pray with the Word. When we read about salvation history, particularly the life of Christ, the wisdom of our Creator is revealed. We encounter the Law of God revealed in the Ten Commandments (see Exodus 20:1–17) and the Beatitudes (see Matthew 5:3–12). The Ten Commandments and the Beatitudes direct us toward the true path of happiness. Jesus Christ, the Incarnate Word, walked this earth preaching and teaching about the holy will of the Father. The Paschal Mystery reminds us that the path of righteousness is not always easy and often meets great resistance. Sacred Scripture can help us to make virtuous choices.

Praying with Scripture directs us to the goodness of God. When we participate in the Eucharist, the Sacraments, the Liturgy of the Hours, *lectio divina,* and other prayers based on Sacred Scripture, we come face-to-face with God's saving Word. Grounded in Sacred Scripture, liturgy and prayer challenge us to delve deeper into the absolute and definitive truth of Christ. Praying with the Word of God, both individually and communally, strengthens our ability to recognize the morality of a particular act and to choose what is good. Simply put, when we pray with Sacred Scripture, we unite ourselves more closely with God—Father, Son, and Holy Spirit.

"How I love your law, Lord! / I study it all day long. . . . Your word is a lamp for my feet, / a light for my path" (Psalm 119:97,105).

How do you decide whether a choice is morally right or morally wrong?

© vovan / Shutterstock.com

Article 82: *Lectio Divina*: Praying with Sacred Scripture

Sometimes praying means reciting a memorized prayer. Sometimes praying means talking to God like you would talk to a friend, in a free-flowing conversation. But have you ever tried praying directly with Sacred Scripture? This can be a profound way to allow the Word of God to enter your heart, guide your choices, and bring you closer to God.

Faith in Action
Saint Bernadette, God's Messenger

© De Agostini Picture Library / G. Sioen / The Bridgeman Art Library

Bernadette Soubirous was born to a poor family in Lourdes, France. Her family was extremely poor and lived in a basement cell of a former jail. All her life, Bernadette suffered from asthma. Her poverty and ill health kept her from receiving a thorough practical or religions education. As a result, by the time she was fourteen, she still had not yet made her First Communion, but she always carried her rosary and prayed its traditional scriptural prayers.

One day Bernadette went to gather firewood with her sister and a friend. Suddenly she heard the sound of wind—but nothing moved. She looked toward a nearby cave or grotto, where she could see a dazzling white figure. She called it "a small young lady." Later she learned the Lady's name: the Immaculate Conception. The Lady spoke in Bernadette's own dialect, but Bernadette had never heard these words before and did not know what they meant.

In a later visit, the Lady asked Bernadette to dig into the ground. A spring gushed up. The Lady asked that a chapel be built on this spot so that people might come to pray. We now know this Lady as Our Lady of Lourdes. Her shrine at Lourdes is now a worldwide center for healing and prayer.

And Bernadette? She went to a convent school to learn to read and write and then became a nun. She died at age thirty-five. Bernadette never claimed to be anything but a messenger. She once referred to herself as God's broom, taken out from the corner to be used and then put away once more.

Responding to Sacred Scripture's command to "be still" (Psalm 46:11) to hear the "light silent sound" (1 Kings 19:12) of God's voice, the Benedictine monks developed the prayer form known as *lectio divina*. **Lectio divina** (Latin for "divine reading") is a slow, contemplative praying of Sacred Scripture that allows the Word of God to penetrate our hearts, leading us to a deeper relationship with the Lord. Within monastic communities the practice of divine, or holy, reading, along with manual labor and participation in liturgical life, is the foundation of the monastery and of the life of the monk.

Pope Benedict XVI explained how *lectio divina* benefits the larger Church: "If it is effectively promoted, this practice will bring to the Church—I am convinced of it—a new spiritual springtime" ("Address of His Holiness Benedict XVI to the Participants in the International Congress Organized to Commemorate the 40th Anniversary of the *Dogmatic Constitution on Divine Revelation 'Dei Verbum'*"). *Lectio divina* is not only a spiritual practice of not only monasticism but also the entire Church. In fact, *lectio divina,* "where the Word of God is so read and meditated that it becomes prayer, is thus rooted in the liturgical celebration" (CCC, 1177).

lectio divina
A Latin term meaning "divine reading." *Lectio divina* is a form of meditative prayer focused on a Scripture passage. It involves repetitive readings and periods of reflection and can serve as either private or communal prayer.

© Dawna Stafford / iStockphoto.com

The Four Rungs of *Lectio Divina*

In the twelfth century, a Carthusian monk named Guigo II wrote *The Ladder of Monks,* a book that describes four stages, or rungs, of *lectio divina:*

- *lectio* (reading)
- *meditatio* (meditation)
- *oratio* (prayer)
- *contemplatio* (contemplation)

Practicing *lectio divina* can better prepare us to hear the Sunday Gospel. Find the Gospel reading for the coming Sunday and pray with it, using the steps described in the section "Lectio Divina Made Easy."

lectio
Slow and attentive reading of a passage from Sacred Scripture.

meditatio
Reflecting on a Scripture passage to understand what God intends to communicate.

oratio
Speaking to God in prayer.

contemplatio
A form of prayer in which one simply and silently rests in the presence of God.

actio
Action and life changes that result from *lectio divina*.

The first stage, *lectio*, involves the slow and attentive reading of a particular passage from Sacred Scripture. The Prologue to the Rule of Saint Benedict explains that the deliberate, reverent reading of the Scriptures cultivates the ability to "listen carefully . . . with the ear of your heart."

Moving to the second stage, *meditatio*, we meditate on the chosen Scripture passage to understand what God is trying to communicate to us. Through meditation on the mysteries of Christ, we gain knowledge of his love and deepen our union with him. Meditation engages the intellect by allowing the Word of God to interact with our thoughts, memories, desires, and hopes. When we ponder the words of Sacred Scripture, we can discover God's intended message.

Following meditation we enter the third stage, *oratio*, where we simply let our hearts speak to God in prayer. Through prayer we respond to what we have received in meditation. We allow the Word of God to touch and change our real selves.

In the fourth and final stage, *contemplatio*, we simply and silently rest in the presence of God—Father, Son, and Holy Spirit—who loves us. Contemplation puts all words and thoughts aside to experience the transforming embrace of God.

The journey through these four stages of *lectio divina* results in *actio*, Latin for "action." What happens during *lectio divina* changes us. It affects how we live our lives and may call us to further action regarding ourselves, the Church, or the world.

Lectio Divina Made Easy

The following simple steps can help you to engage in the ancient practice of *lectio divina*:

1. **Choose** one of the Scripture readings from the Eucharistic Liturgy of the day or from the upcoming Sunday.
2. **Find** a comfortable and quiet place to pray.

3 **Take** a few moments of silence to settle your inner thoughts.

4. **Read** the Scripture passage slowly and attentively.

5. **Focus** on a word or phrase from the Scripture reading. Memorize or repeat it several times.

6. **Communicate** with God in prayer.

7. **Experience** God's calming and loving presence.

The best way to get comfortable with this form of praying with Sacred Scripture is to practice. Use the steps above with the following Scripture passages:

- Genesis 45:4–8 (Joseph reunites with his brothers.)
- Jeremiah 1:4–10 (Jeremiah is called by God.)
- Mark 4:35–41 (Jesus calms a storm at sea.)
- Mark 2:1–12 (Jesus heals a paralyzed man.)

Also, keep a journal handy in case you feel like writing down something that touches your heart. If at first you find yourself easily distracted, do not worry about it. Simply continue following the steps. The more you return to this style of prayer, the more comfortable with it you will become.

A Way to Learn about God and Self

Lectio divina is like a classroom where God is the teacher and we are the students. The ancient practice of divine reading teaches us about God and self. At the heart of *lectio divina* is God, our Teacher, who truly loves us and longs to reveal himself to us in the sacred pages of the Bible. As his beloved students, we are called to offer ourselves to him, allowing his Word to inform even the darkest corners of our lives. We are called to consecrate our entire lives—our wills, memories, hopes, and dreams—to him.

> **How can the prayer form of *lectio divina* give you inner peace and draw you closer to God?**

devotional prayers
Also known as devotions, these are personalized prayers that have developed outside, but should lead to, the liturgy of the Church.

Via Dolorosa
Latin for "way of sorrow," referring to the path Jesus journeyed in the last hours of his life, which is commemorated in the devotion of the Stations of the Cross.

Article 83: Two Devotional Prayers Based in Sacred Scripture

In *lectio divina* we pray directly with a passage from Scripture. Over the centuries we have developed many other ways to pray that are based on Scripture. You might recognize the Stations of the Cross and the Rosary as two popular devotional prayers that arise from Sacred Scripture. **Devotional prayers** are personalized prayers that have developed outside the Liturgy of the Church but should lead us to the Liturgy.

The Stations of the Cross

The life, Passion, and Death of Jesus are the focus of many traditional devotions of the Church. One notable devotion, the Stations of the Cross, centers on the Passion of Christ. The Stations of the Cross are rooted in the Scripture accounts of the persecution and Crucifixion of Jesus. The Stations originated during the Middle Ages, to allow pilgrims who could not travel to the Holy Land to commemorate Jesus' suffering on the route to Calvary. Today's Stations of the Cross traditionally commemorate fourteen stops, or stations, along the **Via Dolorosa**, Latin for "way of sorrow":

1. Jesus is condemned to death.
2. Jesus bears his cross.
3. Jesus falls the first time.
4. Jesus meets his mother.
5. Simon of Cyrene helps Jesus to carry his cross.
6. Veronica wipes the face of Jesus.
7. Jesus falls a second time.
8. Jesus meets the women of Jerusalem.
9. Jesus falls a third time.
10. Jesus is stripped of his garments.
11. Jesus is nailed to the cross.
12. Jesus dies on the cross.
13. Jesus is taken down from the cross.
14. Jesus is placed in the tomb.

When we meditate on the chief scenes of Christ's Passion and Death, beginning with his condemnation and ending with the placement of his body in the tomb, we commemorate the sacrifice of Jesus and can better experience God's redemptive love. In the traditional Stations of the Cross, stations 3, 4, 6, 7, and 9 do not have clear scriptural foundations, but they are supported by Sacred Tradition. The traditional Stations of the Cross enrich our spiritual lives by inviting us to experience the Word of God in a unique way.

As Pope in 1991, Saint John Paul II introduced a new devotion as an alternative to the traditional stations. His Scriptural Way of the Cross more closely reflects Christ's Passion as recounted in the Gospels:

© Bill Wittman / www.wpwittman.com

1. Jesus is in the garden at Gethsemane.
2. Jesus is betrayed by Judas and is arrested.
3. Jesus is condemned by the Sanhedrin.
4. Jesus is denied by Peter.
5. Jesus is judged by Pilate.
6. Jesus is scourged and crowned with thorns.
7. Jesus bears the cross.
8. Jesus is helped by Simon the Cyrenian to carry the cross.

Some parishes and other groups pray the Stations of the Cross outdoors, walking to different locations to pray each station. How would this short pilgrimage help you to meditate on Jesus' Passion and his walk to Calvary?

Live It!
Stations of the Cross

Have you noticed the Stations of the Cross in your church or school chapel? Most Catholic churches have paintings or statues representing the traditional Stations on their walls. The next time you are in your church or chapel, take time to pause before each station, study how it depicts an event in Jesus' final journey, and say a short prayer. If you would like to pray more deeply with the Stations of the Cross, many websites and publishers offer resources that include a brief Scripture reading, reflection, and prayer for each station. Ask your teacher or campus ministry team to recommend a Stations of the Cross resource that especially appeals to young people.

9. Jesus meets the women of Jerusalem.
10. Jesus is crucified.
11. Jesus promises his Kingdom to the good thief.
12. Jesus speaks to his mother and the disciple.
13. Jesus dies on the cross.
14. Jesus is placed in the tomb.

The Rosary

Within the Church's Tradition, we find several devotions that focus on Mary, the Mother of God. The most popular devotion to Mary involves praying the **Rosary**. Sacred Scripture is the basis of the Rosary. The Rosary's prayers and mysteries of Jesus on which we reflect are rooted in Scripture.

Praying the Rosary is another way we can integrate Sacred Scripture into our prayer life. If you are not familiar with praying the Rosary, ask someone who knows how to pray it to show you how.

When we pray the Rosary, we recite five sets of ten Hail Marys. Each set is called a decade. Each new decade begins with one Lord's Prayer and concludes with a Glory Be. We trace these prayers along a small chain of beads with a crucifix, called a rosary. While praying the Rosary, we meditate on the mysteries of the life of Jesus. These mysteries are also grouped into sets of five—the five Joyful, five Sorrowful, five Glorious, and five Luminous Mysteries. One recitation of the Rosary is dedicated to each set of mysteries. The mysteries of the Rosary are based on events recounted in Sacred Scripture and transmitted through Tradition. The Joyful Mysteries center on Jesus' birth, the Sorrowful Mysteries on his Death, the Glorious Mysteries on his Resurrection, and the Luminous Mysteries on his public ministry.

Does your family pray the Rosary together? What can you do to make the Rosary a regular part of your prayer life?

© Peter Zelei / iStockphoto.com

The Joyful Mysteries

- The Annunciation
- The Visitation
- The Birth of Our Lord
- The Presentation of Jesus in the Temple
- The Finding of Jesus in the Temple

The Sorrowful Mysteries

- The Agony in the Garden
- The Scourging at the Pillar
- The Crowning with Thorns
- The Carrying of the Cross
- The Crucifixion

The Glorious Mysteries

- The Resurrection of Jesus
- The Ascension of Jesus into Heaven
- The Descent of the Holy Spirit on the Apostles (Pentecost)
- The Assumption of Mary into Heaven
- The Crowning of Mary as Queen of Heaven

Rosary
A devotional prayer that honors the Virgin Mary and helps us meditate on Christ's life and mission. We pray the Rosary using rosary beads, which are grouped into "decades." Each decade consists of praying the Lord's Prayer followed by ten Hail Marys and the Glory Be while meditating on an event from Christ's life and mission.

Pray It!

Hail, Holy Queen

During the Rosary, we say the Lord's Prayer, the Hail Mary, and the Glory Be several times each. To finish the Rosary, we conclude with another prayer that asks Mary to intercede on our behalf: the "Hail, Holy Queen." Any time you feel a need for extra support and comfort, pray these words to call on Mary, Queen of Heaven, our Advocate:

Hail, holy Queen, mother of mercy, our life, our sweetness, and our hope. To you do we cry, poor banished children of Eve. To you do we send up our sighs, mourning and weeping in this vale of tears. Turn then, most gracious advocate, your eyes of mercy toward us, and after this our exile show to us the blessed fruit of your womb, Jesus. O clement, O loving, O sweet Virgin Mary.

The Luminous Mysteries

- The Baptism of Jesus
- Jesus Reveals Himself in the Miracle at Cana
- Jesus Proclaims the Good News of the Kingdom of God
- The Transfiguration of Jesus
- The Institution of the Eucharist

Article 84: Individual and Communal Prayer with Sacred Scripture

We are blessed to have the Holy Spirit to guide us and teach us how to pray. We can pray on our own and also with other people—at school, in our families, and with our church youth groups. We can also pray with friends, with our sports teams, and in countless other ways. When we gather as small Christian communities and in other groups, such as at school or in our parishes, we are called to make Sacred Scripture the basis for our prayer.

Primary Sources

Join Mary in Contemplating Christ

With so many Hail Marys, the Rosary can seem like a prayer that focuses on Mary, not on Christ. Pope Saint John Paul II reminds us that when we pray the Rosary, we actually join Mary in contemplating Christ:

Mary lived with her eyes fixed on Christ, treasuring his every word: "She kept all these things, pondering them in her heart" (Lk 2:19; cf. 2:51). . . . [Those memories] were always with her, leading her to reflect on the various moments of her life at her Son's side. In a way those memories were to be the "rosary" which she recited uninterruptedly throughout her earthly life.

. . . Mary constantly sets before the faithful the "mysteries" of her Son, with the desire that the contemplation of those mysteries will release all their saving power. In the recitation of the Rosary, the Christian community enters into contact with the memories and the contemplative gaze of Mary.

(*Rosarium Virginis Mariae,* 11)

Every time we gather as a faith community, we find strength in the "supreme good of knowing Christ Jesus" (Philippians 3:8). We develop this profound knowledge when we read Sacred Scripture.

© Bob Daemmrich/ The Image Works

How does communal prayer—that is, prayer with other people—help you to make moral and practical decisions?

Chapter Review

1. Why does the Church exhort Christians to read Sacred Scripture?

2. What is *lectio divina*?

3. Name and describe the four stages of *lectio divina*.

4. How can the reading of Scripture influence our moral life?

5. What is a devotional prayer?

6. How is Sacred Scripture used in the devotional prayers of the Stations of the Cross and the Rosary?

Glossary

A

actio Action and life changes that result from *lectio divina*. *(article 82)*

allegory A literary form in which something is said to be like something else, in an attempt to communicate a hidden or symbolic meaning. *(article 23)*

analogy of faith The coherence of individual doctrines with the whole of Revelation. In other words, as each doctrine is connected with Revelation, each doctrine is also connected with all other doctrines. *(article 21)*

anawim A Hebrew word for the poor and marginalized. *(article 62)*

Annunciation The event in which the Archangel Gabriel visits the Virgin Mary to announce that she is to be the Mother of the Savior. *(article 63)*

antichrist A pseudo-messianism whereby a human being puts himself or herself in the place of God or declares himself or herself to be a new messiah. *(article 73)*

apocalyptic literature A literary form that uses dramatic events and highly symbolic language to offer hope to a people in crisis. *(article 75)*

apostate A person who was a believer but has abandoned his or her faith. *(article 74)*

Apostolic Succession The uninterrupted passing on of apostolic preaching and authority from the Apostles directly to all bishops. It is accomplished through the laying on of hands when a bishop is ordained in the Sacrament of Holy Orders as instituted by Christ. The office of bishop is permanent, because at ordination a bishop is marked with an indelible, sacred character. *(article 12)*

Ark of the Covenant A sacred chest that housed the tablets of the Ten Commandments, placed within the sanctuary where God would come and dwell. *(article 46)*

Asia Minor An area corresponding roughly to modern-day Turkey. *(article 75)*

B

Baal . . . Asherah Two Canaanite gods of earth and fertility that the Israelites worshipped when they fell away from the one true God. *(article 43)*

Babylonian Exile The period in Israelite history during which the Israelites of the ancient kingdom of Judah were held in captivity as slaves in Babylon. The period began with the Babylonians' destruction of the Temple and the city of Jerusalem in 587 BC and lasted until 539 BC. *(article 47)*

Beatitudes The teachings of Jesus that begin the Sermon on the Mount and that summarize the New Law of Christ. The Beatitudes describe the actions and attitudes by which one can discover genuine happiness, and they teach us the final end to which God calls us: full communion with him in the Kingdom of Heaven. *(article 63)*

Beloved Disciple A faithful disciple in the Gospel of John who is present at critical times in Jesus' ministry. The Beloved Disciple may have been the founder of the Johannine community. *(article 66)*

biblical exegesis The critical interpretation and explanation of Sacred Scripture. *(article 21)*

biblical inerrancy The doctrine that the books of Sacred Scripture are free from error regarding the truth God wishes to reveal through Scripture for the sake of our salvation. *(article 15)*

breviary A prayer book that contains the prayers for the Liturgy of the Hours. *(article 78)*

C

canon The collection of books of the Bible that the Church recognizes as the inspired Word of God. *(article 18)*

canticle From the Latin *canticum,* meaning "song." It usually refers to biblical hymns (other than the Psalms), such as those found in the Song of Solomon in the Old Testament and the hymns of Mary (see Luke 1:46–55) and Zechariah (see 1:68–79) in the New Testament. By extension, *canticle* is sometimes used to describe other hymns in the liturgy. *(article 62)*

charism A special gift or grace of the Holy Spirit given to an individual Christian or community, commonly for the benefit and building up of the entire Church. *(article 80)*

Christological Having to do with the branch of theology called Christology. Christology is the study of the divinity of Jesus Christ, the Son of God and the Second Divine Person of the Trinity, and his earthly ministry and eternal mission. *(article 23)*

conscience The "inner voice," guided by human reason and Divine Law, that enables us to judge what is good and what is evil. To make good judgments, one needs to have a well-formed conscience. *(article 8)*

contemplatio A form of prayer in which one simply and silently rests in the presence of God. *(article 82)*

contextualist approach The interpretation of the Bible that takes into account the various contexts for understanding. These contexts include the senses of Scripture, literary forms, historical situations, cultural backgrounds, the unity of the whole of Sacred Scripture, Sacred Tradition, and the analogy of faith. *(article 26)*

continency, continence Abstinence from all sexual activity. *(article 4)*

contingency A state in which something relies or depends on something else. *(article 7)*

corruption Decomposition or decay. *(article 65)*

covenant A solemn agreement between human beings or between God and a human being in which mutual commitments are made. *(article 10)*

D

Deposit of Faith The heritage of faith contained in Sacred Scripture and Sacred Tradition. It has been passed on from the time of the Apostles. The Magisterium takes from it all that it teaches as revealed truth. *(article 13)*

devotional prayers Also known as devotions, these are personalized prayers that have developed outside, but should lead to, the liturgy of the Church. *(article 83)*

Divine Inspiration The divine assistance the Holy Spirit gave the authors of the books of the Bible so the authors could write in human words the message of salvation God wanted to communicate. *(article 15)*

Divine Revelation God's self-communication through which he makes known the mystery of his divine plan. Divine Revelation is a gift accomplished by the Father, Son, and Holy Spirit through the words and deeds of salvation history. It is most fully realized in the Passion, Death, Resurrection, and Ascension of Jesus Christ. *(article 9)*

Doctor of the Church A title officially bestowed by the Church on saints who are highly esteemed for their theological writings, as well as their personal holiness. *(article 7)*

dogma Teachings recognized as central to Church teaching, defined by the Magisterium and considered definitive and authoritative. *(article 13)*

E

Ecumenical Council A gathering of the Church's bishops from around the world to address pressing issues in the Church. Ecumenical Councils are usually convened by the Pope or are at least approved by him. *(article 8)*

Emmanuel A Hebrew word meaning "God is with us." *(article 50)*

epistle Another name for a New Testament letter. *(article 73)*

Essenes A group of pious, ultraconservative Jews who left the Temple of Jerusalem and began a community by the Dead Sea, known as Qumran. *(article 25)*

Eucharist, the The celebration of the entire Mass. The term can also refer specifically to the consecrated bread and wine that have become the Body and Blood of Christ. *(article 18)*

Eucharistic Prayer The part of the Mass that includes the Consecration, beginning with the Preface and concluding with the Great Amen. *(article 77)*

Evangelists From a Greek word meaning "messenger of good news," the title given to the authors of the Gospels of Matthew, Mark, Luke, and John. *(article 57)*

exegete A scholar specializing in critical explanation of biblical texts. *(article 22)*

F

Fathers of the Church (Church Fathers) During the early centuries of the Church, those teachers whose writings extended the Tradition of the Apostles and who continue to be important for the Church's teachings. *(article 6)*

fidelity Faithfulness to obligation, duty, or commitment. *(article 48)*

foreshadow To represent or prefigure a person before his or her life or an event before it occurs. *(article 9)*

fundamentalist approach The interpretation of the Bible and Christian doctrine based on the literalist meaning of the Bible's words. The interpretation is made without regard to the historical setting in which the writings or teachings were first developed. *(article 26)*

G

garden at Gethsemane An olive grove near the Mount of Olives, where Jesus gathered with the Apostles to pray before his Crucifixion on Calvary. *(article 65)*

Gentiles Non-Jewish people. *(article 60)*

Gnostic Referring to the belief that salvation comes from secret knowledge available to only a select few. *(article 18)*

Gnosticism A group of heretical religious movements that claimed salvation comes from secret knowledge available only to the elite initiated in that religion. *(article 73)*

Golgotha A Hebrew word meaning "place of the skull," referring to the place where Jesus was crucified. *(article 61)*

Gospel Translated from a Greek word meaning "good news," referring to the four books attributed to Matthew, Mark, Luke, and John. The Gospels are the principal source for accounts of Jesus Christ's life and teaching and work of salvation. *(article 57)*

Gregorian chant A monophonic, unaccompanied style of liturgical singing that takes its name from Pope Gregory the Great. *(article 77)*

H

hallowed Holy, sacred, or revered. *(article 79)*

Hebrew people The descendants of Abraham and Sarah who became known as the Israelites after the Exodus and who later were called Judeans or Jews. *(article 28)*

Hellenism The acceptance of Greek culture, language, and traditions. *(article 30)*

herald One who proclaims or announces a saving message. As a verb, the word means to proclaim or announce a saving message. *(article 47)*

Holy Communion Another name for the Sacrament of the Eucharist. *(article 77)*

homily A brief liturgical sermon that explains the Scripture readings, helps the People of God accept Sacred Scripture as the Word of God, and encourages them to put the teachings of Scripture into practice in their daily lives. *(article 77)*

hymns Poetic song lyrics written to honor God. *(article 52)*

I

idolatrous Worshipping false gods. *(article 44)*

Incarnation From the Latin, meaning "to become flesh," referring to the mystery of Jesus Christ, the Divine Son of God, becoming man. In the Incarnation, Jesus Christ became truly man while remaining truly God. *(article 2)*

Infancy Narratives The accounts of Jesus' birth and early childhood. *(article 63)*

J

Johannine Related to the Apostle John or the New Testament books attributed to him. *(article 66)*

judges The eleven men and one woman who served the Hebrew people as tribal leaders, military commanders, arbiters of disputes, and enliveners of faith. *(article 44)*

K

kerygma A Greek word meaning "proclamation" or "preaching," referring to the announcement of the Gospel or the Good News of divine salvation offered to all through Jesus Christ. *Kerygma* has two senses. It is both an event of proclamation and a message proclaimed. *(article 58)*

L

lament A cry for God's intervention in difficult situations. Many of the Psalms are laments. *(article 52)*

Law of Moses The first five books of the Old Testament, which are also called the books of law or the Torah. God gave Moses the tablets summarizing the Law (see Exodus 31:18), which is why it is also called the Law of Moses, or the Mosaic Law. *(article 29)*

lectio Slow and attentive reading of a passage from Sacred Scripture. *(article 82)*

lectio divina A Latin term meaning "divine reading." *Lectio divina* is a form of meditative prayer focused on a Scripture passage. It involves repetitive readings and periods of reflection and can serve as either private or communal prayer. *(article 82)*

literary forms (genres) Different kinds of writing determined by their literary technique, content, tone, and purpose. *(article 24)*

liturgy The Church's official, public, communal prayer. It is God's work, in which the People of God participate. The Church's most important liturgy is the Eucharist, or the Mass. *(article 77)*

Liturgy of the Hours Also known as the Divine Office, the official public, daily prayer of the Catholic Church. The Divine Office provides standard prayers, Scripture readings, and reflections at regular hours throughout the day. *(article 78)*

Logos A Greek word meaning "Word." *Logos* is a title of Jesus Christ found in the Gospel of John that illuminates the relationship between the three Divine Persons of the Holy Trinity. (See John 1:1,14.) *(article 66)*

M

Magi From the Greek for "priest" or "learned one," refers to the wise men from the East who visited the newborn Jesus in Bethlehem. *(article 60)*

Magisterium The Church's living teaching office, which consists of all bishops, in communion with the Pope, the bishop of Rome. *(article 8)*

Magnificat This is the first Latin word (from *magnus,* meaning "great," and *facere,* meaning "to make") and the title of the prayer of Mary in response to the Annunciation of the birth of Jesus in the Gospel of Luke (see Luke 1:46–55). *(article 62)*

manna The breadlike food that God miraculously provided for the Chosen People during their wandering in the desert. *(article 40)*

martyrdom Witness to the saving message of Christ through the sacrifice of one's life. *(article 71)*

Matthean Related to the author of the Gospel of Matthew. *(article 60)*

meditatio Reflecting on a Scripture passage to understand what God intends to communicate. *(article 82)*

messianic hope The Jewish belief and expectation that a messiah would come to protect, unite, and lead Israel to freedom. *(article 50)*

messianic secret A theme in the Gospel of Mark that portrays the disciples and others as recognizing Jesus' identity as the Messiah. However, Jesus directed them not to tell anyone else. *(article 61)*

Middle Ages Also known as the medieval period, the time between the collapse of the Roman Empire in the late fifth century AD and the beginning of the Renaissance in the fourteenth century. *(article 7)*

miracles Signs or wonders, such as healing or the control of nature, that can only be attributed to divine power. *(article 64)*

monarchy A government or a state headed by a single person, such as a king or queen. As a biblical term, it refers to the period of time when the Israelites existed as an independent nation. *(article 45)*

morality Refers to the goodness or evil of human acts. The morality of an act is determined by the nature of the action, the intention, and the circumstances. *(article 81)*

N

Nag Hammadi manuscripts Fourth-century writings, discovered in 1945 near the village of Nag Hammadi in Upper Egypt, that are invaluable sources of information regarding Gnostic beliefs, practices, and lifestyle. Gnosticism was an early Church heresy claiming that Christ's humanity was an illusion and the human body is evil. *(article 25)*

natural revelation The process by which God makes himself known to human reason through the created world. *(article 5)*

Near East In biblical times the region commonly known today as the Middle East, including the modern countries of Iraq, Iran, Syria, Lebanon, Israel, and Jordan. *(article 35)*

Nicene Creed The formal statement or profession of Christian belief originally formulated at the Council of Nicaea in 325 and amplified at the Council of Constantinople in 381. *(article 33)*

O

opus dei A Latin phrase meaning the "work of God." *(article 78)*

oral tradition The handing on of the message of God's saving plan through words and deeds. *(article 16)*

oratio Speaking to God in prayer. *(article 82)*

Original Sin From the Latin *origo,* meaning "beginning" or "birth." The term has two meanings: (1) the sin of the first human beings, who disobeyed God's command by choosing to follow their own will and thus lost their original holiness and became subject to death, (2) the fallen state of human nature that affects every person born into the world, except Jesus and Mary. *(article 6)*

P

parables Short stories that use everyday images to communicate religious messages. Jesus used parables frequently in his teaching as a way of presenting the Good News of salvation. *(article 64)*

Paraclete A term meaning "advocate" or "helper," used in the Gospel of John to describe the Holy Spirit, the Third Divine Person of the Trinity, whom Jesus promised to the disciples as an advocate and counselor. *(article 69)*

Parousia The second coming of Christ as judge of all the living and the dead, at the end of time, when the Kingdom of God will be fulfilled. *(article 31)*

Paschal Lamb In the Old Testament, the sacrificial lamb shared at the Seder meal of the Passover on the night the Israelites escaped from Egypt; in the New Testament, the Paschal Lamb is Jesus, the Incarnate Son of God who dies on a cross to take away "the sin of the world" (John 1:29). *(article 59)*

Paschal Mystery The work of salvation accomplished by Jesus Christ mainly through his Passion, Death, Resurrection, and Ascension. *(article 12)*

Passion The suffering of Jesus during the final days of his life: his agony in the garden at Gethsemane, his trial, and his Crucifixion. *(article 61)*

Passover The night the Lord passed over the houses of the Israelites marked by the blood of the lamb, and spared the firstborn sons from death. It also is the feast that celebrates the deliverance of the Chosen People from bondage in Egypt and the Exodus from Egypt to the Promised Land. *(article 39)*

patriarch The father or leader of a tribe, clan, or tradition. Abraham, Isaac, and Jacob were the patriarchs of the Israelite people. *(article 10)*

Pauline letters Thirteen New Testament letters attributed to Saint Paul or to disciples who wrote in his name. The letters offer advice, pastoral encouragement, teaching, and community news to early Christian communities. *(article 72)*

Pentateuch A Greek word meaning "five books," referring to the first five books of the Old Testament. *(article 29)*

Pentecost The fiftieth day following Easter, which commemorates the descent of the Holy Spirit on the early Apostles and disciples. *(article 71)*

personification A literary technique that uses human characteristics to describe nonhuman realities. *(article 55)*

pharaoh A ruler of ancient Egypt. *(article 38)*

polytheistic Belief in many gods and goddesses. *(article 43)*

prayer Lifting up of one's mind and heart to God or the requesting of good things from him. The five basic forms of prayer are blessing, praise, petition, thanksgiving, and intercession. In prayer we communicate with God in a relationship of love. *(article 79)*

primeval history The time before the invention of writing and recording of historical data. *(article 33)*

Promised Land The land (Canaan) God promised to the children of Abraham. *(article 36)*

prophecy A message communicated by prophets on behalf of God, usually a message of divine direction or consolation for the prophet's own time. Because some prophetic messages include divine direction, their fulfillment may be in the future. *(article 47)*

prophet A person God chooses to speak his message of salvation. In the Bible, primarily a communicator of a divine message of repentance to the Chosen People, not necessarily a person who predicted the future. *(article 10)*

psalmody From the Greek word *psalmos,* meaning "a song sung to a harp," and *aeidein,* meaning "to sing." The word has multiple meanings: the art of singing psalms, the arranging or composing of psalms for singing, or a collection of psalms for singing or reciting. *(article 77)*

Psalter The Book of Psalms of the Old Testament, which contains 150 Psalms. *(article 19)*

Q

Qoheleth A Hebrew word for *Ecclesiastes,* meaning "preacher" or "one who convokes an assembly." *(article 52)*

Quelle Also called the Q Source, a theoretical collection of ancient documents of the teachings of Jesus shared among the early followers of Christianity; believed by Scripture scholars to be a source for the Gospels of Matthew and Luke. *(article 59)*

R

rabbi An honored teacher in the Jewish tradition. *(article 60)*

redact To edit or adapt written material to serve a particular purpose. *(article 24)*

redemption, redemptive From the Latin *redemptio,* meaning "a buying back," referring, in the Old Testament, to Yahweh's deliverance of Israel and, in the New Testament, to Christ's deliverance of all Christians from the forces of sin. *(article 13)*

remnant A prophetic term for the small portion of people who will be saved because of their faithfulness to God. *(article 49)*

Rosary A devotional prayer that honors the Virgin Mary and helps us meditate on Christ's life and mission. We pray the Rosary using rosary beads, which are grouped into "decades." Each decade consists of praying the Lord's Prayer followed by ten Hail Marys and the Glory Be while meditating on an event from Christ's life and mission. *(article 83)*

S

Sacred Tradition *Tradition* comes from the Latin *tradere,* meaning "to hand on." Sacred Tradition refers to the process of passing on the Gospel message. It began with the oral communication of the Gospel by the Apostles, was written down in Sacred Scripture, and is interpreted by the Magisterium under the guidance of the Holy Spirit. *(article 12)*

salvation From the Latin *salvare,* meaning "to save," referring to the forgiveness of sins and assurance of permanent union with God, attained for us through the Paschal Mystery—Christ's work of redemption accomplished through his Passion, Death, Resurrection, and Ascension. Only at the time of judgment can a person be certain of salvation, which is a gift of God. *(article 2)*

salvation history The pattern of specific events in human history in which God clearly reveals his presence and saving actions. Salvation was accomplished once and for all through Jesus Christ, a truth foreshadowed and revealed throughout the Old Testament. *(article 9)*

Samaritan An inhabitant of Samaria, in the central hill country of Palestine. The Samaritans rejected the Jerusalem Temple and worshiped instead at Mount Gerizim. The New Testament mentions the Jewish rejection of Samaritans in both the Parable of the Good Samaritan (see Luke 10:29–37) and the account of Jesus' speaking with the Samaritan woman at the well (see John 4:1–42). *(article 62)*

Satan The fallen angel or spirit of evil who is the enemy of God and a continuing instigator of temptation and sin in the world. *(article 79)*

scholastic theology The use of philosophical methods to better understand revealed truth. The goal of scholastic theology is to present the understanding of revealed truth in a logical and systematic form. *(article 7)*

scribes Jewish legal scholars or teachers of Jewish Law. In the New Testament, they are associated with the Pharisees and the High Priests as opponents of Jesus. *(article 60)*

Semitic A term referring to Semites, a number of peoples of the ancient Near East—the region commonly known today as the Middle East—from whom the Israelites descended. *(article 35)*

servant leadership A type of leadership based on humble service to all God's people. *(article 46)*

sign The Johannine name for a miracle of Jesus. *(article 66)*

Sinai Covenant The covenant established with the Israelites at Mount Sinai that renewed God's covenant with Abraham's descendants. The Sinai Covenant establishes the Israelites as God's Chosen People. *(article 41)*

stump of Jesse A phrase taken from Isaiah 11:1 that traces Jesus' lineage to Jesse's son, King David. *(article 50)*

synoptic Gospels From the Greek for "seeing the whole together," the name given to the Gospels of Matthew, Mark, and Luke, because they are similar in style and content. *(article 59)*

Syrophoenecian A person from the Phoenician cities of Tyre and Sidon. Jews considered Syrophoenecians "outsiders" because of their idolatrous practices. *(article 61)*

T

temptation An invitation or enticement to commit an unwise or immoral act that often includes a promise of reward to make the immoral act seem more appealing. *(article 79)*

Ten Commandments Sometimes called the Decalogue, the list of ten norms, or rules of moral behavior, that God gave Moses and that are the basis of ethical conduct. *(article 41)*

theocracy A nation in which God is recognized as the head of the state and its divine ruler. *(article 45)*

theophany God's manifestation of himself in a visible form to enrich human understanding of him. An example is God's appearance to Moses in the form of a burning bush. *(article 9)*

Torah A Hebrew word meaning "law," referring to the first five books of the Old Testament. *(article 29)*

Trinity From the Latin *trinus,* meaning "threefold," referring to the central mystery of the Christian faith that God exists as a communion of three distinct and interrelated Divine Persons: Father, Son, and Holy Spirit. The doctrine of the Trinity is a mystery that is inaccessible to human reason alone and is known through Divine Revelation only. *(article 9)*

V

Vatican Council II The Ecumenical or general Council of the Roman Catholic Church that Saint John XXIII convened as Pope in 1962 and that continued under Venerable Pope Paul VI until 1965. *(article 2)*

venerate Treat with deep reverence and devotion. *(article 57)*

Via Dolorosa Latin for "way of sorrow," referring to the path Jesus journeyed in the last hours of his life, which is commemorated in the devotion of the Stations of the Cross. *(article 83)*

vocation A call from God to all members of the Church to embrace a life of holiness. Specifically, it refers to a call to live the holy life as an ordained minister, as a vowed religious (sister or brother), or in a Christian marriage. Single life that involves a personal consecration or commitment to a permanent, celibate gift of self to God and one's neighbor is also a vocational state. *(article 1)*

W

wisdom literature The Old Testament books of Proverbs, Job, Ecclesiastes, Sirach, and the Wisdom of Solomon. *(article 10)*

written tradition Under the inspiration of the Holy Spirit, the synthesis in written form of the message of salvation that has been passed down in the oral tradition. *(article 16)*

Y

Yahweh The most sacred of the Old Testament names for God, which he revealed to Moses. It is frequently translated as "I AM" or "I am who am." *(article 39)*

Index

Acknowledgments

The first "Salt and Light" excerpt on page 68 is from the New Revised Standard Version of the Bible, Catholic Edition (NRSV). Copyright © 1993 and 1989 by the Division of Christian Education of the National Council of the Churches of Christ in the United States of America. All rights reserved.

The "Salt for the Earth and Light for the World" excerpt on page 68 is from the *New Jerusalem Bible (NJB)*. Copyright © 1985 by Darton, Longman and Todd, London; and Doubleday, a division of Bantam Doubleday Dell Publishing Group, New York. All rights reserved.

The second "Salt and Light" excerpt on page 68 is from the Good News Translation® (Today's English Version, Second Edition). Copyright © 1992 by the American Bible Society. All rights reserved. Bible text from the Good News Translation (GNT) is not to be reproduced in copies or otherwise by any means excerpt as permitted in writing by the American Bible Society, 1865 Broadway, New York, NY 10023 (*www.americanbible.org*).

All other scriptural quotations in this book, including "The Similes of Salt and Light" on page 68, are from the *New American Bible, revised edition* © 2010, 1991, 1986, 1970 Confraternity of Christian Doctrine, Inc., Washington, D.C. All Rights Reserved. No part of this work may be reproduced or transmitted in any form or by any means, electronic or mechanical, including photocopying, recording, or by any information storage and retrieval system, without permission in writing from the copyright owner.

The excerpts marked *Catechism* and *CCC* are from the English translation of the *Catechism of the Catholic Church* for use in the United States of America, second edition. Copyright © 1994 by the United States Catholic Conference, Inc.—Libreria Editrice Vaticana (LEV). English translation of the *Catechism of the Catholic Church: Modifications from the Editio Typica* copyright © 1997 by the United States Catholic Conference, Inc.—LEV.

The poetic lines of Saint John of the Cross on page 14 are from *The Collected Works of Saint John of the Cross*, revised edition, translated by Kieran Kavanaugh and Otilio Rodriguez (Washington, DC: ICS Publications, 1991), pages 358–359. Copyright © 1964, 1979, 1991 by the Washington Province of Discalced Carmelites. Used with permission of ICS Publications, 2131 Lincoln Road NE, Washington, D.C. 20002-1199, USA, *www.icspublications.org*.

The prayers on pages 14, 42, 115, and 155 are from *The Catholic Youth Prayer Book*, by Mary Shrader, Lauré Krupp, Robert Feduccia Jr., and Matthew J. Miller (Winona, MN: Saint Mary's Press, 2007), pages 13, 13, 13, and 25, respectively. Copyright © 2007 by Saint Mary's Press. All rights reserved.

The excerpt on page 102 and the quotation on page 248 are from the English translation of Saint Jerome's *Commentary on Isaiah from The Liturgy of the Hours* © 1974, International Commission on English in the Liturgy Corporation (ICEL) (New York: Catholic Book Publishing Corp., 1975), volume IV, page 1448. Copyright © 1975 by the Catholic Book Publishing Corp. All rights reserved. Used with permission of the ICEL.

The excerpts and quotation on pages 107, 211, and 212 are from the English translation of *The Roman Missal* © 2010, ICEL. (Washington, DC: USCCB, 2011), pages 527, 355, and 578, respectively. All rights reserved. Used with permission of the ICEL. Published with the approval of the Committee on Divine Worship, USCCB.

The mission statement of the Sisters of Our Lady of Sion on page 108 is from the CCJ Hillingdon News Archive, at *www.ccj-hillingdon.org.uk/archive/sisters.htm.*

The excerpts and quotation on pages 117 and 236 are from the *United States Catechism for Adults*, by the USCCB (Washington, DC: USCCB, 2006), pages 70 and 31, respectively. Copyright © 2006 USCCB. All rights reserved. No part of this work may be reproduced or transmitted in any form or by any means, electronic or mechanical, including photocopying, recording, or by an information storage and retrieval system, without permission in writing from the copyright holder. Used with permission of the USCCB.

The excerpt on page 148 is from *St. Augustine's City of God and Christian Doctrine*, book, 17, chapter 8, at *www.ccel.org/ccel/schaff/npnf102.toc.html.*

The quotation by Archbishop Romero on page 153 was found at *www.consortiumnews.com/2010/031810b.html.*

The excerpt on page 159 is from *Abraham Joshua Heschel: Essential Writings*, selected by Susannah Heschel (Maryknoll, NY: Orbis Books, 2011), pages 62 and 64. Copyright © 2011 by Susannah Heschel.

The excerpt on page 174 is from *God Is Love (Deus Caritas Est)*, number 6, at *www.vatican.va/holy_father/benedict_xvi/encyclicals/documents/hf_ben-xvi_enc_20051225_deus-caritas-est_en.html.* Copyright © 2005 LEV.

The excerpt on page 207 is from *Parables: The Arrows of God*, by Megan McKenna (Maryknoll, NY: Orbis Books, 1994), page 28. Copyright © 1994 by Megan McKenna.

The excerpt on page 218 is from "Angelus," at *www.vatican.va/holy_father/benedict_xvi/angelus/2012/documents/hf_ben-xvi_ang_20120729_en.html.* Copyright © 2012 LEV.

The lists of numbers and colors on page 240 are adapted from *The Book of Revelation*, by Catherine Cory (Collegeville, MN: The Liturgical Press, 2006), pages 12–13. Copyright © 2006 by the Order of Saint Benedict, Collegeville, MN.

The papal quotations on pages 249 and 251 are from *Constitution on the Sacred Liturgy* (*Sacrosanctum Concilium*, 1963), numbers 24 and 121, at *www.vatican.va/archive/hist_councils/ii_vatican_council/documents/vat-ii_const_19631204_sacrosanctum-concilium_en.html*. Copyright © LEV.

The excerpt on page 251 is quoted from Saint Augustine and reprinted here from the *General Instruction of the Liturgy of the Hours*, at *www.fdlc.org/Liturgy_Resources/general_instruction_of_the_liturgy_of_the_hours.htm*.

The quotation from Saint Augustine on page 259 is from "The Rule of Our Holy Father Augustine," number 3, found at *www.enicholl.com/bolton-priory-church/html-files/right-frame-st-augustine.htm*.

The quotation from Saint Benedict on page 260 is from "The Order of Saint Benedict: The Rule of Benedict," chapter 53, found at *www.osb.org/rb/text/rbeaad1.html*.

The quotation from Saint Francis on page 261 is from "The Rule of St. Francis—1223," chapter II, found at *www.thenazareneway.com/rule_of_st_francis.html*.

The quotation by Pope Benedict XVI on page 267 is from "Address of His Holiness Benedict XVI to the Participants in the International Congress Organized to Commemorate the 40th Anniversary of the *Dogmatic Constitution on Divine Revelation 'Dei Verbum*,'" at *www.vatican.va/holy_father/benedict_xvi/speeches/2005/september/documents/hf_ben-xvi_spe_20050916_40-dei-verbum_en.html*. Copyright © 2005 LEV.

The quotation on page 268 is from the "Rule of Saint Benedict: Prologue," found at *www.trappist.net/RuleofStBenedict*.

The excerpt on page 274 is from *Rosary of the Virgin Mary* (*Rosarium Virginis Mariae*), number 11, at *www.vatican.va/holy_father/john_paul_ii/apost_letters/documents/hf_jp-ii_apl_20021016_rosarium-virginis-mariae_en.html*. Copyright © LEV.

To view copyright terms and conditions for Internet materials cited here, log on to the home pages for the referenced websites.

During this book's preparation, all citations, facts, figures, names, addresses, telephone numbers, Internet URLs, and other pieces of information cited within were verified for accuracy. The authors and Saint Mary's Press staff have made every attempt to reference current and valid sources, but we cannot guarantee the content of any source, and we are not responsible for any changes that may have occurred since our verification. If you find an error in, or have a question or concern about, any of the information or sources listed within, please contact Saint Mary's Press.

Endnotes Cited in Quotations from the *Catechism of the Catholic Church*, Second Edition

Unit 1
1. Cf. *1 Corinthians* 6:19–20; 15:44–45.
2. St. Thomas Aquinas, *Summa Theologiae* I, 2, 3.
3. Vatican Council I, *Dei Filius* 2: Denzinger-Schönmetzer, *Enchiridion Symbolorum, definitionum declarationum de rebus fidei et morum* (1965) 3004; cf. 3026; Vatican Council II, *Dei Verbum* 6.
4. Cf. *Ezekiel* 36; *Isaiah* 49:5–6; 53:11.
5. *Dei Verbum* 8 § 1.
6. *Matthew* 28:20.

Unit 2
1. *Dei Verbum* 12 § 3.
2. *Dei Filius* 4: Denzinger-Schönmetzer, *Enchiridion Symbolorum, definitionum declarationum de rebus fidei et morum* (1965) 3017.
3. cf. Origen, Hom. in Ex. 4, 5: J. P. Migne, ed., Patrologia Graeca [Paris, 1857–1866] 12, 320.
4. *Dei Verbum* 12 § 3.
5. Cf. *Revelation* 21:1–22:5
6. Littera gesta docet, quid credas allegoria, moralis quid agas, quo tendas anagogia. Augustine of Dacia, *Rotulus pugillaris*, I: ed. A. Walz: Angelicum 6 (1929) 256.
7. Cf. *Dei Verbum* 14.
8. *Dei Verbum* 15.
9. Cf. St. Augustine, *Quaest. in Hept.* 2, 73: J. P. Migne, ed., Patrologia Latina 34, 623; cf. *Dei Verbum* 16.

Unit 3
1. St. Augustine, Faust 22: J. P. Migne, ed., Patrologia Latina [Paris: 1841–1855] 42, 418.
2. Cf. *Ezekiel* 36; *Isaiah* 49:5–6; 53:11.
3. *Lumen gentium* 6; cf. *Galatians* 4:26; *Revelation* 12:17; 19:7; 21:2, 9; 22:17; *Ephesians* 5:25–26, 29.

Unit 4
1. *Dei Verbum* 18.
2. Cf. Council of Trent (1547); Denzinger-Schönmetzer, *Enchiridion Symbolorum, definitionum et declarationum de rebus fidei et morum* (1965) 1529.
3. St. Rose of Lima, cf. P. Hansen, *Vita mirabilis* (Louvain, 1668).

Unit 5

1. Cf. *Dei Verbum* 21.
2. *Sacrosanctum concilium* 56.
3. Cf. *Dei Verbum* 21.
4. Tertullian, *De orat.* 1: J. P. Migne, ed., Patrologia Latina (Paris: 1841–1855) 1, 1251–1255.
5. St. Thomas Aquinas, *Summa Theologiae* II–II, 83, 9.